Writing, Grammar, and Usage

Carolyn O'Hearn

Pittsburg State University

MACMILLAN PUBLISHING COMPANY • New York

Copyright © 1989 by Macmillan Publishing Company,
a division of Macmillan, Inc.

Printed in the United States of America

All rights reserved. No part of this book may be reproduced or transmitted in any form or by any means, electronic or mechanical, including photocopying, recording, or any information storage and retrieval system, without permission in writing from the Publisher.

Macmillan Publishing Company
866 Third Avenue, New York, New York 10022

Library of Congress Cataloging-in-Publication Data

O'Hearn, Carolyn.
    Writing, grammar, and usage / Carolyn O'Hearn.
      p.   cm.
    Includes indexes:
    ISBN 0-02-3899130-0
    1. English language—Rhetoric. 2. English language—Grammar—1950– 3. English language—Usage. I. Title.
PE1408.038 1989
808'.042—dc19   88-29364
                                                                                  CIP

Printing: 1 2 3 4 5 6 7   Year: 9 0 1 2 3 4 5

Credits

William Hermann. "In Learning Limbo." From *Arizona Republic*, March 23, 1986. Reprinted by permission of the author.
James Joyce. "The Dead." From *Dubliners* by James Joyce. Copyright 1916 by B. W. Huebsch. Definitive text copyright © 1967 by the Estate of James Joyce. All rights reserved. Reprinted by permission of Viking Penguin Inc.
Donald Light, Jr., and Suzanne Keller. From *Sociology*, 2nd edition, by Donald Light, Jr., and Suzanne Keller. Copyright © 1978 by Alfred A. Knopf, Inc. Reprinted by permission of Alfred A. Knopf, Inc.
Carin C. Quinn. "The Jeaning of America—and the World." Copyright © 1978 American Heritage Publishing Company, a division of Forbes Inc. Used with permission from *American Heritage*, April/May 1978.
Jodi M. Robbins. "The Selling of Barbie." From *Bulletin for First Year Composition, 1985-86* (Department of English, Arizona State University). Copyright © 1985 Bellwether Press. Reprinted by permission of Bellwether Press and the author.
Seymour St. John. "The Fifth Freedom." From *Saturday Review*, October 10, 1953. Reprinted by permission of the author.
Sally P. Springer and Georg Deutsch. From *Left Brain, Right Brain*, Revised Edition, by Sally P. Springer and Georg Deutsch. Copyright © 1981, 1985. Reprinted with the permission of W. H. Freeman and Company.
E. Fuller Torrey, M.D. "Witchdoctors and the Universality of Healing." Copyright © 1972 by E. Fuller Torrey. From *The Mind Game: Witchdoctors and Psychiatrists*, Bantam Books, 1973; reprinted as *Witchdoctors and Psychiatrists: The Common Roots of Psychotherapy and Its Future*, Harper & Row, 1986. Reprinted by permission of the author.
Marie Winn. From *The Plug-in Drug* by Marie Winn. Copyright © 1977 by Marie Winn. All rights reserved. Reprinted by permission of Viking Penguin Inc.

Preface

Writing, Grammar, and Usage is a highly versatile text that can adapt easily to a variety of situations and audiences. Written originally for students in basic composition classes, this book can be used by both native and non-native speakers of English in developmental composition classes, in introductory grammar classes, and in tutorial labs.

As the title suggests, a "top-down" organizational structure is employed, beginning with Unit I, "Writing Essays," and then proceeding through Units II, III, and IV, "Sentence Structure," "Word Form," and "Writing Conventions." This organization emphasizes the primacy of content for writers, while recognizing that effective writing requires mastery of form.

Context is an important principle throughout this text. Explanations place concepts of grammar and usage in the context of writing. Numerous exercises give students the opportunity to practice these concepts in *rhetorical context* (practices consist of several sentences on one subject, organized into paragraphs), *social context* (subjects of practices are similar to those students might choose to write about), and *linguistic context* (vocabulary and sentence structure approximate student language). Thus, students can readily see the connections between the text and their own writing and can apply the principles demonstrated in the text to their own writing process, particularly during revision.

Unit I, "Writing Essays," begins with a chapter on writers and the writing process. This chapter introduces students to concepts such as audience and purpose and illustrates their importance in shaping discourse. Other chapters in this unit introduce students to commonly used forms of discourse: description, process, comparison-contrast, and persuasion. Each chapter includes samples of student writing with accompanying commentaries and suggestions for successful writing. The two concluding chapters in this unit provide instruction in summary writing and in other types of text-based writing.

A key organizational feature of Unit II, "Sentence Structure," is the combining of related subjects that are often scattered throughout other texts. This "clustering" of related topics enables students to study a problem principle and its variations at the same time. For example, Chapter 11, "The Forbidden Doubles," deals with double subjects, double comparatives and superlatives, and double (or multiple) negatives. All of the forbidden doubles are derived from the same principle: the writer uses two — or more — signals when only one is required. Thus, "clustering" the forbidden doubles in one chapter is an efficient approach to this problem of English usage. Unit II also presents students with several methods writers may use in revision and explains the implications and consequences of each method. Students learn to consider a variety of options when revising their writing and to choose the method that most precisely conveys what they want to say.

Still another feature of *Writing, Grammar, and Usage* is its recognition that problems of grammar and usage may be either systematic or idiosyncratic. Unit III, "Word Form," provides explanations so students can recognize systematic patterns in their writing. Procedures are established to help students recognize and correct idiosyncratic problems. For example, Chapter 17, "Homonyms and Near-Homonyms," begins with a section, "The Most Troublesome Homonyms" (for example *its/it's* and *your/you're*). Problems with these homonyms are usually systematic because they are based on confusion between possessive pronouns and contractions. On the other hand, difficulties with pairs like *brake* and *break* are idiosyncratic. Writers who confuse such pairs may also confuse other pairs like *coarse* and *course* and *right* and *write*, but there is no underlying pattern to the confusion.

The Word Index at the end of the text directs students to appropriate portions of Unit III, which includes much tabular material for easy reference. The flexibility of the approach used in this unit allows for individualized instruction. It provides students with access to solutions for their particular problems, while omitting unnecessary assignments for those students with different problems.

The text concludes with Unit IV, "Writing Conventions," which includes Chapters 18, 19, and 20, "Punctuation," "Capitalization," and "Spelling Basics." Many of the practices in this unit are in letter form.

ACKNOWLEDGMENTS

In *Writing, Grammar, and Usage*, I have attempted to write a theory-based text for a student audience whose learning abilities are too often underestimated. In doing so, I have been greatly influenced by three texts written for widely different audiences, and I should like to acknowledge the influence of and my debt to the following authors and their works: Frank J. D'Angelo, *Process and Thought in Composition* (Little, Brown); J. J. Lamberts, *A Short Introduction to English Usage* (Krieger); and Martha Kolln, *Understanding English Grammar* (Macmillan).

The materials in *Writing, Grammar, and Usage* were originally written for classes in a developmental reading–composition program at the University of Texas at El Paso. Well over a thousand students have used these materials since they were first introduced into the program in the fall of 1984. I would like to thank those students for their patience, forbearance, enthusiasm, and encouragement. I am especially grateful to the many students who gave me permission to use their writing.

Numerous teachers have used these materials, often making suggestions for improvement. Special thanks to Lawrence Apodaca, Sandra Blystone, Sharon Owen, Ruth Pepin, Nancy Roberts, Maria Rollin, and Dorothy Ward, all of the University of Texas at El Paso, for their support and helpful suggestions. I particularly want to thank Joyce Smith (now at the University of Tennessee at Chattanooga), who not only offered encouragement and advice but also helped proofread and edit on more than one occasion.

Other colleagues at the University of Texas at El Paso were supportive: Robert Esch provided useful information about summary writing; John Dick and Howard Daudistal helped me track down an elusive reference; David Schwalm (now at Arizona State University) offered invaluable advice and assistance; and G. Douglas Meyers cheered and encouraged me.

Many thanks to the following individuals who reviewed *Writing, Grammar, and Usage* in various states of progress: Henry Castillo, Temple Junior College; Carol I. Croxton, University of Southern Colorado; Leo Dangel, Southwest State University; Kitty Chen Dean, Nassau Community College; Sandra Sellers Hanson, LaGuardia Community College; Ted Johnston, El Paso Community College; S. J. Kozikowski, Bryant College; Lewis Meyers, Hunter College; Joyce J. Parris, Asheville–Buncombe Technical Community College; Richard F. Thompson, North Virginia Community

College; and Susan B. Warrington, Phillips County Community College. Their wise and perceptive comments and suggestions improved the text greatly.

Every author needs an editor, and I was fortunate to work with two of the best: Jennifer Crewe (formerly of Macmillan), who sought out the project, and Barbara Heinssen, current English Editor, who guided it to its completion. I am indebted to both for their encouragement, their insight, and their good advice.

Finally, I would like to thank friends and family for their patience and tolerance. I particularly want to thank my good friend, Melinda Rollow, and my mother, Opal Bayley, for listening to the trials and tribulations of a would-be textbook author.

C.O.

Contents

UNIT I
WRITING ESSAYS

Chapter 1 Writers and the Writing Process   3

1.1 Introduction   3
1.2 Stages of the Writing Process   3
   Invention 4   Organization 4   Generation of Text 4   Revision 5   Overlapping Stages of the Writing Process 6
1.3 Throughout the Writing Process   6
   Subject and Thesis 6   Audience 7   Purpose 8
1.4 Variations in the Writing Process   9
   Patricia's Writing Process 9   Robert's Writing Process 11   Arlene's Writing Process 14

Chapter 2 Writing Description   21

2.1 Introduction   21
2.2 Organizing Description   22
2.3 Student Description Paper   23
2.4 Description Activities   29
2.5 Suggestions for Writing Description Successfully   30
2.6 Description Assignments   30

Chapter 3 Writing Process   32

3.1 Introduction   32
3.2 Organizing Process   32
3.3 Student Process Paper   33

3.4 Process Activities   43

3.5 Suggestions for Writing Process Successfully   43

3.6 Process Assignments   44

Chapter 4   Writing Comparison-Contrast   46

4.1 Introduction   46

4.2 Organizing Comparison-Contrast   47

4.3 Student Comparison-Contrast Papers   48

Gisela's Comparison-Contrast Paper (Half-and-Half Method) 48   Raquel's Comparison-Contrast Paper (Point-by-Point Method) 53

4.4 Comparison-Contrast Activities   62

4.5 Suggestions for Writing Comparison-Contrast Successfully   62

4.6 Comparison-Contrast Assignments   62

Chapter 5   Writing Persuasion   65

5.1 Introduction   65

5.2 Organizing Persuasion   65

5.3 Student Persuasion Papers   66

Paulina's Persuasion Paper 66   Arlene's Persuasion Paper 70

5.4 Persuasion Activities   76

5.5 Suggestions for Writing Persuasion Successfully   77

5.6 Persuasion Assignments   77

Chapter 6   Writing Summaries   80

6.1 Introduction   80

6.2 Suggestions for Successful Summary Writing   80

6.3 Summary Assignment   81

6.4 Student Responses   82

6.5 Summary Activities and Assignments   88

Chapter 7 **Readings for Writing** 91

    7.1 Introduction 91

    7.2 Reading Selections 91
        "The Fifth Freedom," Seymour St. John 91
        "In Learning Limbo: Elective Courses Have Resulted in
          No Education at All," William Hermann 94
        "Television Addiction," Marie Winn 98
        "The Selling of Barbie," Jodi M. Robbins 101
        "The Jeaning of America—and the World," Carin C.
          Quinn 104
        "Witchdoctors and the Universality of Healing," Edwin
          Fuller Torrey 107

UNIT II
SENTENCE STRUCTURE

Chapter 8 **Subjects and Verbs** 113

    8.1 Introduction 113

    8.2 Recognizing Subjects 114

    8.3 Recognizing Verbs 114

    8.4 The Basic Pattern of Subject-Verb Agreement 116

    8.5 Present Tense of the Verb to be 118

    8.6 Past Tense of the Verb to be 120

    8.7 Sentences with More Than One Subject 121

    8.8 Recognizing Prepositional Phrases 122

    8.9 Subjects After Verbs 125

    8.10 Review on Subjects and Verbs 127

Chapter 9 **Sentence Boundaries** 129

    9.1 Introduction 129

    9.2 Dependent Clause Sentence Fragments 129

9.3 *More Dependent Clause Sentence Fragments* 133

9.4 *Phrase Fragments* 135

9.5 *Review on Sentence Boundaries* 137

Chapter 10 Clause Boundaries 138

10.1 *Introduction* 138

10.2 *Comma Splices* 139

10.3 *Run-Together Sentences* 142

10.4 *Revising Comma Splices and Run-Together Sentences* 144
Revision Method One (Separate Sentences) 145
Revision Method Two (Compound Sentences) 145
Revision Method Three (Complex Sentences) 146

10.5 *Choosing the Best Method of Revision* 147

10.6 *Choosing the Best Connective* 147

10.7 *Review on Clause Boundaries* 150

Chapter 11 The Forbidden Doubles 151

11.1 *Introduction* 151

11.2 *Double Subjects* 152

11.3 *Double Comparatives and Superlatives* 154

11.4 *Double (or Multiple) Negatives* 157

11.5 *Review on the Forbidden Doubles* 160

Chapter 12 Unbalanced and Illogical Structures 162

12.1 *Introduction* 162

12.2 *Unbalanced Structures* 163

12.3 *Illogical Structures* 165

12.4 *Review on Unbalanced and Illogical Structures* 167

UNIT III
WORD FORM

Chapter 13 Nouns 173

13.1 *Introduction* 173

13.2 *Regular Noun Plurals* 174

13.3 *Variations on the Regular Pattern* 177
Nouns Ending in y 177   Nouns Ending in o 179
Nouns Ending in f 181

13.4 *Irregular Noun Plurals* 183
Class 1 Irregular Nouns (man-men) 184
Class 2 Irregular Nouns (tooth-teeth) 186   Class 3
Irregular Nouns (mouse-mice) 188   Class 4 Irregular
Nouns (deer-deer) 189

13.5 *Possessive Nouns* 191
Singular Possessive Nouns 191   Regular Plural
Possessive Nouns 193   Irregular Plural Possessive
Nouns 194

Chapter 14 Verbs 196

14.1 *Introduction* 196

14.2 *Troubleshooting Verbs* 196

14.3 *Regular Verbs* 197
When to Add -s 197   When to Add -ed 200

14.4 *Variations on the Regular Pattern* 205
Class 1 Variants (teach-taught) 207   Class 2 Variants
(keep-kept) 210   Class 3 Variants (send-sent) 213
Class 4 Variants (feed-fed) 215   Class 5 Variants (find-found; swing-swung) 218   Class 6 Variants
(cut-cut) 220   Variants with No Pattern (say-said) 222

14.5 *Irregular Verbs* 225
Class 1 Irregulars (sing-sang-sung) 229   Class 2
Irregulars (drive-drove-driven) 231   Class 3 Irregulars
(choose-chose-chosen) 234   Class 4 Irregulars (wear-

wore-worn) *238*   *Class 5 Irregulars (know-knew-known) 240   Irregular Verbs with No Pattern (go-went-gone) 243*

14.6   *Verb Terminology*   245
Definition 245   Categories 246   Principal Parts of the Verb 247   Auxiliary Verbs 250

Chapter 15   Pronouns   255

15.1   *Introduction*   255

15.2   *Personal Pronouns*   255
Pronoun Reference 255   Pronoun Shifting 257   Pronoun Function 261

15.3   *Reflexive Pronouns*   267

Chapter 16   Adjectives and Adverbs   272

16.1   *Introduction*   272

16.2   *Adjectives*   272
Comparatives and Superlatives 273   Count and Mass Nouns 276

16.3   *Adverbs*   278

16.4   *Intensifiers and Qualifiers*   283

Chapter 17   Homonyms and Near-Homonyms   285

17.1   *Introduction*   285

17.2   *The Most Troublesome Homonyms*   286

17.3   *More Homonyms*   291

17.4   *Common Near-Homonyms*   303

17.5   *More Near-Homonyms*   310

UNIT IV
WRITING CONVENTIONS

Chapter 18 Punctuation 321

- 18.1 *Introduction* 321
- 18.2 *Signaling Full Stops* 322
  Period 322   Question Mark 322   Exclamation Mark 323   Colon 323   Semicolon 324
- 18.3 *Using Commas* 326
  Using Commas to Separate Simple Elements 327   Using Commas in Pairs and in Series 329   Using Commas After Introductory Elements 331   Using Commas to Separate Nonrestrictive Elements 334
- 18.4 *Using Other Punctuation Marks* 337
  Apostrophe 337   Hyphen 338   Dash 339   Parentheses 339   Underline 340   Quotation Marks 340
- 18.5 *Review on Punctuation* 341

Chapter 19 Capitalization 343

- 19.1 *Introduction* 343
- 19.2 *Rules of Capitalization* 343
- 19.3 *Review on Capitalization* 346

Chapter 20 Spelling Basics 349

- 20.1 *Introduction* 349
- 20.2 *Phonetic Spelling* 350
- 20.3 *College-Related Words Often Misspelled* 352
- 20.4 *Common Words Often Misspelled* 353
- 20.5 *Spelling Rules* 354
  Rule 1. ie and ei 355   Rule 2. Adding Prefixes Without Change 356   Rule 3. Adding Suffixes Without Change 356   Rule 4. Doubling Final Consonants

Before Suffixes 357   Rule 5. Changing y *to* i *Before Suffixes 358   Rule 6. Dropping Final* e *Before Suffixes 358*

20.6   Review on Spelling Basics   360

Word Index   **364**

Subject Index   **367**

UNIT 1

Writing Essays

MANY writers accept without question an unrealistic view of writers and writing ability. According to this view, there are "good" writers and "bad" writers, and this division is preordained and unchangeable: good writers are born good writers and they always write well; bad writers are born bad writers and they always write badly.

In truth, people labeled "good" writers are capable of producing very bad writing, and people regarded as "bad" writers are often capable of good writing—if they make the effort. Often their written product is not good because their writing process is flawed. The best and surest way for writers to improve their writing is to improve their writing process.

Chapter 1 of this unit, "Writers and the Writing Process," provides examples of student writing in various stages of that process. Chapter 2, "Writing Description"; Chapter 3, "Writing Process"; Chapter 4, "Writing Comparison-Contrast"; and Chapter 5, "Writing Persuasion" discuss commonly used types of writing and include more samples of student writing in process. Chapter 6, "Writing Summaries," presents examples of in-class student writing; and Chapter 7, "Readings for Writing," provides several short essays for reading, discussion, summarizing, and other writing assignments.

CHAPTER 1
Writers and the Writing Process

1.1 INTRODUCTION

Writing is a necessity for most college students, but many of them—perhaps the majority—feel uncomfortable about their writing. Often they tell their teachers, particularly their English teachers, "I hate writing papers" or "I'm a terrible writer." Implicit in these statements is the assumption that there is nothing that can be done about the situation—they will always hate writing and they will always be terrible writers. Unfortunately, such statements can become self-fulfilling prophecies. That is, writers who think of themselves as "terrible writers" and who "hate writing" probably will continue to be terrible writers and to hate writing.

To be an effective writer, you need an understanding of the writing process in general and of your own writing process in particular. Once you gain this understanding, you can then revise your writing process, improving it for a more effective writing product.

1.2 STAGES OF THE WRITING PROCESS

There are four major stages in the writing process:

Invention
Organization
Generation of Text
Revision

Most writers are familiar with Organization and Generation of Text, but they may be less aware of Invention and Revision, two stages that are essential in the improvement of the writing process and the written product.

Invention

Invention occurs primarily between the time you are given a writing task and the time you sit down to generate text. "Invention" may be considered another word for thinking. "Discovery" is yet another word for this stage of the writing process, since writing may be a verbal record of exploration, recognition, and realization.

Invention should begin as soon as you are given a writing assignment. Do not wait until the evening before the assignment is due to begin thinking about your paper. If, for example, the paper is assigned on Monday, but you will have no opportunity to generate text until the following weekend, you still have four or five days and nights when both your conscious and your unconscious mind can be working at Invention.

One advantage of Invention is that it can take place at any time—while you are walking to class, driving to the grocery store, taking a shower, eating lunch, or watching television. It can even take place while you are asleep.

Friends and family who are willing to listen as you think aloud about your writing can be very helpful during the Invention stage; an encouraging but somewhat critical audience is the best kind. If family members and friends are not helpful during the Invention stage, try the tutorial services available at your school. If your first tutored experience is not productive, ask specifically for a tutor who has worked with students with writing problems. Some tutors are better at Invention than others.

Organization

Organization occurs when writers attempt to order, or structure, their writing, determining what will come first, second, and so forth. An outline is a form of Organization.

Generation of Text

Generation of Text refers to the act of sitting down with pen and paper, typewriter, or computer and producing text. When someone says, "I have to write a paper tonight," that person is usually referring to the production of text.

Revision

Like Invention, **Revision** should play a major role in the writing process. Revision means a great deal more than simply writing a clean copy of a messy draft. The word Revision literally means "to see again." There are three substeps in the Revision stage: rewriting, editing, and proofreading.

1. **Rewriting** is the writer's response to the "seeing again" that should take place during Revision. It includes developing more completely ideas that may have been sketchily drawn in only a sentence or two in the first draft.

Cutting may be necessary if some ideas cannot be developed adequately or if others are not appropriate to the focus of the paper. Cutting is probably one of the most painful tasks for any writer; excising your own words is the psychological equivalent of taking a scalpel and performing surgery on yourself—without anaesthetic. Nevertheless, learning how and when to cut is an important part of improving your writing.

Restructuring, arranging ideas in the most effective order, may also be necessary. Often writers record their ideas in backward order, beginning with the most important and then listing other, less important, points as they come to mind. The result is a paper that starts strong and then diminishes. In this case, you need to reorder your paper, and usually the change in order will require other internal changes.

Reworking the introduction and conclusion may be required. After rewriting the body of the paper, you will probably need to rewrite your introduction and conclusion so they seem appropriate to the rewritten draft of the paper. You must introduce and conclude the paper you have written—not the paper you **intended** to write or the paper you **think** you have written, but the paper you **have written**.

2. After you have rewritten your paper, you need to edit it. **Editing** requires looking critically at sentence structure and word choice. Reading your paper aloud or having someone read it to you can be helpful at this stage. You might also dictate the paper into a tape recorder and then play it back, listening to what you have written to help distance yourself from your text.

3. **Proofreading** for spelling, punctuation, capitalization and other minor errors is the final stage in Revision. You should make handwritten corrections on the rough draft, so that you can concentrate completely when you produce the final draft. After the final draft is produced, set it aside for as long as possible; then proofread it for copying errors and other mistakes you might have overlooked earlier.

Overlapping Stages of the Writing Process

Any discussion of the writing process must inevitably make it seem more orderly than, in fact, it is, since stages of the process frequently overlap. Invention, for example, may take place at any stage of the writing process, as you discover a new idea or a new angle on an old idea. Organization may also take place throughout the process. As you invent, you structure your ideas, often without realizing it. You may also organize and reorganize during Generation of Text and Revision. Generation of Text may take place simultaneously with Organization and when you add new text during Revision.

Revision, the final stage, may actually take place fairly early on, as you reject some ideas or methods of organization during Invention. Nevertheless, it is a good idea to delay substantial revision until later in the writing process. Writers who write the first sentence of their paper, and then rewrite it and rewrite it, trying to make it perfect before they go to the next sentence, usually find writing frustrating and unproductive.

1.3 THROUGHOUT THE WRITING PROCESS

Throughout the writing process, you need to concern yourself with defining and refining your subject and thesis, your audience, and your purpose.

Subject and Thesis

The **subject** is what you plan to write about. For example, if you decided to write a paper about soap operas, "Television Soap Operas" could be your working title, but you would need to narrow your topic and focus on a specific aspect of television soap operas. Otherwise, you would be writing a book—not a paper.

In the process of narrowing your topic, you would establish the **thesis:** a sentence or two explicitly stating the direction of your paper, your "angle" on television soap operas. To come to this point, however, you will need to probe your attitudes toward soap operas. Following are some statements about soap operas that you may or may not agree with.

1. Soap operas are a waste of time.
2. Soap operas portray life in an unrealistic way.
3. Soap operas offer a heightened reflection of life.
4. Soap operas show people how to deal with problems in personal relationships.
5. Soap operas sell soap.
6. Anyone who watches soap operas is an idiot.
7. Some highly intelligent and successful people are soap opera fans.
8. No matter how bad soap operas are, at least they are better than game shows.

Topics 2 and 3 are probably the most workable for most writers. Since they offer two opposite views of soap operas, writers choosing Topic 2 would develop it one way, and writers choosing Topic 3 would develop it another. For example, to develop Topic 2, numerous examples of the unrealistic nature of soap operas need to be given, and soap operas should be contrasted with the reality of everyday life. To develop Topic 3, examples of realistic situations should be related to similar situations in everyday life.

As you develop your topic, working through the stages of the writing process, you continue to define and refine your subject and thesis. The final written product of your writing process may be a somewhat different paper with a somewhat different thesis than you originally planned.

Audience

Throughout the writing process, you also need to define—and sometimes redefine—your **audience.** A clear sense of audience will help make your writing easier and more effective.

Your audience may be one person or a group of persons. When you are writing a letter, your audience is usually one person, whom you might or might not know. When you write a personal letter to a friend or a family member, you know your audience, but when you write a business letter, often you do not know the person who will read your letter.

If your audience is a group, you need to consider its size and nature. For example, a letter to the editor of a newspaper is actually addressed to the general reading audience. Such an audience includes both men and women and all age groups except children. It also includes people of all educational levels except the illiterate. If the newspaper is published in a large city, its audience will ordinarily include members of a variety of religious and ethnic groups who hold a wide range of political views. If the newspaper is published in a small town, its audience will probably be less varied, particularly with respect to religious and ethnic groups. A range of political views may still be expected, but they may tend to be more conservative in one part of the country, more liberal in another.

If your audience is more specialized, you need to consider the general characteristics of the group in addition to possible variables. For example, if you are writing a letter to the editor of your campus newspaper, then your primary audience is students attending your school, but faculty and staff also read campus newspapers. In addition, the college student audience may vary greatly from one type of institution to another. For instance, if your college is a residential-type school, most students are probably in their late teens or early twenties, and many of them live in dormitories. Relatively few are married, and even fewer have children. Some may own cars, but virtually none own houses. Most of them are full-time students; some of them may have part-time jobs on campus or in local businesses. Very few vote in local elections. In contrast, the college student audience at a commuter-type school will ordinarily be much more varied. The age of students may range from those just graduated from high school to those recently retired. Most students live off campus, commuting to and from school. Many work full-time and attend school on a part-time basis. Many are married and many have children. They are more likely to own cars and houses and to vote in local elections. All of these factors and others not mentioned would affect a letter written to the editor of a campus newspaper.

Purpose

In addition to determining your audience, you also need to determine your **purpose.** The purpose of your writing might be to express feelings and to share experiences, or it might be to inform or to persuade. For example, if you are writing a letter to a personal friend or a family member, your purpose may be to share recent experiences. Even in personal letters about the same experiences, however, your purpose might be different according to your audience. A story about a prank of some kind might be exaggerated somewhat to a friend and diminished to a parent.

Much of the writing that college students and professionals do is informative in nature, but some college writing tasks are not truly informative. For example, when you write an explanation of photosynthesis on an exam in botany, you are demonstrating your mastery of information rather than conveying it to your botany professor, who already knows about photosynthesis. On the other hand, a review of a movie that a teacher has not seen would be truly informative, as would a paper surveying college student attitudes about some campus issue.

Another common purpose is persuasion. When you write a letter to an editor expressing your views on some matter, you may be attempting to persuade others to adopt your views. A letter of application is also persuasive in nature.

1.4 VARIATIONS IN THE WRITING PROCESS

The writing process varies among individual writers. Following are three student papers that illustrate some differences in the writing process. A commentary about the student's writing process is given after each draft.

Patricia's Writing Process

The first writer, Patricia, does a great deal of thinking in advance. When she writes, she has already determined fairly precisely how she is going to say what she wants to say. Although her first draft is her first **written** work, she has devoted considerable time and thought to her writing before committing anything to paper.

Patricia's writing process is often highly successful; however, she has a difficult time when more substantial revision is needed. Once she has committed words to paper, she finds it hard to think of any other way to approach her writing task.

PATRICIA'S IMITATION OF JAMES JOYCE'S DESCRIPTION OF A THANKSGIVING TABLE

Patricia's First Draft

In the center of the table stood two, tall, milk-white candle holders, topped with cherry-red candles, flickering with small orange-blue flames. To the right a large side of rare roast-beef, on a bed of thin sliced mushrooms, lay glistening from the beef-juices, oil, and soft glow of candle light. Beside this was a very deep, circular, clear, brown glass bowl, filled to the rim with pale-green lettuce, bright red tomatoes, and small yellow chunks of colby cheese with the strong aroma of garlic and vinager drifting from it all. To the left of the candles was an enormous oval platter, upon which lay small white potatoes, thick crinkle-cut slices of carrot, and tiny translucent peral onions with touches of parsley scattered through out. Next to this stood a basket, woven out of pale-brown straw, in which lay eight flakey, golden-brown cresent rolls with the faint smell of butter coming from them.

COMMENTARY ON PATRICIA'S FIRST DRAFT

Patricia's first draft is a good imitation of the passage by James Joyce (see Chapter 2 for the original essay). She has problems with spelling and a tendency to use commas excessively, so she needs to proofread her papers carefully. In this draft, she also has some instances of vague pronoun reference, using the word *this* when she needs to be more precise as to what *this* refers.

Patricia's Final Draft

In the center of the table stood two tall milk-white candle holders topped with cherry-red candles, flickering with small orange-blue flames. To the right a large side of rare roast-beef on a bed of thin-sliced mushrooms lay glistening from the beef juices, oil, and soft glow of candle light. Beside this was a very deep circular clear brown glass bowl, filled to the rim with pale-green lettuce, bright red tomatoes, and small yellow chunks of colby cheese with a strong aroma of garlic and vinegar drifting from it all. To the left of the candles was an enormous oval platter, upon which lay small white potatoes, thick crinkle-cut slices of carrot, and tiny translucent pearl onions with touches of parsley scattered throughout. Next to this stood a basket woven out of pale-brown straw, in which lay eight flakey, golden-brown crescent rolls with the faint smell of butter coming from them.

COMMENTARY ON PATRICIA'S FINAL DRAFT

Patricia corrects her errors in spelling and punctuation in her final draft, but she does not revise her vague pronoun use.

Robert's Writing Process

Like Patricia, Robert too expends considerable time and effort before he generates text; however, his first draft is rather uneven, with some parts needing very little further revision while other sections need considerable rework in order for the paper to be a consistent piece of writing.

ROBERT'S DESCRIPTION OF A PICTURE OF HIS BABY SON

Robert's First Draft

A baby, almost twenty six inches long, is sitting on a fluffy, light blue blanket with bunches of tiny white flowers. His hair, sandy blonde with a tint of red to it, is baby fine and lies in a smooth cap close against his head. The deep blue color of his eyes reflects the camera's flash. Those eyes are ringed with long feather soft lashes that are almost too light to see. His perfect round ears are snuggled close to his head and his brow is creased as if listening to his father's voice. The joyful smile on his lips is a testament to the love he feels for that voice. A rosy glow radiates from his pale delicate skin.

His chubby double chin is tucked down onto the bib of his striped overalls as he posses for the camera. The overalls, with their baseball and bat are a visible sign of his father's dreams for his new son's future. He rests his right hand on his knee and his left hand sits casually on his stomach. His left leg appears to be frozen in mid-kick. His little baby feet are wrapped in miniature athletic socks, and they are covered with baby-size sneakers.

From the top of his head to the tips of his tiny tennis-shoed feet, the baby radiates a love for all that is good in his world. He is safe in the knowledge that his father returns his love.

COMMENTARY ON ROBERT'S FIRST DRAFT

Robert's first paragraph, in which he describes the physical characteristics of his son, is well developed and clearly written, but the second paragraph is sketchy. He needs to describe the clothing more accurately, specifically giving color information.

Robert's Final Draft

Two foot two with eyes of blue, the chubby cherub of a babe, happily reclining on a fluffy light-blue blanket that is covered with bunches of tiny white flowers, surveys his newly conquered subjects. Sandy blonde hair tinged with red lies like a smooth-fitting cap, and the tiny shell-like ears snuggle to his head and peek through the strands of silky fine hair. Reflected in the deep blue color of his eyes is the camera's flash; the eyes--large, dark blue, and ringed with long, light-colored, feather-soft lashes that curl upward--command attention. While a rosy glow radiates from his pale, delicate skin, the joyful smile on his lips is a testament to the love, security, and contentment he feels when he hears his father's voice.

Emblazoned with red baseball and bat and the words "Lil' Rookie," the pint-size baseball uniform is a visible sign to the world of his father's dreams for his new son's future. Not only does he wear the blue and white pin-striped rompers and white shirt, but those tiny baby feet are wrapped in miniature white athletic socks and covered with baby-size blue and white sneakers. Casually he rests his left hand on his potbelly stomach, puts his right hand on his knee, pulls up the left leg as if in mid-stride, tucks his chubby double chin over the bib of his striped suit, and says to the world, "Look at me."

From the top of his oblong head to the tip of his tiny, tennis-shoed feet, the baby radiates a love for all that is good in his world. He is safe in the knowlege that his father returns his love.

COMMENTARY ON ROBERT'S FINAL DRAFT

Robert's final draft is much more evenly developed than the first draft. Unlike Patricia, he can respond to suggestions for revision. He too has a problem with spelling and punctuation, and he needs to proofread his paper more carefully for comma problems, specifically their overuse. Sometimes his word choice could be improved: *wrapped, covered,* and *oblong* do not seem to be the best choices in the context of his paper.

Arlene's Writing Process

With Patricia and Robert, it is somewhat difficult for us to see the early stages of their writing process, since they do not commit words to paper until they are fairly well along in the writing process, especially Patricia. It is also possible that they do some preliminary drafting that they never let anyone see. In contrast, Arlene records virtually every step of her writing process and in doing so enables us to see how a first draft, which is really a rather poor piece of writing, finally becomes a good written product.

Notice the changes Arlene makes at each stage. Her first draft is only two paragraphs long, with no introduction or conclusion. In her second draft, she develops a structure for her paper—an introductory paragraph, one paragraph in the body of the paper, and a concluding paragraph. In the third draft, Arlene refines the structure established in her second draft, and in her fourth and final draft, she polishes her style.

ARLENE'S DESCRIPTION OF A PICTURE OF AN ESKIMO

Arlene's First Draft

It looks cold as hell. That was the first thought that came to my mind when I saw this picture. The landscape is vast and barren and is composed entirely of ice and snow. There are numerous jagged crevices apparent on the ice. Aqua blue shadows appear on the ice, mostly in the area where a man is standing. The rest of the ice and snow is a stark white. Only a small piece of sky is visible, and it appears to be a vivid blue and white.

A man is standing patiently in the foreground of the picture. It is obviously bitterly cold and perhaps a sharp breeze is blowing as his hair looks disheveled. He wears a white parka with a black and brown furry hood hugging his face. His stark black hair sticks out from the hood of the parka, and he has deep wrinkles in his face, similar to the crevices in the ice. His black eyes are squinting against the glare of the bright sun on the ice. His face is deeply tanned, and he has a large flat nose and tightly compressed lips. He has no expression on his face. Only the upper half of his body is visible, dressed in the tight-fitting white parka.

COMMENTARY ON ARLENE'S FIRST DRAFT

Arlene provides some good descriptive detail, but she needs to add more. She also needs an introduction and a conclusion.

Arlene's Second Draft

I am going to describe in words a picture, to enable the reader to see the picture in their mind without actually viewing it. The landscape in this picture is vast, barren, and is composed entirely of ice and snow. There are numerous jagged crevices apparent on the surface of the ice, which is a stark, unyielding white. Only a small piece of sky is visible and it is appropriately a sky blue and white which blends with the snow.

A man standing patiently in the foreground of the picture casts aqua-blue shadows upon the ice, with only the upper half of his body visible. It is obviously bitterly cold, with a sharp wind blowing. He is wearing a tight-fitting snow white parka with a black and beige furry hood hugging his face, and stark black hair sticking out in the front of his face. His skin has the look of worn leather, deeply tanned, with deep wrinkles running vertically between his thick black eyebrows. He has black button eyes squinting against the glare of the bright sun on the ice, a large flat nose, and tightly compressed lips. More deep wrinkles are apparent on either side of his mouth.

The man is obviously in his own environment as he does not appear to feel the cold, and shows no emotion on his face. Looking at the man and then at the land, they seem as one because they have many similarities. One such similarity would be the crevices in the icy land and the wrinkles in the man's face. Or perhaps the worn look of the man and of the land.

COMMENTARY ON ARLENE'S SECOND DRAFT

Arlene's second draft shows considerable improvement. It is more well developed than the first draft, and she has added an introduction and a conclusion. Both the introduction and conclusion need revision, and she needs to edit for better sentence structure.

Arlene's Third Draft

The following paragraphs describe a picture selected from a magazine that caught my eye and should enable the reader to visualize the picture in their mind.

The landscape in this picture is vast and barren, composed entirely of ice and snow. There are numerous jagged crevices apparent on the surface of the ice, which is a stark, unyielding white. Only a small piece of sky is visible, and it is appropriately a sky blue and white which blends with the snow.

A man standing patiently in the foreground of this picture casts aqua-blue shadows upon the ice. It is obviously bitterly cold, with a sharp wind blowing. Only the upper half of his body is visible, showing the man wears a tight-fitting snow white parka with a black and beige furry hood hugging his face. His jet black hair emerges from the front of the hood and his skin has the look of worn leather, deeply tanned, with deep wrinkles running vertically between his thick black eyebrows. He has black button eyes squinting against the glare of the bright sun on the ice, a large flat nose, and tightly compressed lips. More deep wrinkles are apparent on either side of his mouth.

    I feel that this man is obviously in his own environment as he does not appear to feel the cold and shows no emotion on his face. The man and the land on which he is standing seem to fit together, they compliment each other. Therefore, I think you can understand why this picture caught and captured my attention.

COMMENTARY ON ARLENE'S THIRD DRAFT

Arlene continues to improve her description paper, but she still has problems with her introduction and conclusion. The conclusion seems rather weak; it needs another sentence or two. The introduction still is not effective.

Arlene's Final Draft

    I was flipping through the pages of a magazine, not really paying much attention to it, when I noticed a picture of an Eskimo man. For some inexplicable reason this picture captured my attention and held it for several minutes. Perhaps if I describe the picture you might understand what it was that made me look so intently.

    The landscape in this picture is vast and barren, composed entirely of ice and snow. There are numerous jagged crevices apparent on the surface of the stark white ice. Only a small portion of the bright blue sky is visible.

A man standing patiently in the foreground of the picture casts aqua-blue shadows upon the ice. It appears to be bitterly cold with a sharp wind blowing, but the man does not give you the impression that he feels the cold and the wind. Only the upper half of his body is visible, showing that the man wears a tight-fitting snow-white parka with a black and beige furry hood hugging his face. A shock of jet black hair juts out from the hood of the parka. His skin has the look of worn leather, deeply tanned, with deep wrinkles running vertically between his thick black eyebrows. This man has black eyes with an Asian cast, squinting against the glare of the bright sun on the ice, a large flat nose which protrudes from his face, and tightly compressed lips. More deep vertical wrinkles are visible on either side of his mouth. His parka-clad arms are bent and appear to be thrust into his pockets.

The fact that this man is obviously in his own environment was the reason this picture caught and captured my attention. The man's features and manner of dress are suited for the harsh surroundings in which he lives. He has adapted to fit the land on which he lives.

COMMENTARY ON ARLENE'S FINAL DRAFT

Arlene finally solves her introduction problem in a very simple way; she straightforwardly tells the reader **how** she happened to choose this picture to describe. This approach also enables her to strengthen her conclusion because she explains there **why** this particular picture caught her eye.

Is Arlene a good writer or a bad writer? Anyone reading only the first draft would probably label her a "bad writer." On the other hand, a reader who had read only the final draft would probably call her a "good writer." The two drafts represent stages of Arlene's writing process, one that requires considerable time and effort on her part, in addition to determination and patience. As the final draft shows, hers is an **effective** writing process capable of generating a good written product.

CHAPTER 2
Writing Description

2.1 INTRODUCTION

Description is primarily sensory in nature; when writers describe, they use the language of the senses—sight, hearing, touch, smell, and taste. The following passage written by James Joyce is a good example of descriptive writing. Titled "The Thanksgiving Table," it is a paragraph taken from a longer work.

THE THANKSGIVING TABLE

A fat brown goose lay at one end of the table and at the other end, on a bed of creased paper strewn with sprigs of parsley, lay a great ham, stripped of its outer skin and peppered over with crust crumbs, a neat paper frill round its shin and beside this was a round of spiced beef. Between these rival ends ran parallel lines of side dishes: two little minsters of jelly, red and yellow, a shallow dish full of blocks of blancmange and red jam, a large green leaf-shaped dish with a stalk-shaped handle, on which lay bunches of purple raisins and peeled almonds, a companion dish on which lay a solid rectangle of Smyrna figs, a dish of custard topped with grated nutmeg, a small bowl of chocolates and sweets wrapped in gold and silver papers and a glass vase in which stood some tall celery stalks. In the centre of the table there stood, as sentries to a fruit stand which upheld a pyramid of oranges and American apples, two squat old-fashioned decanters of cut glass, one containing port and the other dark sherry.

JAMES JOYCE, "THE DEAD"

A good description is filled with specific details, and Joyce provides a variety of kinds of such details in his description: color, shape and size, taste, and touch or texture. He also uses phrases of location and figures of speech.

Unlike Joyce, some writers have difficulty providing sufficient details when they write description—and in other kinds of writing too; their writing lacks **development.** A writer with this problem might have described Joyce's Thanksgiving table as follows:

> The table looked wonderful. It was filled with food. There were all different kinds of food on the table. It was really nice. The food looked really good, but there was so much of it. Everyone commented about how pretty everything looked.

Writers who do this sort of thing do not really develop their ideas; instead they make a generalization—a judgment—about the attractiveness of the table and the amount of food on it, and then they repeat the generalization in as many ways as they can. Notice how vague and repetitious this kind of writing is.

> The table looked wonderful....
> It was really nice....
> Everyone commented about how pretty everything looked....
>
> It was filled with food....
> There were all different kinds of food on the table....
> The food looked really good, but there was so much of it....

It is true that Joyce was a professional literary man, but Patricia, in her imitation of Joyce's passage, also provided the writer with many specific descriptive details. (See Chapter 1 for Patricia's imitation.)

 ORGANIZING DESCRIPTION

In addition to providing a wealth of details in his passage describing the Thanksgiving table, Joyce also orders those details carefully. He is describing a rectangular horizontal surface, and he chooses to begin at the ends of the table and to work systematically toward the center.

A similar scene with a small circular table would require a different organizational pattern, perhaps clockwise or counterclockwise. The description might begin at the outside of the table and proceed clockwise or counterclockwise toward the center, or the description might begin at the center and then proceed outward.

Following are some methods of organizing description. When writing description, you must choose the best approach; you should not simply provide random details in no particular order.

clockwise	counterclockwise
inside to outside	outside to inside
left to right	right to left
top to bottom	bottom to top
foreground to background	background to foreground

2.3 STUDENT DESCRIPTION PAPER

Kimberly's Description Paper

Kimberly's description paper is a good example of the problems that writers encounter when they write description. Her first draft is only two short paragraphs, lacking in accurate details, and not well organized. In her second draft, she demonstrates that she has a good sense of color, but she does not describe location well. In her third draft, she establishes a method of organization, foreground to background. Her final draft refines the third draft.

Kimberly's First Draft

Image that you are sight seeing in the mountains while all the Aspen tree's leaves are a beautiful lemon color. The air is cool and refreshing on your face as the light breeze russles through the trees. Down below in a valley between the mountains flows a deep blue river.

Looking far across the smooth ice cold water stands towering dark evergreen trees. The rough terrain that lies on the stretching mountains ahead eventually fades out into the ice blue sky where the birds fly free.

COMMENTARY ON KIMBERLY'S FIRST DRAFT

Kimberly provides some good detail in her first draft, but she needs much more. She demonstrates a precise sense of color, specifying that the leaves are *"lemon" yellow* rather than just *yellow* and that the river is *"deep" blue* rather than just *blue*, but she gives little spatial information—that is, information that tells **where** something is in relation to something else. She needs to add more detail, particularly about spatial relationships. She also needs to avoid relying on the vague pronoun *you* and focus on what the scene actually shows rather than what someone might feel when looking at the scene.

Kimberly's Second Draft

The beauty of the earth is shown here with the Aspen trees blending in with the blue pool of water. The rocky shoreline starts the beginning of acres of evergreen trees. Skattered homes lie within the evergreens as the roof tops are very faint. As the stretching mountains continue they begin to fade away to meet the sky.

Lofty Aspen trees hold their branches with dangling lemon yellow leaves. The contrast of the brown branches and yellow leaves shines bright with the blue water lying behind them. The deep blue lake sparkles in the sunlight with ripples going across to the other side. Rocks and sticks among other things border the shoreline. Cabins and houses are scarcely skattered throughout the towering dark evergreen trees. Beyond this point are stretching mountains with a very rough terrain. Various colors such as the yellow Aspen trees, faint evergreens, and the chocolate brown texture of the facing side of the mountain are hazey. The mountain tops are both smooth and hilly and rigid edged. As they begin to fade out there begins another lake that feeds into the river. The ice blue sky adds the finishing touch by outlining the mountains.

As a overall view of the picture a valley between two mountains is very beautifully ornate part of the earth.

COMMENTARY ON KIMBERLY'S SECOND DRAFT

Kimberly's second draft shows considerable improvement over her first draft. She provides more detailed information, but spatial relationships are still not clear. The organization of her paper also needs improvement, since it seems to jump back and forth rather than moving through the scene in an orderly, coherent manner. Providing an introduction and revising her rather confusing conclusion would also strengthen her organization. Kimberly's word choice is sometimes unprecise to the point that it creates confusion (for example, the words *stretching, begins,* and *beautifully ornate*). She needs to employ more precise language.

Kimberly's Third Draft

The elegant mountain lake scene shows its beauty during the fall season. Aspen trees stand out against a background of deep blue water. Across the lake, a rocky shoreline borders acres of towering evergreen trees. Beyond the evergreens lies two mountain ranges which complete the scene.

Lofty Aspen trees hold their thin branches with dangling lemon yellow leaves. The brown branches are very long and thin with much space between them. Little round leaves of the Aspen trees are what gives them their color and beauty. Beyond the bright yellow trees is a deep blue lake. In the sunlight, sparkles shine from the water where ripples are seen sliding to the far side of the lake.

Rocks, sticks, and green brush border the shoreline at the far side of the lake. Directly behind the brush begin thickets of tall evergreen trees. Unlike the Aspen trees, the evergreens are built quite compact. The bottom branches are fairly long and grow more narrow toward the top ending with a point. Evergreens have needles instead of leaves; therefore, the closeness of them gives the trees a solid deep color. Rooftops of sparseley scattered cabins are seen peeking out through the evergreens.

Beyond the evergreens at the base of the mountain, various colors show through the hazey moist atmosphere. The bright yellow of the Aspen trees, the rich green of the evergreens, and the soft browns of the rocky plauteaus blend in harmony. As the mountain comes to a peek, the terrain becomes rough and the evergreens scarce.

Beyond this mountain range a second majestic range stands guard in dusty blue splendor. Another valley lies within these mountains, cradeling yet another lake far in the distance. The ice blue sky outlines the craggy summit of the mountain top very definitely, showing every soft curve and jagged edge.

This mountainous scene creates a peaceful view of nature's calm. From the spirited aspens close at hand, across the placid lake to the far shore, moving through the evergreens and up the slopes of the restful mountains, the eye follows visions of glory into the depth of the endless sky.

COMMENTARY ON KIMBERLY'S THIRD DRAFT

Kimberly has improved her content and organization greatly. Now she needs to focus on sentence structure and word choice. She should combine some of her short, choppy sentences and work still more on appropriate word choice. Her conclusion has a nice sweeping rhythm to it, but words such as *spirited, restful,* and *glory* are not appropriate to the context. She also misspells several words.

Kimberly's Final Draft

The elegant mountain lake scene shows its beauty during the fall season. Aspen trees stand out against a background of deep blue water and across the lake, a rocky shoreline borders acres of towering evergreen trees. Behind the evergreens lie two mountain ranges which complete the scene.

In the foreground, lofty aspen trees hold their thin branches with dangling lemon yellow leaves. The brown branches are very long and thin with much space between them, but the little round yellow leaves give them their color and beauty. Beyond the bright yellow trees is a deep blue lake whose ripples sparkle in the sunlight as they slide to the far side of the lake.

Rocks, sticks, and green brush border the shoreline at the far side of the lake. Directly behind the brush begin thickets of tall evergreen trees. Unlike the Aspen trees, the evergreens are built quite compact; bottom branches are fairly long and grow more narrow toward the top, ending with a point. Since evergreens have needles instead of leaves, the thickness of the needles gives the trees a solid deep green color. Rooftops of sparsely scattered cabins can be seen peeking out through the evergreens.

Beyond the evergreens at the base of the mountain, various colors show through the hazy moist atmosphere. The bright yellow of more aspen trees, the rich green of the evergreens, and the soft browns of the rocky plateaus blend in harmony. As the mountain comes to a peek, the terrain becomes rough and the evergreens scarce.

Behind this mountain range a second majestic range stands guard in dusty blue splendor. Another valley lies within these mountains, cradling yet another lake far in the distance. The ice blue sky outlines the craggy summit of the mountain top very definitely, showing every soft curve and jagged edge.

This mountainous scene creates a peaceful view of nature's calm. From the whispering aspens close at hand, across the placid lake to the far shore, moving through the evergreens and up the slopes of the peaceful mountains, the eye follows visions of grandeur into the depth of the endless sky.

COMMENTARY ON KIMBERLY'S FINAL DRAFT

No paper is ever perfect, but Kimberly's final draft is certainly ready to be submitted for evaluation. *Quite compact* should be *quite compactly* and she has misspelled mountain *peak* as "peek."

DESCRIPTION ACTIVITIES

1. Re-read the Joyce passage at the beginning of this chapter more carefully. Put a *C* above all words or phrases which suggest color, *S-S* for shape and size, *T* for taste, and *T-T* for touch or texture. Put an *L* above phrases of location and an *F* above figures of speech. Then list them as follows: color, shape and size, taste, touch or texture, phrases of location, figures of speech. Some words or phrases might be listed twice.

2. Write an imitation of Joyce's passage. You might choose to describe your own kitchen or dining room table covered with food, or perhaps a buffet table at a reception or a wedding. Other choices would be a table in a nice restaurant, in a cafeteria, or in a fast-food restaurant. The scene need not be attractive. Sometimes the unattractive is more interesting and easier to describe than the attractive.

3. Describe a scene similar to the one described by Joyce: a flat surface covered with objects. Some possible topics would be a cluttered desk; a coffee table covered with ornaments, magazines, and newspapers; a shelf holding a collection of china, figurines, dolls, or trophies; or the top of a dresser or a chest of drawers with ornaments and/or grooming items neatly arranged or haphazardly disorganized. Again, the scene need not be attractive; an untidy surface with items scattered about haphazardly may be more interesting and easier to describe than a neat and orderly one.

4. Describe a picture. Choose something neither too complicated nor too simple. Make a list like the one you made for Joyce's passage. List as many details as you can; then ask your classmates and friends to look at the same picture, pointing out details you may have missed.

SUGGESTIONS FOR WRITING DESCRIPTION SUCCESSFULLY

1. Choose a subject that can be described adequately in a few hundred words. You cannot really describe a country or a state or even a city adequately in a short paper, but you could describe a garden or a room in a house.

2. Make a list of details.

3. Use precise language.

4. Choose an appropriate method of organization.

DESCRIPTION ASSIGNMENTS

1. Write a letter to your best friend or a member of your family in which you describe some place currently important in your life that this person has not seen. For example, you might describe your dorm room to your best friend from high school who is attending another college and has never visited your campus. Your purpose is to share your experience.

2. Your family (or a group of friends) recently held a social occasion (for example, a wedding or an anniversary party) and a favorite relative or close friend was unable to attend because he or she was in the hospital (or out of town or in the military). Write a letter describing the occasion, specifically the setting. Include as much sensory detail as you can. Your purpose is to share your experience.

3. Your campus newspaper runs a column called "Campus Gourmet," in which guest columnists write reviews of local restaurants. Write a review of a restaurant you visited recently, including as much sensory detail as possible. Your purpose is to inform, but you are also recommending the restaurant as a place to visit or one to avoid. Your audience is primarily students at your school. Consider your knowledge of that audience as you are writing your review.

4. Your local campus newspaper runs a column called "Campus Sites," describing various locations and scenes on campus, especially those not open to everyone. Write a description of such a

place; possible topics might be the athletes' dressing room, the food preparation area in the cafeteria, the room in the library where overdue books are processed. Another possibility would be a site often overlooked or ignored; for example, a quiet corner behind the library or a small lounge area on the top floor of the administration building. Your purpose is to inform.

5. Develop your own assignment along the lines of those suggested previously. Define your audience and your purpose.

CHAPTER 3
Writing Process

3.1 INTRODUCTION

Process deals with **how**, and examples of process thinking and writing surround us. When one person gives another directions on how to get from Place A to Place B, process is exemplified. If the person being directed gets lost, the instructions may have been faulty or they may not have been followed properly.

Science textbooks are filled with process explanations—**how** electricity works, **how** volcanoes are created, **how** the circulatory system operates, **how** photosynthesis works. The media brings us news that scientists have discovered a new process dealing with superconductivity, or that a theory concerning continent formation has been revised, or that there is a new understanding of how hurricanes or tornadoes are created. We are also informed of how plane crashes, car wrecks, or other accidents occur. During presidential elections, we are reminded of how the electoral college works.

Another common type of process is the instruction. Recipes and "do-it-yourself" procedures are process instructions. So are technical manuals that explain how to overhaul airplane engines. Anything that is manufactured has an instruction, or series of instructions, that must be followed during the manufacturing process. If it has to be maintained in any way—disassembled, cleaned, repaired, painted, reassembled—then another series of instructions exists. Such instructions may be very brief, or they may require hundreds, even thousands, of pages.

3.2 ORGANIZING PROCESS

Most process instructions generally follow an outline similar to the one shown here:

PROCESS INSTRUCTION OUTLINE
- **I.** Introduction
  - **A.** Identification of the process
  - **B.** Reasons for doing this process
- **II.** Equipment and materials needed to complete the process
- **III.** The stages of the process
  - **A.** The first stage of the process
    - Step 1
    - Step 2
    - Step 3 . . .
  - **B.** The second stage of the process
    - Step 1
    - Step 2
    - Step 3 . . .
  - **C.** The third stage of the process
    - Step 1
    - Step 2
    - Step 3 . . .
- **IV.** Conclusion
  Rewards of the process; what the reader has after completing the process

 STUDENT PROCESS PAPER

Richard's Process Paper

Richard writes a process paper about making chile rellenos, a popular Mexican dish. He begins with a combination outline/first draft; in his second draft, he develops what was merely outlined in his outline/first draft. In his third and final draft, he refines his essay. Although Richard submits his third draft for evaluation, he really needs to write at least one more draft, since the third draft still shows a number of weaknesses.

Richard's Outline/First Draft

```
            The making of Chile Rellenos
Equipment. Frying pan, bowls, spatula, electric
mixer, can opener, tongs, cutting board, knife,
serving tray, spoon, blender, plate, stove
```

Supplies. Eggs (1 doz.), chiles (1 can), cheese or meat (1 Sq cheese or 1/2 lb meat), flour, salt, pepper, cinnamon, sugar, whole peeled tomatoes (1 can), lard, parsley,

Steps - Take the canopener and begin by opening the can of whole green chiles. Carefully lay the chiles on a plate being careful not to break them. There should be approximately twenty chiles per can. Now take the block of cheese, and slice it into 1" x 2" strips using a knife. Take these pieces and gently stuff the whole chiles. When you finish with this first part, place the stuffed chiles aside on a plate.

Next get a large deep bowl and a smaller one also. Take the dozen eggs and break them in half placing the yolks in the smaller bowl and the whites in the larger one. Using the electric mixer beat the whites alone for approximately ten minutes or until you can turn the bowl upside down and have the whipped whites cling to the bowl. Now add the yolks to the fluffy mixture and beat it so as to mix the two together.

Taking a plate, place about 1/4 to 1/2 cup of flour on it and then take the stuffed chiles and roll them in the flour until fully covered. At this time you want to begin to get about a cup of lard to heat up in the frying pan. You also want to get the serving plate ready so you can put the finished chiles in it.

When the lard is hot enough, begin to dip a single chile in the batter and place it in the frying pan. Do this to as many chiles as will fit into the pan. Continue to cook the rest of them and when lightly browned on both sides take them out and put them on the serving plate.

When you are done, take and open the can of whole peeled tomatoes. Pour them in the blender and then begin to add about 1/2 tablespoon of salt, a sprinkle of cinnamon, four tablespoons of sugar, and a dash of pepper to the tomatoes. You then blend the sauce until it is liquified thoroughly. Finally, take this mixture and and pour it in a saucepan and heat it up to a simmer. The meal can now be served by Placing the chiles on a dinner plate with some tomato sauce spooned over the top.

COMMENTARY ON RICHARD'S OUTLINE/FIRST DRAFT

Richard has chosen an appropriate topic for a process paper. He begins his writing process with a mixture of an outline and a first draft. He lists the equipment and supplies needed in outline form, but he presents the steps in paragraph form. Richard needs to use paragraph form throughout his essay, but his approach is appropriate at this early stage of the writing process.

Richard's Second Draft

Chile Rellenos

Making Chile Rellenos can be much easier than most people suppose. To prepare this common Mexican dish, you will need a can of whole green chiles which have already been cleaned of the stem and the seeds which are inside the chile. Each can includes approximately twenty chiles. A dozen eggs, one block of whichever cheese you prefer, one can of whole peeled tomatoes, about a half cup of flour, a cup of lard, salt and pepper, one-quarter cup of sugar, and last but not least a teaspoon of cinnamon.

You begin by taking a can opener and opening the can of whole green chiles. Once opened, take the chiles out and place them on a plate carefully separating them. Make sure not to tear them as they have a small pocket inside of them which has been made by removing the stem. Now take the block of cheese and using a small knife cut the cheese into one-inch by two-inch strips. After you finished cutting the cheese take the strips and begin to stuff them into the pocket in the chile. Again, be careful not to tear the chile when you stuff it. Organize the chiles on a plate and set them aside.

Next, take the dozen eggs and a large deep bowl and break the eggs in half separating the whites into the bowl and the yolks into a medium size cup. Using an electric mixer, beat the egg whites for about ten minutes or until they are so fluffy that they stick to the bowl like jello when you turn it over. When you get this result, add the egg yolks and mix them into the mixture. Set the bowl next to the chiles.

Place a half cup of flour on a plate and take

the stuffed chiles and roll them in the flour so as to coat them entirely with it. Again, organize the coated chiles on the place.

At this time you want to get a cup of lard and begin heating it up at medium heat in a large frying pan. Meanwhile, get two large serving plates ready so you have somewhere to put the fried chiles when they are done. Also, organize the plate of stuffed flour-covered chiles next to the bowl of whipped eggs so as to make it easier to dip the chiles into the eggs and then into the frying pan.

By now the lard should be hot enough. Using some tongs take a chile and dip it into the egg batter and then place it in the frying pan. The pan should be large enough to fit about three maybe four chiles at a time. Let the chiles cook for about three minutes and then using a spatula turn them over. They should be fried until they are nice and golden brown. As you finish each chile place it on the serving plate and then add another chile to the frying pan. As always, be careful not to burn yourself with the frying pan and watch out for spattering lard.

When you finish frying make sure that you have turned off the stove.

Place the finished chiles aside to cool off. You can now start on the tomato sauce which is made as a topping for the chiles.

First, open the can of whole tomatoes. Pour

the contents into a blender and then add a quarter cup of sugar, a teaspoon of cinamon, and a dash of salt and pepper. Blend all of these at high speed for a minute and when finished pour the mixture into a medium-sized saucepan. Place the saucepan on the stove and heat up to a simmer.

While you wait for the sauce to heat up, you can commence the funnest part of cooking--the clean-up. Place everything you've used in the sink and add some dishwashing soap. Fortunately, in making Chile Rellenos, you do not use as many utensils as you would for other more extravagant dishes.

Check the sauce and if it is simmering you are then ready to sit down and enjoy the fruits of your labor.

Take a couple of chile rellenos and place them on a plate and then spoon some sauce over them. If you wish, the rellenos can be served with either rice and/or beans, both of which compliment this delicious dish.

COMMENTARY ON RICHARD'S SECOND DRAFT

Richard's paper is now entirely in paragraph form, but his first paragraph is rather confusing. He needs to take his first sentence and develop it into an introductory paragraph. The purpose of the second sentence about the chiles is not clear, the sentence about the ingredients is one long sentence fragment, and the necessary utensils (listed in the outline) have been omitted. In the third paragraph, the analogy to jello seems confusing rather than clarifying. Richard also occasionally forgets to tell his readers when to remove pans from the burner, and he needs to strengthen the conclusion.

Richard's word choice also needs improvement, since it is often repetitious or inappropriate: "whole green chiles *which* have already been cleaned of the stem and the seeds *which* are inside the chile," "*Organize* the chiles," "*organize* the coated chiles," "*you want to get* a cup of lard," "*organize* the plate of stuffed flour-covered chiles," "*a couple of* chile rellenos."

Richard's Third/Final Draft

Making chile rellenos can be much easier than people suppose. The old-fashioned way of preparing the whole green chile peppers, the main ingrediant of this common Mexican dish, is to roast the peppers over an open flame until toasted and then remove the stem and the seeds which are on the inside of the chile. However, by buying a large can of whole green chiles which have already been prepared, you can eliminate the process of having to roast and prepare the chiles yourself.

To prepare this dish, you will need a large can of whole green chiles which contains approximately twenty chiles. You will also need a dozen eggs, a medium size block of cheese, whichever type you prefer, a half cup of flour, a cup of lard, a quarter cup of sugar, a can (large) of whole peeled tomatoes, a bit of salt and pepper, and a teaspoon of cinnamon. These are all of the ingrediants needed to make the rellenos.

The utensils which will be needed include an electric can-opener, an electric mixer, a blender, a large deep mixing bowl, a large frying pan, a large saucepan, a cutting board, a measuring cup, a regular knife, a pair of tongs, a rubber and a metal spatula, a teaspoon and a tablespoon, a serving plate, and two regular plates.

Begin by taking the electric can-opener and opening the can of whole green chiles. Once opened, take the chiles out and place them on a plate, carefully separating them. Make sure not to tear them as they have a small pocket inside of them which has been made by removing the stem and seeds. Now take the block of cheeses and using the regular knife cut the cheese into one-inch by two-inch strips. After you finish cutting the cheese, take the strips and begin to stuff them into the pocket in the chile. Place the stuffed chiles on a regular plate and set them aside.

Next, take the dozen eggs and the large deep bowl and break the eggs in half, separating the whites into the bowl and the yolks into a regular glass. Using the electric mixer, beat the egg whites for ten minutes or until they are so fluffy that they cling to the mixing bowl when you turn the bowl upside down. When you get this result, add the egg yolks and mix them into the mixture. Set the bowl next to the plate of stuffed chiles.

Take a plate and place a half cup of flour on it using the measuring cup. Take the stuffed chiles and roll them individually in the flour so as to coat them entirely. When you finish, set the flour coated chiles aside.

At this time, get a cup of lard with the measuring cup and place it in the large frying pan, then place it on the stove, and heat it up at a medium heat. Meanwhile, get two large serving plates ready so you have somewhere to put the fried chiles when they are done. Also, place the plate of stuffed flour-coated chiles next to the bowl of whipped eggs so as to make it easier to dip the chiles into the eggs and then into the frying pan.

By now the lard in the frying pan should be hot enough. Be very careful not to burn yourself with the frying pan or the hot lard inside. Using some tongs take a chile and dip it into the egg batter and then place it in the frying pan. The pan should be large enough to hold three or four chiles at a time. Let the chiles cook for about three minutes and then using a spatula turn them over. They should be fried until they are a nice golden-brown color. As you finish each chile, place it on the serving plate and then add another chile to the frying pan using the same step as before.

When you are finished with the frying pan, after all the chiles are done, remove it from the stove and turn-off the gas. Place the frying pan and all the utensils used so far in the sink and add some dishwashing liquid. This will help you to start the clean-up process. Take the plate of finished chiles and set it aside to cool off. Now you can start on the tomato sauce which is made as a topping for the chiles.

First, open the can of whole peeled tomatoes using the can-opener. Pour the contents into the blender and then add a quarter cup of sugar, a teaspoon of cinnamon, and a bit of salt and pepper. Blend all of these at high speed for a minute and then pour the mixture into the large saucepan. Place the saucepan on the stove and heat to a simmer at medium heat.

While you wait for the sauce to heat up, you can begin to wash the items you have in the sink.

Once the sauce is at a simmer you are then ready to sit down and enjoy the fruits of your labor. Take the saucepan off the stove, turn the stove off, and place the saucepan on one of the stove's cool burners.

The chile rellenos can be served with rice and beans, both of which compliment this dish, or they can be served by themselves with the tomato sauce. When you finish, you can easily tell, that by eliminating the process of preparing chile peppers, it really isn't as hard to make chile rellenos as most people suppose it to be.

COMMENTARY ON RICHARD'S THIRD/FINAL DRAFT

Richard chose to submit this draft for evaluation, but he really needed to do another revision. His paper is much improved over the earlier drafts, but there are still a few parts that need further explanation. In the eighth paragraph, he comments that the lard should be "hot enough," but does not explain what that statement means. In paragraph ten, he instructs the cook to "Place the saucepan on the stove and heat to a simmer at medium heat." The sentence sounds as if the saucepan is being heated rather than the mixture within it, and "simmer" is not defined. Similarly, in his conclusion, he states that the chile rellenos can be "served with rice and beans," or they can be "served by themselves with the tomato sauce." The implication is that tomato sauce cannot be used if rice and beans are being served.

Richard's introduction also needs some revision. He assumes in the introduction that his readers have always wanted to make chile rellenos but have avoided doing so because the preparation was too complicated. Probably many readers do not really know what chile rellenos are; neither do they know that there is a traditional—but rather complicated—method of preparation that contrasts with the easier one Richard plans to explain. Richard returns to this point in his conclusion, which also requires some revision.

Richard has improved his word choice, but he still relies on vague and repetitious language. Notice how often he uses the word *regular* without ever defining what it means.

3.4 PROCESS ACTIVITIES

1. Watch someone do a process, writing down each step as it is completed. Then do the process yourself, following the instructions you have written down—and only what you have written, not what you remember.

2. As you do a process, write down each step as it is completed. Then have someone else do the process, following the instructions you have written down—and only what you have written. The person should not have observed you doing the process; he or she must rely only on what you have written.

3.5 SUGGESTIONS FOR WRITING PROCESS SUCCESSFULLY

1. Choose an appropriate topic; avoid topics that are too complicated or too simple. For example, building a house would be too complicated, but building a dog house or a storage shed might not be. Conversely, a too-simple topic gives you nothing to write about. You might write a paper about concocting an exotic punch, but there's not much to say about preparing instant iced tea.

2. Assume only general knowledge on the part of your audience; sometimes a writer who knows a great deal about a subject will use terminology and refer to tools that are unfamiliar to most readers. If you are a master electrician accustomed to giving explanations to apprentice electricians, you may find it difficult to adjust yourself to a less knowledgeable audience.

3. Avoid abstractions: how to write a paper, how to give a speech, how to win at bridge. Such topics seldom work.

4. Cluster related steps together in well-developed paragraphs; you are writing a process essay, not an insert in a "do-it-yourself" kit.

5. Avoid recipe style; again remember you are writing a process essay, not a cookbook. Recipe style omits many words and is not stylistically appropriate in an essay.

RECIPE STYLE	ESSAY STYLE
Put pan in oven.	Put the pan in the oven.
Mix until smooth.	Mix the batter until it is smooth.
Serves four.	This dish provides enough food for generous servings for four people.

6. Do not try to write any process entirely from memory.

3.6 PROCESS ASSIGNMENTS

1. Recently, a member of your family called to tell you that an appliance/bicycle/car had broken down or needed some kind of routine maintenance or cleaning. Keeping the item repaired/maintained/cleaned was always your job, but you are not there to do it. Write a letter explaining how to repair/maintain/clean the item in question. Remember, you are not there to show the person how to follow this process, and the person has never done the process or watched you do it. Your purpose is to inform.

2. Your campus newspaper runs a column called "Campus Cook," in which guest columnists explain how to prepare their favorite dishes. Write a guest column; remember you are writing an essay, not a recipe. Consider the nature of your audience, particularly the money and facilities available. Your purpose is to inform.

3. Your local newspaper runs a column called "Good Grooming," which contains various hints about appearance. Write a guest column in which you explain a grooming procedure. Consider the nature of the audience of the local newspaper. Your purpose is to inform.

4. Your local newspaper runs a column called "Automobile Maintenance and Repair." Write a guest column in which you explain how to do a routine maintenance task or a simple auto repair. Consider your audience and the tools, equipment, and supplies that would be available to them. Your purpose is to inform.

5. Your local newspaper runs a column called "Handyperson." Write a guest column in which you explain how to do a routine household maintenance or repair task. Consider your audience and the tools, equipment, and supplies that would be available to them. Your purpose is to inform.

6. Your local newspaper runs a column called "Making It," which provides instructions about needlework, crafts, and sewing. Write a guest column in which you explain how to make a fairly simple and inexpensive item. Consider your audience and the tools, equipment, and supplies that would be available to them. Your purpose is to inform.

7. Using the following topics, create a writing process assignment. Your purpose is to inform an audience that has no special knowledge.

How to build _____
How to repair _____
How to clean _____
How to assemble _____ _____

How to make _____
How to prepare _____
How to operate _____
How to cook _____

CHAPTER

4 Writing Comparison-Contrast

4.1 INTRODUCTION

We apply the principles of **comparison** and **contrast** virtually every day of our lives. In the grocery store, we engage in comparison: "A is cheaper than B; I like B better, but I am short of money today so I will buy A. When I get paid on Friday, I will buy B." We compare products, we compare restaurants, we compare movies and television shows, and we compare cars. We compare friends and relatives and former, present, and possible future companions or spouses.

Newspapers, magazines, and television are filled with comparison-contrast: "John Smith is a better pitcher/quarterback than Rick Adams"; "Network A's Friday evening detective show is more poorly written than Network B's Thursday evening detective show"; "The horror movie showing at theater A has more gratuitous sex and violence than the horror movie showing at theater B." Political discussions are also filled with comparison-contrast: "Candidate A has a better housing program than Candidate B." So, too, are historical commentaries: "President A was a more effective war leader than President B." As you can see, we employ or encounter comparison-contrast in virtually every facet of life.

Whenever we use comparison-contrast, there must be both similarities and differences. There must be a basic likeness; otherwise, there is no true basis for comparison. Two pitchers or two quarterbacks are compared—not a pitcher and a quarterback. There must be differences. If the two things being compared are exactly alike, there is little to be said. For that reason, identical twins are frequently not a good subject for comparison-contrast; the more alike they are, the more difficult it is to write a good comparison-contrast paper. On the other hand, fraternal twins, particularly two brothers or sisters, often are a good choice, especially if there are marked differences in appearance and personality.

4.2 ORGANIZING COMPARISON-CONTRAST

There are two basic methods of organizing comparison-contrast: Half-and-Half, or Point-by-Point. Following are outlines of both methods.

HALF-AND-HALF OUTLINE
  I. Introduction

  II. Subject A
      Point 1
      Point 2
      Point 3

  III. Subject B
      Point 1
      Point 2
      Point 3

  IV. Conclusion

POINT-BY-POINT OUTLINE
  I. Introduction

  II. Point 1
      Subject A
      Subject B

  III. Point 2
      Subject A
      Subject B

  IV. Point 3
      Subject A
      Subject B

  V. Conclusion

Notice that in both the point-by-point and half-and-half methods, the same points are covered for both subjects. Writing about one set of points for one subject and another for the second subject is not comparison-contrast.

STUDENT COMPARISON-CONTRAST PAPERS

Following are two student comparison-contrast papers that use the two different methods of organization. Gisela uses the half-and-half method to compare two cars; Raquel employs the point-by-point method to compare living in a campus dormitory with living in an apartment.

Gisela's Comparison-Contrast Paper (Half-and-Half Method)

Gisela compares two cars that she and her husband have owned, writing of a situation that confronts many car owners at some point in their lives when changes in life-style create changes in transportation needs.

Gisela's First Draft

<u>Volvo versus Toyota</u>

Before my husband and I had children, we owned two cars: a sports car which had just enough room to carry us and my handbag, and a Toyota Corolla which we used when we needed to take luggage, friends, or sports equipment along. After the birth of our son we realized that a small Toyota and an even smaller sportscar could not carry us, a baby, and baby travelling equipment at the same time. We started to look around for a car which would adjust to our new situation and found it: a Volvo. We sold the sportscar and kept the Toyota. The Volvo and the Toyota supplement each other to fit our needs.

When travelling we definitely prefer the Volvo. It's huge trunk can easily hold five big suitcases, change of clothes for two children for two days in an extra bag, and diverse little sacs filled with diapers, food, drinks and other necessities. In summer the car's air-conditioner keeps us cool through many hours of driving, and the cruise-control which is adjusted at about 60 mph prevents us from getting a traffic ticket for speeding. The chassis which gives the Volvo the reputation of being the safest car in the world, makes us feel safe. The car's square design makes it appear bulky and heavy, but the economical fuel injected four cylinder engine which powers it, gets a respectable 29 miles per gallon on the highway. In summary, the Volvo satisfies us in every aspect and lives up to our expectations.

That is not the case with our Toyota. It is much smaller than the Volvo and the trunk holds only three small suitcases, while all the little odds and ends need to be placed into the passenger area. We usually use the Toyota to go shopping, because the trunk is just big enough to hold about ten grocery bags. Those trips to the grocery store are especially uncomfortable and exhausting in the summertime, because the car doesn't have an air conditioner. Since we don't use our Toyota for longer trips, a cruise control is not really needed. The second purpose of our little car is to take my husband to work. We decided to use the Volvo when transporting our children because the Toyota, with its light small frame, just lacks the safety we would like to have for our children. Our concern for their safey overrides my husbands need for comfort. The fact that the Toyota's engine is not fuel-injected doesn't add to it's efficiency. Our little car gets fewer miles per gallon than the Volvo.

After the birth of our second child it became apparent that the Volvo wasn't as big as we thought it was after all. It is amazing, how two carseats, mounted in the backseat, reduce space. The Volvo is just getting too small for our family needs, and as a result of that we have started to look around for a Minivan, and have decided to keep the Toyota.

COMMENTARY ON GISELA'S FIRST DRAFT

Gisela's paper is interesting, but her treatment of the two cars seems rather uneven; she writes much more about the Volvo than she does the Toyota. She needs to add more information to her discussion of the Toyota. Since the comparison-contrast operates within a narrative (story) framework, she needs to reverse the order of presentation, putting the Toyota first and then the Volvo. This order would be more logical, since they owned the Toyota before they bought the Volvo. Gisela comments in her conclusion that they may have to trade the Volvo and keep the Toyota, but she does not capitalize on the contradiction and irony inherent in their trading the car they like and keeping the one they find unsatisfactory.

Gisela's Second/Final Draft

<u>Volvo versus Toyota</u>

Before my husband and I had children, we owned two cars: a sportscar which had just enough room to carry us and my handbag, and a Toyota Corolla which we used when we need to take luggage, friends, or sports equipment along. After the birth of our son we realized that a small Toyota and an even smaller sports car could not carry us, a baby, and baby travelling equipment at the same time. We started to look around for a car which would adjust to our new situation and found it: a Volvo. We sold the sportscar and kept the Toyota. The Volvo and the Toyota complement each other to fit our needs.

    The little Toyota is too small in order to be used as a family car. The trunk holds only three small suitcases, while all the other little odds and ends which would be needed on a long journey would have to be placed in the passenger area. We only use the Toyota for short trips, and for that reason we don't really need a cruise control. The Toyota's first job is to take us to the grocery store, which is an uncomfortable and exhausting trip in the summertime, because the car doesn't have an air-conditioner. The second purpose of our little car is to take my husband to work. We decided to use the Volvo when transporting our children because the Toyota, with its light small frame, just lacks the safety we would like to have for our children. Our concern for their safety overrides my husband's need for comfort. The fact that the Toyota's engine is not fuel-injected doesn't add to its efficiency. Our little car gets fewer miles per gallon than the Volvo. Actually we complain a lot about the Toyota, but it is a reliable commuter car and we are relatively satisfied with it.

On the other hand the Volvo surpasses our little car in every aspect. When travelling we definitely prefer the Volvo. Its huge trunk can easily hold five big suitcases, change of clothes for two children for two days in an extra bag, and diverse little sacks filled with diapers, food, drinks and other necessities. In summer the car's air-conditioner keeps us cool through many hours of driving, and the cruise control, which is adjusted at about 60 mph, prevents us from getting a traffic ticket for speeding. The chassis, constructed of solid steel beams, which surround both sides of the car, makes us feel safe. The car's square design makes it appear bulky and heavy, but the economical fuel-injected, four-cylinder engine which powers it, gets a respectable 29 miles per gallon on the highway. In summary, the Volvo satisfies us in every aspect and lives up to our expectations.

After the birth of our second child, it became apparent that the Volvo wasn't as big as we thought it was after all. It is amazing, how two carseats, mounted in the backseat, reduce space. The Volvo is just getting too small for our family needs, and as a result of that we have started to look around for a Minivan. We haven't made up our minds yet, because of a lack of money we would have to trade the newer and more expensive Volvo against the new car and keep the Toyota. It will be a hard choice, because we really enjoy the Volvo.

COMMENTARY ON GISELA'S SECOND/FINAL DRAFT

Gisela chose to submit her second draft for evaluation, but the paper really needs another revision. Her attempt to reverse the order of presentation in her second draft proves unsuccessful because she does not change the internal material. She begins her discussion of the Toyota with comments about its unsuitability for long trips; that beginning was effective as a transition following the discussion of the Volvo in her first draft, but it seems irrelevant and inappropriate in this draft because the discussion of the Toyota now comes first. For some reason, she eliminates the material about the number of grocery sacks the trunk can hold, an appropriate detail, and keeps the material about the three small suitcases, an inappropriate detail. She needs another draft to make the internal discussion consistent with the paper as it is now organized.

Gisela might benefit from writing an outline at this point. She did not write one originally, and the absence of an outline may be the reason that she finds it difficult to make a structural revision. She also needs to strengthen her conclusion; perhaps she is not comfortable with irony, but she still needs to add another sentence or two in order to avoid a trailing-off effect.

Raquel's Comparison-Contrast Paper (Point-by-Point Method)

Raquel writes about a choice that many college students have to make, whether to live in a campus dormitory or in an apartment. She chooses to use the point-by-point method of comparison.

Raquel's Outline

Living in the dorm vs living in an Apartment

Thesis: Out of town undergraduate college students should live on campus while attending school.

I. Subsistence & Economic
   - Means of subsisting

II. Financial (Housing)   Economical
   - No utilities bills
   - No monthly dwelling fee - flat fee per semester
   - Maintence

III. Rules/Regulations   Safety at Campus
   - Visitors, Pets
   - Curfew
   - Decorations

IV. Communication   Cultures
   - aware of University procedures/functions (Possible for extra curricular activities)
   - Friendships
   - No transportation problems to/from school

V. Reasons for residing on campus while attending a university

   Economical Reasoning $

   Participation

   Awareness

Must learn the locality

COMMENTARY ON RAQUEL'S OUTLINE

Raquel's thesis demonstrates that she is clear about what she wants to write, but her outline seems somewhat confused. She lists appropriate matters for discussion, but the organization is not always logical; for example, she lists transportation problems under "Communication."

WRITING COMPARISON-CONTRAST

Raquel's First Draft

Out of town and out of state college undergraduate students should live on campus while attending school. Times will be rough for the new student when arriving on campus for the first time. During this period, the student will feel both lost and lonely; however, by residing in a dormitory this problem can be eliminated by his participation in campus activities. A student can save money, learn to respect, abide the housing rules & regulations, and share an intensive skill in communication with several residents while living on campus.

Financially speaking, living on campus is more economical for students than if they were to reside off campus. There are no monthly bills like utilities, room rental, or board when living in a dormitory. Maintence is also free. The student only worries about depositing a small fee for room reservation before each school year and payments are made in two installments. Installment # 1 is made at registration and the second is paid at midsemester. Prices for room and board range from $900.00 to $1200.00 respectfully; however, the price reflects the type of room, number of meals the students will have per week and the locality of the dormitory on campus. If a student resides off campus he will have to pay a larger fee, for example, a deposit for his apartment plus he must sign a lease for his residency there. Besides paying monthly bills for utilities, housing and transportation the student must worry about groceries.

Living on campus is no different than living at home. A student's room may be decorated as he wishes, but he may not paint the walls to his liking. Visitors may come and leave, but if they intend to stay overnight with the student, they must be registered with the Residential Assistant on duty for security purposes. Dormitories on campus usually have curfew on weekdays and weekends when doors to the dormitory are locked at 12pm and 1am respectfully for security, but by ringing the doorbell, located at the front of each dormitory entrance, the student will be admitted by the Residential Assistant or Dorm mother. When a student resides off campus, he can have as many visitors at his room and he can come and leave as he pleases, but there are no precautionary security measures. Consequently, both campus and apartment life require the student to abide to their rules and regulations while living on its premises.

Communication among other students is most favorable when living on campus. Not only does one learn of other students culture, but he also has a chance to live in it and share ideas. There is also more awareness on what is happening at the university and the student can take part in its activities, whereas, if he resided off campus a student is somewhat limited to campus participation. Last when residing on campus there are hardly any problems in transportation for the student. He doesn't have to worry about driving out in the rain, leaving his home early to beat the traffic, or running out of gas while driving to school. Merely, he only sets his alarm, awakens, eats breakfast and walks to his classes.

In conclusion, after viewing some of the problems confronted by most commuters attending college, I strongly suggest that undergraduate students live on campus. By living on campus they will help eliminate themselves from problems like campus unawareness, transportation, grocery bills and an increase in room rental (apartments) fees. Students will become exposed to different communicative skills with students from around the U. S. A. and other countries & Friendship will become meaningful when sharing ideas and residing together. Therefore, out of town undergraduates should live on campus while attending school.

COMMENTARY ON RAQUEL'S FIRST DRAFT

Raquel makes some good points in this draft, but some parts are confusing and vague. She needs to provide more specific information about costs in paragraph two. Paragraph three needs revision for clarity; the first sentence in the paragraph is not really true: "Living on campus is no different than living at home." It also does not seem relevant to the paper because the comparison-contrast is between living on campus and living in an apartment, not living on campus and living at home.

Raquel also needs to edit for appropriate and precise word

choice. The last sentence of her introductory paragraph is quite confusing because of word-choice problems: "A student can save money, learn to *respect, abide* the housing rules & regulations, and share an *intensive skill in communication* with *several* residents while living on campus." She also uses *respectfully* when she means *respectively* in paragraphs two and three.

Raquel's Second/Final Draft

Living in the dorm vs. living in an apartment

Out of town and out of state college undergraduate students should live on campus while attending school. Times will be rough for the new student when arriving on a campus for the first time. During this period, the student will feel both lost and lonely; however, by residing in a dormitory this problem can be eliminated by his participation in campus activities. By becoming a campus resident, the student can save an estimated $1,000.00 per semester for both room and board, he can enrich his communicative skills with other students who reside in the dormitory, and last he will develop responsibility and respect for himself and others around him.

Financially speaking, living on campus is more economical for a student than if he were to reside off campus. There are no monthly bills like utilities, room rental, or board when living in a dormitory. Maintence is also free. The student only worries about depositing a small fee of $50.00 for room reservation, which is applied towards payment before each school year, and payments are made in two installments. Installment # 1 is made at registration and the second is paid at mid-semester. The cost for room and board range from $900.000 to $1200.000 per semester; however, the cost reflects the type of dormitory one is residing in, the locality of the dormitory on campus, and the type of meal package he decides to purchase. For example, if a student chooses to live in the campus' most modern dormitory with private bath and telephone; he will pay about $300.00 more per semester than a student residing in an older dormitory with community baths and telephones per floor or wing. Students who reside alone usually pay an extra $75.00 to $150.00 per semester depending on his housing arrangement. Since a meal ticket is issued out to campus residents, students have their choice from a 12-meal ticket or 18 meal ticket at the college's dining facility. By receiving a 12 meal ticket the student is allowed to 2 meals per day for six day in a week; moreover, a 18 meal ticket is for 3 meals per day for 6 days in the week. The difference between the cost of the tickets is $60.00 per semester.

If a student resides off campus he will have to pay a larger fee, for example, a deposit ranging from $150.00-$250.00 for his apartment which can not be applied towards payment, but all or a portion is returned to him at the end of his housing contract. A student renting an apartment must sign either a three or six month lease for his residence at the complex. Besides paying monthly bills which average from $75.00-$150.00 for utilities, $200.00-$250.00 for groceries; the student must also pay a rental fee ranging from $210.00-$350.00 per month for his housing.

Living on campus may not be so different from living at home because a student may decorate his room as he wishes, but he may not paint the walls to his liking. Visitors may come and go, but if they intend to stay overnight with the student they must be registered with the Residential Assistant on duty for security pruposes. Dormitories on campus usually have a curfew on weekdays (12 pm) and weekends (1 A. M.) when doors to the dormitory are locked for security, but by ringing the doorbell, located at the front of each dormitory entrance, the student will be admitted by the Residential Assistant or Housing Director. When a student resides off campus, he can have as many visitors at his apartment without registering them and he can come and go as he pleases; thus, there is no security at the complex as at university. Consequently, both campus and apartment life require that the student abide to their housing rules, example-breakage or damages to walls, doors, furniture, etc. while living on the premises shall be charged to the resident.

Communication between other students is most

favorable when living on campus. Not only does the student learn of other students' cultures, but he also has a chance to live in it. There is more awareness on the happenings at the university, and the student can take part in its activities, whereas, if he resides off campus its more difficult for communication and participation.

Last when residing on campus there aren't alot of problems with transportation. The student doesn't have to worry about driving out in the rain, leaving his home early to beat the traffic, or running out of gas while driving to school. Nevertheless, he only sets his alarm, awakens, eats breakfast, and walks to his classes.

In conclusion, after viewing some of the problems confronted by most commuters attending college, I strongly suggest that undergraduate students live on campus. By living on campus the student will be better aware of activities or functions occurring and may even participate in them. Second he will save an estimated $1000.00 or more for housing. Last he may develop meaningful friendships with other residents.

COMMENTARY ON RAQUEL'S SECOND/FINAL DRAFT

Raquel chose to submit her second draft for evaluation, but the paper really needs more revision. She has added specific information about costs, but that material is now out-of-proportion to the rest of the paper. The paragraphs on living conditions and communication are still underdeveloped and confusing, but she makes some good points about the advantages of not having to drive to school. Since Raquel handles specific cost-type information fairly well but seems to have difficulties with more vague concepts such as living conditions and communication, perhaps she should eliminate those from her paper. She could then include transportation costs in her discussion and focus entirely on a comparison-contrast of the costs of living on campus versus living in an apartment. Such a change in the content and structure of the paper would probably require two drafts—one a structural revision and another to refine details and word choice.

4.4 COMPARISON-CONTRAST ACTIVITIES

1. Read the sports page of a newspaper, or read a sports magazine. List the types of comparisons, and classify each article according to its method of organization: half-and-half or point-by-point.

2. Find two editorials or two letters to the editor that express contrasting points of view; list the points on which they differ.

3. Watch a television news broadcast during which people of contrasting points of view appear together. List the points of difference.

4.5 SUGGESTIONS FOR WRITING COMPARISON-CONTRACT SUCCESSFULLY

1. Choose appropriate subjects; they must have something in common, but they also must have significant differences.

2. Outline your paper using both methods of organization; often one method is more effective for a particular topic than the other.

3. Limit your topic; do not try to compare and contrast **everything** about your subjects.

4.6 COMPARISON-CONTRAST ASSIGNMENTS

1. You have just received a letter from a friend who is going to move to your hometown, the city where you now live, or to a city where you lived previously. Your friend is moving reluctantly because his or her spouse or parents have been transferred—or a

[Handwritten margin note: Calif & Texas / earthquakes / & hurricanes]

similar reason. Write a letter in which you compare and contrast the city or town where your friend is currently living with the city or town he or she is moving to. You might want to discuss size, climate, recreational activities, educational institutions, professional opportunities, and similar issues. Your purpose is to inform, but you may also want to encourage your friend to be more positive about the move.

2. You have broken up with a boyfriend/girlfriend/spouse and have begun a relationship with someone new. Write a letter to your best friend comparing and contrasting the relationship just ended with the new relationship. Your purpose is to share your experience and express your feelings.

3. You and a friend or family member want to take friends or parents to a nice restaurant to celebrate a special event (for example, a promotion, an engagement, a wedding, or an anniversary). You must make reservations in advance, and your friend or family member is not in town. Write a letter in which you compare and contrast the two restuarants, so he or she can help you make the decision about which one to choose. Consider issues such as price, service, setting, quality of food, preferences of the individual(s) being treated, and the like. Your purpose is to inform.

4. Your campus newspaper runs a column called "Campus Gourmet." Write a guest column in which you compare-contrast two fast-food restaurants close to campus (for example, two hamburger places, two pizza parlors, or two fried chicken places). You may want to consider convenience, price, cleanliness, speed, quality of service, and quality of food. Your purpose is to inform, but you may want to persuade your readers that one restaurant is better than the other.

5. Your campus newspaper runs a column called "The Smart Shopper." Write a guest column in which you compare-contrast two retail establishments (for example, two department stores or two appliance stores). Your purpose is to inform, but you may want to persuade your audience that one store is better than the other.

6. Your local newspaper runs an "Entertainment" section that includes columns about movies, plays, television shows, and local establishments. Write a guest column about one of the following. Your purpose is to inform, but you may want to persuade your audience that one is better than the other.

a. Compare-contrast two night clubs, two bowling alleys, two pool halls, or similar such establishments.
b. Compare-contrast two television shows: soap operas, detective shows, or situation comedies.
c. Compare-contrast two television news broadcast anchors (local or national), two weather reporters, two disk jockeys, or two talk show hosts.
d. Compare-contrast two rock groups, two country western stars, or two classical musicians.
e. Compare-contrast two movies: horror shows, comedies, epics, dramas, or detective stories.

7. Your local newspaper runs a column called "Sports Observer." Write a guest column in which you compare-contrast two sports, two athletes who play the same position (for example, two quarterbacks), or two athletes as examples of sportsmanship (one positive, the other negative).

8. Your high school newspaper regularly runs a guest column, often written by a recent graduate. The current editor, the younger sister of a friend of yours, has asked you to write a column in which you attempt to prepare graduating high school seniors for what to expect when they reach college. By comparing and contrasting high school and college, you hope to advise them of pitfalls to avoid.

CHAPTER 5
Writing Persuasion

5.1 INTRODUCTION

When we write **persuasion**, we write to convince our readers to accept our point of view, or to take a particular action that we support, or perhaps to cease something we oppose.

Newpaper editorials are often persuasive in nature, as are letters to the editor. A letter of application is persuasive. So is a letter to a professor asking for more time to complete a paper, or a letter to a department chair requesting permission to substitute one course for another, or a letter to a dean asking that a course requirement or suspension be waived.

5.2 ORGANIZING PERSUASION

Unlike process and comparison-contrast, which ordinarily use variations of the basic organizational methods presented in the outlines in Chapters 3 and 4, persuasion can be organized in a variety of ways. The following outline may be helpful to you in organizing your persuasive writing, but it should not be followed rigorously.

PERSUASION OUTLINE
  I. Introduction
     A. Statement of the situation/problem
     B. Thesis statement
     C. Listing of supporting points

  II. Point 1
     A. Controlling statement (topic sentence)
     B. Evidence supporting this statement
        1. Example 1

  2. Example 2
  3. Example 3
 III. Point 2
  A. Controlling statement (topic sentence)
  B. Evidence supporting this statement
   1. Example 1
   2. Example 2
   3. Example 3
 IV. Point 3
  A. Controlling statement (topic sentence)
  B. Evidence supporting this statement
   1. Example 1
   2. Example 2
   3. Example 3
 V. Conclusion
  A. Restatement of the situation/problem
  B. Restatement of the thesis

5.3 STUDENT PERSUASION PAPERS

Following are two papers on the same topic: early marriage. Both are written by women arguing against early marriage and using their own experience as an example, but one paper is effective while the other is not.

Paulina's Persuasion Paper

Paulina seems to have difficulty making an objective, convincing argument, primarily because she is not able to detach herself from her personal experience in order to put it in a larger context. She also makes no substantive revisions between her first and second drafts, perhaps because she really does not want to write about her subject.

Paulina's First Draft

  Getting married at an early age is not what kids think it's going to be. Even though it does sound romatic, living the rest of your lives with the one you love does sound great. Now the reality hits shortly after saying "I do."

If the parents aren't too happy about the idea, you'll of coarse be off to a bad start. Let's say they don't mind & have both agreed well your first problem will be where to live, with both of you still going to school some one will have to quite and start working whose going to have to make this sacrifice because it will be and you'll realize this later on in life. Next problem in line where will you live, you can't afford a place of your own so usually it will be the husband's parents. That will take a lot of adjusting as his mother will be doing all the things you were hoping to do in your fantasy of the perfect wife. There will be alot of tension when you try to be assertive and demand a chance to take care of your husband. He will of coarse expect you to be more understanding of his mother and more problems. Don't worry it won't just be coming from his parents but yours also. Although the parents don't mean to cause problems somehow it's not much consulation when you're going through it.

Money is one of the biggest problems going. Once you can afford moving out you have to keep on a very tight budget as here are a lot more bills coming.

Next we have kids, well the younger you are the worse it is. There is however one good fact that is you'll be able to hopefully mature with your child. Only watch out they might beat you. Now you have children & money problems. The kids have needs you couldn't possible imagine.

I know cause I got married at 17 years and its hard although I did not have children til two years later, it didn't make it easier. What you need to do is get your schooling, traveling and going out nighty out of your system. Then you'll be able to handle these situations better. Wait till you're older.

COMMENTARY ON PAULINA'S FIRST DRAFT

Paulina has chosen a good topic for a persuasive paper, and her personal experience should be an advantage to her in writing the paper. A major problem is that she assumes that everyone who marries young is female, in school, and will live with her husband's parents; she makes her own experience a universal one. Instead, she should use it as a source of specific examples of the difficulties involved in early marriage. Citing the experience of others she knows who married early would also add to the validity of her argument. As it is, the paper seems chatty and rambling, an impression heightened by her frequent and vague use of the pronoun *you*.

Paulina's Second/Final Draft

Getting married at an early age is not what young people think it will be. Years ago if a person was not married by the age of fifteen they were considered to be "over the hill." Fortunatly times have changed; although they're not getting married that young they do get married straight out of high school alot of them which can cause many problems.

Lots of times one or the other spouse may want to continue their education and it makes it difficult financially as there are so many expenses that were taken for granted when living at home. One of the worst problems a young couple can and does have is money. Because of these situations they might be forced to live with one of the parents until they can get on their feet. Although the parents suggest living at home to try to help out it sometimes leads to more problems for the young couple starting out.

One other problem which can occur is when children are born when you yourself are too young. It can be rough because once a child is born it needs alot of attention and patience of which as easy as it sounds can be very nerve racking. Children have a great deal of needs that if you're not emotionally ready you will not be able to handle them causing more problems to a marriage.

Although I haven't really touched on the majority of problems that could arise in young marriage, these two are soom you might be facing.

I know this because I did get married at the age of seventeen and it was hard although we did not have children right away it didn't make it easier. You still need to get use to each others likes and dislikes and consider their feelings as well as yours. What you need to do is first finish your schooling, traveling, and going out nightly out of your system. Then you will be more mature to handle these situations.

COMMENTARY ON PAULINA'S SECOND/FINAL DRAFT

Paulina chose to submit this draft for evaluation, but the paper is still quite weak. She has corrected some of the errors in mechanics in the first draft, and she has cut down on her use of the pronoun *you*, but these are merely surface changes that do not resolve the basic problems pointed out in the response to the first draft. In fact, Paulina should probably have abandoned this topic and tried another. Her own experience, which should have been an advantage to her in writing the paper, seems in fact to be a disadvantage. Perhaps this topic is too close and too personal and too painful for her to write about it effectively.

Arlene's Persuasion Paper

Unlike Paulina, Arlene writes an effective persuasive paper opposing early marriage. She seems to be able to distance herself from her personal experience in order to put it into a larger context. Like Paulina, Arlene uses herself as an example, but she presents her own experience as merely typical.

Arlene's First Draft

I have known several people who married at what most people consider to be a young age, 18 years old. I married at the age of 22, which I consider too young. Speaking from personal experience, the disadvantages of early marriage greatly outweigh the advantages. I think the majority of people should wait until after age 25 to marry, so he or she has had time to become more emotionally stable and perhaps grow up. An advantage of delaying marriage is that it is much easier to start and finish a college education within four years and establish a career. Plus, it is easier to support one person financially. Finally, a person will have time to enjoy being single without being tied down in a marriage.

Young people usually do not know exactly what they want out of life. If they do know, it is oftentimes hard to obtain that goal and even harder if you are married. The majority of young people do not have a realistic view of life, and when two young people get married, they do not automatically know exactly what their goals are and how they are going to achieve them. For example, when I was married I had no idea of what career I wished to pursue, nor did my husband.

Quite often, people who marry young either drop out of high school or delay beginning their college education and thus establishing a career. Some teenagers in high school think being married is very romantic and is like playing house, and in turn may lead them to drop out of high school. Soon, they come to the realization that being married so young has many disadvantages. For example, young married couples usually have to work right out of high school and therefore delay their college education indefinitely. If they decide to continue their education by either obtaining a GED or enrolling in a university, they usually have to work part-time or full-time to support themselves, and more often than not, a young family. Therefore, they can only be a part-time student, and when you are a part-time student, graduating from college is a very distant goal.

Another point to consider is that it is easier to support one person instead of two. A single person can live in a studio apartment or a dorm room, will eat less, and will only have to worry about having one car. A single person could perhaps live at home for a few years, but if you marry young, most parents would prefer you to move to your own home.

Finally, a person should enjoy being young and single, and without any encumbrances. When you marry young you will always think that the grass is greener on the other side and wonder what you missed. Resentment is prevalent in young marriages. A spouse may decide that he was left out of the social scene by marrying young and tries to recapture it, which leads to the destruction of the marriage. It may be hard for young people to realize that they have a responsibility to their spouses, whether financial or emotional.

Therefore, I think the disadvantages of early marriage greatly outweigh the advantages. A college education, even a high school education, is much easier to obtain when you are single, it is easier to support yourself, and you can enjoy your youth while you have no encumbrances. In my experience as a legal assistant, a great number of people who marry while still in high school or before the age of 25 are divorced before the age of 30, and have many regrets. Most people I have talked with, if they could live their lives again, would not have married before age 25.

COMMENTARY ON ARLENE'S FIRST DRAFT

Arlene has chosen an appropriate topic for a persuasive paper, she has organized her draft well, and she has made some good points. Her paper would be more convincing if she supported those points with specific examples. If she feels uncomfortable writing about her own experience, she could use as examples the experiences of some of the people she referred to in her conclusion.

Arlene's Second/Final Draft

I believe that the disadvantages of early marriage greatly outweigh the advantages. I have known several people who married at what most peopple consider to be a young age, 18 years old. I married at the age of 22, which I consider too young. I think the majority of people should wait until after age 25 to marry, so they have had time to become more emotionally stable and perhaps to grow up. An advantage of delaying marriage is that it is much easier to start and finish a college education within four years and establish a career. Another point to consider is that it is easier to support one person financially. Finally, a person will have time to enjoy being single without being tied down in a marriage.

Young people usually do not know exactly what they want out of life. If they do know, it is often times hard to obtain that goal and even harder if they are married. The majority of young people do not have a realistic view of life, and when two young people get married, they do not automatically know exactly what their goals are and how they are going to achieve them. For example, when I was married, I had no idea of what career I wished to pursue, nor did my husband. My husband and I started working immediately after graduating from high school just so that we could have spending money. We did not think of our future at all. I did not realize exactly what I wanted out of life until I was about 25 years old. By that time I was married with two children and had to work full-time. Because of my family responsibilities, it will be much harder to obtain my goal.

Quite often, people who marry young either drop out of high school or delay beginning their college education and thus establishing a career. Because some teenagers in high school think being married is very romantic and is like playing house, they may drop out of high school. Soon, they come to the realization that being married so young has many disadvantages. For example, young married couples usually have to work right out of high school and therefore delay their college education indefinitely. If they decide to continue their education by either obtaining a GED or enrolling in a university, they usually have to work part-time or full-time to support themselves and more often than not, a young family. Therefore, they can only be part-time students, and for part-time students graduating from college is a very distant goal. Using myself as an example, I was married at age 22, had two children by the time I was 25, was divorced by age 26, and did not start school until I was 24. I will always have to be a part-time student because I have a family to support.

Another point to consider is that it is easier to support one person instead of two. A single person can live in a studio apartment or a dorm room, will eat less, and will only have to worry about having one car. A single person could perhaps live would prefer you to move to your own home. A friend of mine married when she was 19 years old, and her parents demanded that she and her husband move to their own home and support themselves. They did not realize how much it would cost to live on their own, and finally divorced because of financial pressures.

Finally, a person should enjoy being young and single, and without any encumbrances. By marrying young you will always think that the grass is greener on the other side and wonder what you missed. Resentment is prevalent in young marriages. A spouse may decide that he was left out of the social scene by marrying young and tries to recapture it, which leads to the destruction of the marriage. My husband felt that way and began staying out all night at bars, trying to feel as if he were single and with no responsibilities. That was the major reason for our divorce. Many young people do not realize that they have a responsibility to their spouse, whether financial or emotional.

In conclusion, I think the disadvantages of early marriage greatly outweigh the advantages. A college education, even a high school education, is much easier to obtain when you are single, it is easier to support yourself, and you can enjoy your youth while you have no encumbrances. In my experience as a legal assistant, a great number of people who marry while still in high school or before the age of 25 are divorced before the age of 30, and have many regrets. Most people I have talked with, if they could live their lives again, would not have married before age 25.

COMMENTARY ON ARLENE'S SECOND/FINAL DRAFT

Arlene's second draft is not perfect, but it is ready to submit for evaluation. There are some mistakes that a more careful final proofreading should have caught, including typing errors and inadvertently omitted material. In her last paragraph, she switches to the pronoun *you* and addresses the reader directly, a device that seems appropriate and effective in this context.

5.4 PERSUASION ACTIVITIES

1. Read editorials and letters to the editor in newspapers and magazines. Most of these will be persuasive in nature. Categorize what you read as effective or ineffective. What are the characteristics of effective persuasive writing? What are the characteristics of ineffective persuasive writing?

2. Perhaps someone in your personal or professional life is causing you a certain amount of anxiety or distress. List the arguments you could make to this person that would persuade him or her to do what you want.

3. Listen to children in grocery stores and department stores trying to persuade their parents to buy them something they want or perhaps to allow them do something they want to do. What kind of arguments do they use? Are they effective? Why or why not?

5.5 SUGGESTIONS FOR WRITING PERSUASION SUCCESSFULLY

1. Choose your subject carefully. Subjects like "abortion" or "gun control" rarely work well. More specific subjects such as a suggested change at your college or where you work would be more effective.

2. Avoid arguments based solely on fairness or "what's right." Others may have different standards than yours.

3. Propose solutions when you can; otherwise, your paper may sound more like a complaint than a piece of persuasive writing.

5.6 PERSUASION ASSIGNMENTS

1. In the stereotyped view of many, the "typical" college student is eighteen years old and living away from home for the first time, probably in a college dormitory. The student's major interest is the opposite sex, and his or her major occupations are attending football and basketball games and partying, often with the assist of alcohol and/or drugs. Write a guest editorial for your local newspaper in which you attempt to refute this stereotype as it concerns the "typical" student at your college. Provide specific examples, using yourself and other students you know.

2. Car insurance is an expense that most adults have to bear. It is particularly burdensome for many young adults whose incomes are fairly low but who must pay high premiums because of their age. One controversial feature concerning car insurance for young adults is that young males must pay a higher premium until the age of 25, but the higher premium applies to young females only to the age of 21. The insurance industry argues that statistics show that young males have more car accidents, often with alcohol or speeding involved, than young females. Opponents argue that this is an example of blatant sex discrimination. You have recently heard that the U.S. House of Representatives may hold hearings on this matter. Write a letter to your representative in which you take a position on this issue and argue for your point of view. Be sure to consider opposing arguments and refute them. If possible, suggest compromises and alternate approaches.

3. A local radio station, K– –, is sponsoring a contest with the grand prize being a trip to Hawaii for two. Entrants must write an essay on the topic "Why K– – is the best radio station in _____." The judges will be the general manager and the advertising manager of the radio station, the general manager of a local television station, a college professor who specializes in the study of electronic media (radio and television), a local high school teacher, and two regular listeners chosen at random. You may wish to include some of the following in your essay: type of music played, disk jockeys, newscasts, special programs (for example, talk shows), contests, or other appropriate details. Be specific; cite examples.

4. You are in danger of being placed on scholastic suspension because of poor grades. You feel that your poor grades are the result of overscheduling in the past, when you tried to take too many hours of classes and work too many hours at the same time. Write a letter to the Dean of Students, who will be making the final decision, in which you attempt to convince him or her to give you another semester to bring up your grades. You admit that your poor grades were the result of a misjudgment on your part in the past and that you understand the nature of that misjudgment. Since then you have adapted your schedule to provide for an appropriate mixture of time devoted to work and to school. This new schedule should enable you to maintain a satisfactory academic performance in the future. Provide specific details.

5. Write a guest editorial for your campus newspaper in which you discuss a campus problem such as registration, parking, safe lighting, library hours, or bookstore policies. Explain what the problem is and propose what you regard as a sensible solution.

6. Write a letter to the editor of your local newspaper in which you discuss a local problem such as poor garbage collection service, inadequate parking, excessive watering of lawns, unsightly areas, or some similar topic of concern to you. Explain what the problem is and propose what you regard as a sensible solution.

7. Write a guest column for a magazine addressed to the national college audience in which you discuss an issue in education that concerns you and many other college students. Explain the issue and take a stance.

8. Create your own persuasive writing assignment. Define your subject and your audience.

CHAPTER 6 Writing Summaries

6.1 INTRODUCTION

A **summary** is an abbreviated version of a longer piece of writing, a miniature reflection of the original text. The length of the summary in relation to the original may vary according to the requirements of the situation. There are summaries called **abstracts** that may summarize in one page or one paragraph a book of several hundred pages.

Summaries are widely used in business, industry, and the sciences. Busy executives do not have the time to read all the reports addressed to them; they may require that summaries accompany such reports, or they may delegate the task of summarizing the reports to a staff member. Scientists do not have the time to read everything written that might relate to their field, so they read summaries of other scientists' research to determine what may be relevant to their own work.

Summarizing is also important for college student writers. When you take class notes or write an essay exam, you are engaging in a summary-type activity, providing yourself or someone else with an abbreviated version of a lecture or assigned chapters in a textbook. If you are assigned a book review to write, part of that review will include a summary of what you have read.

6.2 SUGGESTIONS FOR SUCCESSFUL SUMMARY WRITING

DO
1. Do summarize the entire passage.

DO NOT
1. Do **not** summarize only part of the passage.

CHAPTER 6
Writing Summaries

6.1 INTRODUCTION

A **summary** is an abbreviated version of a longer piece of writing, a miniature reflection of the original text. The length of the summary in relation to the original may vary according to the requirements of the situation. There are summaries called **abstracts** that may summarize in one page or one paragraph a book of several hundred pages.

Summaries are widely used in business, industry, and the sciences. Busy executives do not have the time to read all the reports addressed to them; they may require that summaries accompany such reports, or they may delegate the task of summarizing the reports to a staff member. Scientists do not have the time to read everything written that might relate to their field, so they read summaries of other scientists' research to determine what may be relevant to their own work.

Summarizing is also important for college student writers. When you take class notes or write an essay exam, you are engaging in a summary-type activity, providing yourself or someone else with an abbreviated version of a lecture or assigned chapters in a textbook. If you are assigned a book review to write, part of that review will include a summary of what you have read.

6.2 SUGGESTIONS FOR SUCCESSFUL SUMMARY WRITING

DO
1. Do summarize the entire passage.

DO NOT
1. Do **not** summarize only part of the passage.

vice, inadequate parking, excessive watering of lawns, unsightly areas, or some similar topic of concern to you. Explain what the problem is and propose what you regard as a sensible solution.

7. Write a guest column for a magazine addressed to the national college audience in which you discuss an issue in education that concerns you and many other college students. Explain the issue and take a stance.

8. Create your own persuasive writing assignment. Define your subject and your audience.

2. Do reflect accurately what the author says.

3. Do focus on the main ideas.

4. Do use quotations to support summary statements.

5. Do quote the author's words exactly and enclose them in quotation marks.

6. Do paraphrase—restate the author's ideas in your own words.

2. Do **not** intrude your opinions, or add information not presented in the original.

3. Do **not** focus on examples, ignoring the main ideas.

4. Do **not** copy the original passage virtually word for word.

5. Do **not** quote inaccurately or use the author's exact words without quotation marks.

6. Do **not** use the author's words, changing them only slightly.

6.3 SUMMARY ASSIGNMENT

Read carefully the following passage taken from an introductory sociology text written by Donald Light, Jr., and Suzanne Keller. Focus your attention on the key ideas of the passage that the authors present. Then write a summary of the passage in approximately 200 words. Include, in condensed form, all the major points necessary for understanding the passage.

A black student is bused to a school in a white neighborhood across town and finds himself the subject of unwanted controversy. An urban middle-class couple with a five-figure income is shocked to discover they can't afford to buy a house within commuting distance of the city. A bank employee who embezzled thousands of dollars by programming a computer to divert pennies to his account is caught but given only a suspended sentence. Liberal, free-thinking parents are bewildered when their son joins a fundamentalist religious sect. "Why?" they ask themselves.

We tend to think that what happens to us is the result of something we did or something "they" did to us, ignoring the social forces that shape us. In different ways, all of these individuals are caught up in sociological events that are beyond their direct control. But these forces are not beyond understanding. It takes what C. Wright Mills called "sociological imagination" to perceive the larger forces that shape our lives—and to stop blaming ourselves or others for our frustrations.

The sociological eye looks beyond individual psychology and unique events to the predictable patterns and regular occurrences of social life. A sociologist would be more interested in the effects of marijuana on teen-age dating behavior than in the habits of one individual who smokes. A sociologist would be more interested in how best-selling novels come to be published, how they are circulated, and which groups read them and why than in what merits or flaws a particular novel has. A sociologist would be more interested in the similarities and differences among families that produce a schizophrenic child than in the case history of a particular child.

There is nothing mysterious or cold-blooded about the sociological perspective. It is one way of examining our social lives in order to make sense and meaning out of the forces that shape our individual destinies. It complements the perspectives and angles of visions that we already have at our command. In this first chapter, we will discuss how the sociological perspective is used and the meaning of social facts. We will also consider the main theoretical orientations in sociology, the origins of sociology, its relations to other disciplines, and its uses in contemporary society.

DONALD LIGHT, JR., AND SUZANNE KELLER, *SOCIOLOGY*

6.4 STUDENT RESPONSES

Following are examples of student responses to the preceding summary assignment. The first three summaries are quite weak; the last two are considerably better. It should be emphasized that these summaries were written in class at the beginning of the term and that these particular students had been given no instruction in summary writing. Under those conditions, none of the students wrote especially good summaries, but the difficulties they had are illustrative of the problems that writers often have in writing summaries.

After each summary, a commentary discusses the major problems of that summary; the commentary does not address issues of grammar, usage, or mechanics. Summaries have been scored on a scale of 1 to 10; consider whether or not you agree with the assigned score.

WRITING SUMMARIES 83

Summary 1 *Score: 2*

Discussing the Social life of certain individuals. In this Passage we find discrimination of blacks. There is also a sign of inflation, where a middle class couple cannot afford a house, and going on to acts against the law, a person who is caught doing a serious crime is just given a suspended sentence. Another case is when children growup and start living their own lifes, Parents get shocked by that, especially when serious changes occur. Sociologists are more interested in the unormal than in the normal social life of a person. People need help once in a while, when things are not going the right way.

COMMENTARY ON SUMMARY 1

This summary has three serious problems: first, it focuses almost entirely on the first paragraph of the essay; second, it does not summarize but merely restates that first paragraph; third, it draws conclusions not found in the original, "People need help once in a while, when things are not going the right way."

Summary 2 *Score: 3*

An Urban middle-class couple with a five-figure income is shocked to discover they can't afford a house within commuting distance to the city. A bank employee who embezzled thousands of dollars by programming a computer to divert pennies to his account is caught and given only a suspended sentence. Liberal, free-thinking parents are bewildered when their son joins a religious sect. All are somewhat common everyday type occurances which effect many people.

However, the person to whom an incident happened feels that it was the result of somthing we did or something "they" did to us. They ignore the social forces that shape us and fail to realize that they are caught up in sociological events that are beyond their direct control.

The sociological eye looks beyond individual psychology and unique events to the predictable patterns and regular occurences of social life.

A sociologist would be more interested in the similarities and differences among families that produce a schizophrenic child than in the case history of a particular child.

This may seen sort of nasty, or cold-blooded on the part of the sociologist, but it helps us to make sense of the social forces which determines each of our destinies.

In this first chapter, we will discuss how the sociological perspective is used and the meaning of social facts.

We will also consider the main theoretical orientations in sociology, the origins of sociology, it's relations to other disciples, and its uses in contemporary society.

COMMENTARY ON SUMMARY 2

This summary merely restates much of the original's first paragraph, while the rest of the summary is simply a lifting of the author's words from the first sentence or two of each paragraph of the original. The last two short paragraphs repeat virtually word-for-word the last two sentences of the last paragraph of the original passage.

Summary 3   *Score: 3.5*

The ways of our society influence the way we think. Discrimination is everywhere. The cost of living is sky-high, poverty is everywhere. People arents being honest. They're selling from one another. The law is weakening and not doing its job. People are joining sects & cults where someone else does they're thinking and run thier lives like the leader demands. In different ways all these individuals are caught up in society and have no direct control. This is sociological imagination. It is the forces out in the world that shape our lives.

 The sociological eye looks beyond individual psychology, & events to the predicatable patterns & occurance of social life. He is interested in what <u>causes</u> one to do think, or act.

COMMENTARY ON SUMMARY 3

Much of this summary is the writer's reaction to the passage and the conclusions he or she has drawn from reading it. The writer makes gross generalizations based on the examples provided in the first paragraph.

The two student summaries that follow were given the same score, but they are quite different in other respects. You might want to consider whether you think one is better than the other and why.

Summary 4 *Score:* 7

    This passage, taken from a text in freshman Sociology, discusses what sociologists look for in a society. They do not look at the individual, but what causes the individual to do certain things. In the beginning of the passage, it discusses what may happen to a person just because of social forces. We do not always realize it is social force, but instead we blame ourselves. We are told that we are "caught up on sociological events that are beyond direct control." The sociologist wants only to look at those forces and understand them.

    We are also told in this passage that the sociologist looks for the predictable patterns and regular occurrences of social life. This, again, means looking beyond the individual. The sociological perspective, as it is said in the passage, is not mysterious or cold-blooded. Instead of being mysterious or cold-blooded, "it compliments the perspectives and angles of visions we already have at our command".

    So, after reading the passage from the text, it could be summarized by generally saying it is mainly about the sociological outlook on society and not the individual.

COMMENTARY ON SUMMARY 4

This writer obviously understands the passage and does a fairly credible job of summarizing it. His or her major problem is a tendency toward repetition. The phrase *the passage* occurs five times. The last two sentences of the second paragraph also illustrate this tendency toward repetition: "The sociological perspective, as it is said in the passage, is not *mysterious or cold-blooded.* Instead of being *mysterious or cold-blooded,* 'it compliments the perspectives and angles of vision we already have at our command.'" Note that in the last sentence the writer quotes appropriately, although misspelling *complements*. In fairness, it must be repeated that the summary was an in-class writing assignment and the writer had no chance to revise.

Summary 5 *Score:* 7

When something happens to an individual that he particularly didn't want to happen to him, he often ask himself, "Why?" These individuals tend to think they did something wrong or someone did something to them. Actually these people are caught up in a larger force that shapes all our lives. They need to stop blaming themselves and others for these unwanted events.

A sociologist looks beyond unique events and people and towards group occurrences. For example, a sociologist would look at group behaviors or people that smoke marijuana instead of just one individual's habits who smoke. In this way sociologists can make sense of the forces that shape individuals destinies. It helps add to our own views that we already have of our society and ourselves.

COMMENTARY ON SUMMARY 5

This summary is much more fluent than Summary 4, but it does not mention important concepts like "sociological imagination" or "sociological perspective," and it gives only one example from the original: "people who smoke marijuana instead of just one individual's habits who smoke." Note that this writer uses **abstract** style; that is, he or she does not refer to "the passage" or "the author." In some instances, abstract style is appropriate, but more commonly writers make some reference to the fact that they are summarizing and quoting a text.

6.5 SUMMARY ACTIVITIES AND ASSIGNMENTS

1. Read carefully the following passage taken from a book written by Sally P. Springer and Georg Deutsch. Focus your attention on the key ideas in the passage that the authors present. Then write a summary of the passage in approximately 200 words. Include, in condensed form, all the major points necessary for understanding the passage. You may want to refer to Section 6.2, Suggestions for Successful Summary Writing.

Note. In the passage being summarized, mark in each paragraph the sentence or sentences that contain the main idea(s) of the paragraph. Then make an outline based on those sentences.

WHAT PAW DOES YOUR DOG SHAKE HANDS WITH?

The most obvious sign of lateralization in humans is handedness. Thus investigators have looked for paw or limb preferences in animals as evidence of brain lateralization, and they have found that many species do show such preferences. Cats typically use one paw in tasks that involve reaching for an object. Monkeys too use one limb predominantly in unimanual tasks. Even mice show consistent preferences in a task in which they must use one paw at a time to reach for food.

Although the pattern of limb preference in a given animal bears some resemblance to hand preference shown by human beings, there is an important difference. Approximately 50 percent of the cats, monkeys, and mice show a preference for the right paw, and 50 percent show a preference for the left paw. This is strikingly different from the breakdown found in human beings—90 percent right-hand preference, 10 percent left-hand preference.

The 50-50 split in animals has led some investigators to propose that paw preferences are the result of chance factors. According to this hypothesis, the limb first used by an animal is determined by chance. The additional dexterity gained as a result of the experience increases the probability that the same limb will be used again. This kind of use-dexterity loop rapidly produces preferences for that limb in the animal under consideration. Some support for such a mechanism has come from geneticist Robert Collins' work with paw preference in mice.

Collins compared the predictions of the chance, environmental model of paw preference with predictions that follow from the assumption that paw preference has a genetic basis. If a trait is under genetic control, it should be possible to select for it. That is, if individuals with the trait are selectively mated, each successive generation should show a higher incidence of the trait. If the trait is determined by chance, however, no such increase across generations should occur.

Collins began his study by mating mice that shared the same paw preference. In the next generation, he mated those offspring who showed the same paw preference as the parents. After repeating the selective inbreeding three times, Collins looked at the proportion of left-pawed and right-pawed offspring in the last generation. He found a 50-50 split, the same proportion he had started with in generation 1.

Collins interpreted his data as evidence against genetic control of lateral preference in mice and argued that chance is the determining factor in such preferences. His data, of course, speak only to the question of the basis for paw preference in mice. Selective inbreeding studies have not been reported for other animals. However, we can say with some assurance that the favored paw in animals showing a preference is equally likely to be the left or the right. Human beings appear to be the only animals with lateral preferences strongly biased in one direction.

SALLY P. SPRINGER AND GEORG DEUTSCH,
LEFT BRAIN, RIGHT BRAIN

2. Using the Suggestions for Successful Summary Writing and the sample student summaries in this chapter, evaluate your summary on a scale of 1 to 10 and write a commentary on it. Then revise for a score of 10.

3. Chapter 7 provides several more essays for further summary practice. All of them are approximately 1,000 words long; write a summary of approximately 250 words of one or more of the essays.

CHAPTER 7
Readings for Writing

7.1 INTRODUCTION

Much of the writing that college students must do requires response to their reading. The response may be a fairly simple and straightforward task, like writing a summary, or it may be a complex and sophisticated project such as writing a research report using a variety of books, articles, and other sources.

7.2 READING SELECTIONS

Following are several short pieces of writing for you to read, respond to, and write about. At the end of each selection are questions for discussion and suggestions for writing.

THE FIFTH FREEDOM

More than three centuries ago a handful of pioneers crossed the ocean to Jamestown and Plymouth in search of freedoms they were unable to find in their own countries, the freedoms we still cherish today: freedom from want, freedom from fear, freedom of speech, freedom of religion. Today the descendants of the early settlers, and those who have joined them since, are fighting to protect these freedoms at home and throughout the world.

And yet there is a fifth freedom—basic to those four—that we are in danger of losing: the *freedom to be one's best*. St. Exupery[1] describes a ragged, sensitive-faced Arab child, haunting the streets of a North African town, as a lost Mozart: he would never be trained or developed. Was he free? "No one grasped you by the shoulder while there was still time; and nought will awaken in you the sleeping poet or musician or astronomer that possibly inhabited you from the beginning." The freedom to be one's best is the chance for the development of each person to his highest power.

How is it that we in America have begun to lose this freedom, and how can we regain it for our nation's youth? I believe it has started slipping away from us because of three misunderstandings.

First, the misunderstanding of the meaning of democracy. The principal of a great Philadelphia high school is driven to cry for help in combating the notion that it is undemocratic to run a special program of studies for outstanding boys and girls. Again, when a good independent school in Memphis recently closed, some thoughtful citizens urged that it be taken over by the public-school system and used for boys and girls of high ability, that it have entrance requirements and give an advanced program of studies to superior students who were interested and able to take it. The proposal was rejected because it was undemocratic!

Out of this misunderstanding comes the middle-muddle. Courses are geared to the middle of the class. The good student is unchallenged, bored. The loafer receives his passing grade. And the lack of an outstanding course for the outstanding student, the lack of a standard which a boy or girl must meet, passes for democracy.

The second misunderstanding concerns what makes for happiness. The aims of our present-day culture are avowedly ease and material well-being: shorter hours; a shorter week; more return for less accomplishment; more soft-soap excuses and fewer honest, realistic demands. In our schools this is reflected by the vanishing hickory stick and the emerging psychiatrist. The hickory stick had its faults, and the psychiatrist has his strengths. But the trend is clear: Tout comprendre c'est tout pardonner.[2] Do we really believe that our softening standards bring happiness? Is it our sound and considered judgment that the tougher subjects of the classics and mathematics should be thrown aside, as suggested by some educators, for doll-playing? Small wonder that Charles Malik, Lebanese delegate at the U.N., writes: "There is in the West"—in the United States—"a general weakening of moral fiber. [Our] leadership does not seem to be adequate to the unprecedented challenges of the age."

The last misunderstanding is in the area of values. Here are some of the most influential principles of teacher education over the past fifty years: there is no eternal truth; there is no absolute moral law; there is no God. Yet all of history has taught us that the denial of these ultimates, the placement of man or state at the core of the universe, results in a paralyzing mass selfishness; and the first signs of it are already frighteningly evident.

Arnold Toynbee[3] has said that all progress, all development come from challenge and a consequent response. Without challenge there is no response, no development, no freedom. So first we owe to our children the most demanding, challenging curriculum that is within their capabilities. Michelangelo did not learn to paint by spending his time doodling. Mozart was not an accomplished pianist at the age of eight as the result of spending his days in front of a television set. Like Eve Curie,[4] like Helen Keller,[5] they responded to the challenge of their lives by a disciplined training: and they gained a new freedom.

The second opportunity we can give our boys and girls is the right to failure. "Freedom is not only a privilege, it is a test," writes du Nouy. What kind of a test is it, what kind of freedom where no one can fail? The day is past when the United States can afford to give high school diplomas to all who sit through four years of instruction, regardless of whether any visible results can be discerned. We live in a narrowed world where we must be alert, awake to realism. These are hard words, but they are brutally true. If we deprive our children of the right to fail we deprive them of their knowledge of the world as it is.

Finally, we can expose our children to the best values we have found. By relating our lives to the evidences of the ages, by judging our philosophy in the light of values that history has proven truest, perhaps we shall be able to produce that "ringing message, full of content and truth, satisfying the mind, appealing to the heart, firing the will, a message on which one can stake his whole life."[6] This is the message that could mean joy and strength and leadership—freedom as opposed to serfdom.

SEYMOUR ST. JOHN

NOTES

1. Antoine de Saint Exupery (1900–1944), French writer and aviator.
2. "To understand all is to forgive all."
3. Modern British historian (1889–1975), author of *A Study of History* and *Civilization on Trial*.

4. French author. Daughter of Pierre and Marie Curie, discoverers of radium.
5. Deaf and blind from the age of two, Helen Keller (1880–1968) became a writer and lecturer.
6. Also from Charles Malik, Lebanese delegate to the U.N.

Questions for Discussion

1. What are the five freedoms described by the author?

2. According to St. John, the loss of the fifth freedom is being caused by what three misunderstandings? Can you think of further examples of the three misunderstandings he cites? Are there any other misunderstandings in addition to the ones he mentions?

3. What are the three opportunities that St. John says we should give our children? Can you think of other opportunities we should give our children?

Writing Assignments

1. Write a summary of approximately 250 words of "The Fifth Freedom." Review Chapter 6, "Writing Summaries," if necessary.

2. Write a short paper in which you respond to and evaluate "The Fifth Freedom." Do you agree with what St. John says? If so, why? Give specific examples from your own experience or reading. Do you disagree with what St. John says? If so, why? Give specific examples from your own experience or reading.

IN LEARNING LIMBO: ELECTIVE COURSES HAVE RESULTED IN NO EDUCATION AT ALL

We educate a few of our high school children for freedom and we educate a few for slavery. Most we educate for nothing at all. We learned how to educate for freedom and slavery from the ancients. Educating for nothing we seem to have invented all by ourselves.

We give our children various tests during their grade school years, and those with low scores (usually children from homes of little affluence; children who have small frame of reference for learning) are likely to be guided into vocational training, the modern version of the sort of practical, task-oriented education the Greeks and Romans considered appropriate for slaves.

Grade school students whose test results are high are led

into an education very much like one the ancients felt was proper for a free person; an education completely different from a slave's education.

The Greeks and Romans believed that, unlike a slave, a free person's education should not be a "practical" education. The Roman word for free was "liber," and a "liberal" education was an education not so much in learning to *do* as in learning to *think*. A slave was educated in specifics and a free person was educated in abstractions.

Then, as now, a liberal education consisted of classes in language, history, philosophy, mathematics and the sciences— all subjects that were useless in most respects for performing specific, wage-earning tasks, but very good in exercising the mind in the kind of complex reasoning the ancients felt a free person was called upon to do on a daily basis (of course, a liberal education also gave, and gives, one the sort of general grounding that makes it possible to quickly learn skills necessary for making a living—most free people in ancient times had to make a living eventually, just as they must today).

A liberal education was designed to ensure that one would be willing and able to participate effectively in community affairs. The "liber" person had studied history and understood how issues of the past relate to issues of the present. He had studied philosophy and understood the philosophical foundations of his government. The moral lessons of literature were ingrained within him and he was able to apply them to community life, and personal life as well.

About 15 percent of our high school children are given something very much like the old liberal education. They spend all four of their high school years taking "solid" classes: English, history, a foreign language, math, social studies and science. They do not negate the value of the old regimen by taking either vocational classes or "elective" classes in place of solid classes.

The curriculum in modern American high schools is, then, what we might call a real plan, an agenda for education, for those children who are taking a schedule of classes much like the old liberal curriculum, and for young people in a vocational education program (we may not agree with the goals of vocational education, but we must grant that it is a distinct plan for education). Together, children in vocational education and in classes constituting a liberal education account for perhaps 40 percent of our high school-age population.

What about the rest—the majority of American high school students?

The rest are in learning limbo. They tested high enough that they are not sent off to auto shop and hairdressing classes, but through indifference on their own part, their parents and the school, they are allowed to opt out of a four-year liberal education curriculum they are perfectly capable of handling, and choose a curriculum that is no education at all.

Certainly, they must take about half of a liberal education—language, history, math and science courses mandated by the state as requirements for graduation. In the typical American high school, of the 18 to 22 credits needed to graduate, only half of them must be in required classes. Once those required classes are taken, most American high school students drift off into the elective curriculum.

Most large American high schools offer a variety of elective classes that is astounding. Calligraphy, modern dance, jewelry making, film history, weight lifting—the list is endless. The appeal of these classes can be very great, but their cumulative worth is practically nothing.

Many educators believe that the high school years provide barely enough time in which to give our children an education appropriate to a "liber" person. They believe that not only should all four years of high school be spent in an intense liberal education program, but so should the college years. The fact that few of us devote our college years to a strictly liberal education is, these educators say, bad enough—but that so many children spend only half of their time in high school in liberal studies strikes them as a disaster.

Most of our high school children are being badly shortchanged. They don't get enough language, history, math and science to make anything like a real education. The elective classes they take may be fun, but they go nowhere.

The results of giving so many of our children so innocuous an education are plain for all to see. We have a population poorly trained to be "liber." Only a small percentage of our citizens are given the sort of education that prepares one to live in a free society.

We wonder why fewer than 50 percent of American adults exercise their right to vote. They do not vote, they do not take part in helping shape our society, because they were not educated to do so.

"Liber" men and women in ancient times learned that only

through obeying and upholding the laws of the land could a free country survive. An astronomical crime rate among our citizenry tells us that we have not impressed this belief upon a huge segment of our population.

Perhaps the saddest thing about depriving our children of a "liber" person's education is that we are depriving them of the great bonus such an education carries with it.

Studying literature and history makes one aware of the greatest artistic achievements done by the best minds of all time—aware and appreciative.

We wonder why our children read few good books and why they enjoy watching television shows that are so bad. We shouldn't wonder. They have been educated for nothing else.

It is widely remarked that we are at a crossroads in American education; certainly the national debate about which educational road to take is loud and persistent.

The education road once called "slavery" and now called "vocational education" is well marked and easy to travel. It is a part of our ancient heritage, however, that is prime for destruction.

The educational road traveled by free men and women is also well marked. It is wide too, with room for all to travel on. Most of our children are on no road at all. They wander about in an educational wilderness and it is time to get them back on track.

WILLIAM HERMANN

Questions for Discussion

1. In "In Learning Limbo," Hermann compares and contrasts what different types of education? What points does he make? What method of organization does he use?

2. What is the origin of the word *liberal*, specifically in relation to education?

3. What does Hermann mean when he says that the majority of high school students are "in learning limbo"?

4. Together, St. John's "The Fifth Freedom" and Hermann's "In Learning Limbo" paint a rather gloomy picture of American education today. Do you think this picture is justified? If so, why? If not, why not? Both essays were written some years ago; do you think that things are changing for the better? If so, why? If not, why not?

Writing Assignments

1. Write a summary of approximately 250 words of "In Learning Limbo." Refer to Chapter 6, "Writing Summaries," if necessary.

2. Write a short essay in reaction to "In Learning Limbo." Do you agree with what Hermann says? If so, why? Give specific examples from your own experience or your reading. Do you disagree with what Hermann says? If so, why? Give specific examples from your own experience or reading.

3. Think back to your own high school experience. How would you describe and categorize it? Write an essay in which you use your own experience as an example of one of the types of education that Hermann describes in his essay.

4. Write a short paper in which you compare and contrast St. John's "The Fifth Freedom" and Hermann's "In Learning Limbo."

TELEVISION ADDICTION

The word "addiction" is often used loosely and wryly in conversation. People will refer to themselves as "mystery book addicts" or "cookie addicts." E. B. White writes of his annual surge of interest in gardening: "We are hooked and are making an attempt to kick the habit." Yet nobody really believes that reading mysteries or ordering seeds by catalogue is serious enough to be compared with addictions to heroin or alcohol. The word "addiction" is here used jokingly to denote a tendency to overindulge in some pleasurable activity.

People often refer to themselves as being "hooked on TV." Does this, too, fall into the lighthearted category of cookie eating and other pleasures that people pursue with unusual intensity, or is there a kind of television viewing that falls into the more serious category of destructive addiction.

When we think about addiction to drugs or alcohol, we frequently focus on negative aspects, ignoring the pleasures that accompany drinking or drug-taking. And yet the essence of any serious addiction is a pursuit of pleasure, a search for a "high" that normal life does not supply. It is only the inability to function without the addictive substances that is dismaying, the dependence of the organism upon a certain experience and an increasing ability to function normally without it. Thus a person will take two or three drinks at the end of the day not merely for the pleasure drinking provides, but also because he "doesn't feel normal" without them.

An addict does not merely pursue a pleasurable experience and need to experience it in order to function normally. He needs to *repeat* it again and again. Something about that particular experience makes life without it less than complete. Other potentially pleasurable experiences are no longer possible, for under the spell of the addictive experience, his life is peculiarly distorted. The addict craves an experience and yet he is never really satisfied. The organism may be temporarily sated, but soon it begins to crave again.

Finally a serious addiction is distinguished from a harmless pursuit of pleasure by its distinctly destructive elements. A heroin addict, for instance, leads a damaged life: his increasing need for heroin in increasing doses prevents him from working, from maintaining relationships, from developing in human ways. Similarly an alcoholic's life is narrowed and dehumanized by his dependence on alcohol.

Let us consider television viewing in the light of the conditions that define serious addictions.

Not unlike drugs or alcohol, the television experience allows the participant to blot out the real world and enter into a pleasurable and passive mental state. The worries and anxieties of reality are as effectively deferred by becoming absorbed in a television program as by going on a "trip" induced by drugs or alcohol. And just as alcoholics are only inchoately aware of their addiction, feeling that they control their drinking more than they really do ("I can cut it out any time I want—I just like to have three or four drinks before dinner"), people similarly overestimate their control over television watching. Even as they put off other activities to spend hour after hour watching television, they feel they could easily resume living in a different, less passive style. But somehow or other while the television set is present in their homes, the click doesn't sound. With television pleasures available, those other experiences seems less attractive, more difficult somehow.

A heavy viewer (a college English instructor) observes: "I find television almost irresistible. When the set is on, I cannot ignore it. I can't turn it off. I feel sapped, will-less, enervated. As I reach out to turn off the set, the strength goes out of my arms. So I sit there for hours and hours."

The self-confessed television addict often feels he "ought" to do other things—but the fact that he doesn't read and doesn't plant his garden or sew or crochet or play games or have conversations means that those activities are no longer as desirable as his television viewing. In a way a heavy viewer's life is as imbalanced by his television "habit" as a drug addict's or an alcoholic's. He is living in a holding pattern, as it were, passing up the activities that lead to growth or development or a sense of accomplishment. This is one reason people talk about their television viewing so ruefully, so apologetically. They are aware that it is an unproductive experience, that almost any other endeavor is more worthwhile by any human measure.

Finally it is the adverse effect of television viewing on the lives of so many people that defines it as a serious addiction. The television habit distorts the sense of time. It renders other experiences vague and curiously unreal while taking on a greater reality for itself. It weakens relationships by reducing and sometimes eliminating normal opportunities for talking, for communicating.

And yet television does not satisfy, else why would the viewer continue to watch hour after hour, day after day? "The measure of health," writes Lawrence Kubie, "is flexibility . . . and especially the freedom to cease when sated." But the television viewer can never be sated with his television experiences—they do not provide the true nourishment that satiation requires—and thus he finds that he cannot stop watching.

MARIE WINN, *THE PLUG-IN DRUG*

Questions for Discussion

1. In "Television Addiction," Marie Winn compares watching television to what kinds of addiction? List the points of comparison the author uses. What method of organization does she use?

2. Do you think television addiction is the serious problem that Winn presents it to be, or is she overstating her case? Give reasons for your reaction.

3. Are there other kinds of activities like television viewing that have the same potential for addiction?

Writing Assignments

1. Write a summary of approximately 250 words of "Television Addiction." Refer to Chapter 6, "Writing Summaries," if necessary.

2. After reading Winn's essay, you have concluded that a friend or relative suffers from television addiction. You are alarmed and want to point out to this individual the dangers of this type of addiction. Using Winn's essay as a model and a source of ideas, write a letter to your friend or relative in which you define television addiction, quoting from and paraphrasing Winn's essay as appropriate. Then attempt to convince your reader that he or she is indeed a television addict and should attempt to change his or her ways. Outline your letter first, using both the half-and-half method and the point-by-point method, and choose the one you think is more effective.

3. After reading Winn's essay, you have concluded that a friend or relative suffers from an addiction similar to but different from television addiction. You are alarmed and you want to point out to this individual the dangers of his or her addiction. Using Winn's essay as a model and a source of ideas, write a letter to your friend or relative in which you define addiction, quoting from and paraphrasing Winn's essay as appropriate. Then attempt to convince your reader that he or she is indeed an "addict" and should attempt to change his or her ways. Outline your letter first, using both the half-and-half method and the point-by-point method, and choose the one you think is more effective.

4. Assume that a friend or relative has written you a letter claiming that you are a television addict or that you suffer from a similar addiction. Write a letter in response refuting the accusation; consider the points made in Winn's essay and point out how you do not fit the definition. Or admit that you are an addict, and devise a plan for breaking yourself of your addiction.

THE SELLING OF BARBIE

Advertising can be a very tricky business. One would think that commercials for products should be aimed at their consumers, the people who purchase them. Not always so. Toy companies, in particular, aim their advertising indirectly at parents, the actual purchaser of most toys, through their children. Perhaps the most successful and enduring example of this type of marketing approach is Mattel's Barbie commercials.

Barbie is one of the most popular dolls on the market primarily because of her "grown-up" appeal to little girls. Commercials portray Barbie as a glamorous young woman, on an endless succession of dates with Ken, never in the same outfit twice. Such a lifestyle holds tremendous appeal to girls aged six through twelve, the target audience of Barbie commercials. Girls in this age group, not yet old enough for dating or a sophisticated wardrobe, can take part in these aspects of adult life vicariously through their Barbie dolls. The marketers of Barbie seek to offer young girls an idealized version of adult life, one absent of any responsibility. For example, Barbie and her boyfriend, Ken, are never portrayed as married. Thus she is free from the mundane chores of working, cleaning, having a family. She offers every little girl her fantasy—fancy cars, big houses, an endless supply of clothes, and Ken, the everpresent suitor.

Mattel's commercials are also successful because they are shown during "children's prime time," Saturday morning cartoon hours. These spots are aimed directly at children, even though kids themselves have relatively little purchasing power. Toy companies know that children are their best salesmen. Even the most steadfast parents will occasionally cave in to such heart-wrenching appeals as "But I *need* a Barbie townhouse. Please? PLEASE!" By appealing directly to children, Mattel can tailor its commercials to the irrational whims and fancies of young girls. The company doesn't have to deliver a sound, logical sales pitch to parents because little girls sell doll houses in a way Mattel never could, by whining and tantrum throwing.

Aiming these ads directly at children enables Mattel to engage in many subtle deceptions. Kids simply do not understand or listen to such phrases as "assembly required" and "sold separately." By displaying Barbie fully outfitted along with related products that are completely assembled, Mattel plants instant and unrealistic expectations in the minds of young viewers. When a child sees Barbie and Ken lounging in an inflatable pool next to their camper, which just happens to be parked beside their Dreamhouse, she seldom understands that, if her parents buy Barbie, all she receives is a half-naked doll. However, since the desire has been planted by Mattel's commercials, she will persuade her parents to buy a battery of Barbie accessories, again acting unwittingly as an agent for Mattel.

These selling techniques may be unfair, deceptive, and exploitative of children, but one cannot question their success. Rare is the girl who does not have a Barbie doll. Having only the doll, no wardrobe, no Country Cabin, no Beauty Parlor is even more uncommon. Girls fall for Mattel's approach hook, line, and sinker. Mattel relies on Americans' need to instantly gratify their little girls' every wish and desire. Their marketing walks a fine line between selling and deceiving. The little cherub who requests a Barbie Townhouse for Christmas cannot comprehend that her Townhouse is assembled painstakingly from the ground up and that Mommy and Daddy are the construction crew. Are these ads fair to kids or their parents? No. Are they effective? Mattel's sales figures shout a resounding "yes."

JODI M. ROBBINS

Questions for Discussion

1. Have you ever owned a Barbie doll? Have you ever bought one? Do you know someone who owns a Barbie doll? Was the purchase of the Barbie doll triggered in the way that Robbins describes in her essay?

2. Is there a similar item receiving the same kind of commercial exposure as the Barbie doll? What is it? What are the commercials like?

3. Robbins argues that the Barbie doll commercials are deceptive, but are other commercials aimed at adults also deceptive? Give some examples of commercials that you consider misleading.

Writing Assignments

1. Write a summary of approximately 250 words of "The Selling of Barbie." Refer to Chapter 6, "Writing Summaries," if necessary.

2. Write an essay in reaction to "The Selling of Barbie." Using Robbins' essay as a model, choose a popular commercial or series of commercials for a product that parents purchase for their children, and discuss a similar situation. Use Robbins' essay as a source to quote from and paraphrase, but describe a different product.

3. Using Robbins' essay as a model, choose a popular commercial or series of commercials for a product that adults purchase for themselves, and discuss a similar situation.

4. Write an essay in which you argue that parents and/or other adult consumers are responsible for their own choices.

5. Winn's "Television Addiction" and Robbins' "The Selling of Barbie" make negative comments about television and its effects on viewers. Write an essay in which you present the arguments that the two authors make against television. Then either agree or disagree with what they say, offering specific examples of the negative effects of television from your own experience or reading. Or write an essay in which you argue that the authors have overstated their case and point out some of the benefits of television.

THE JEANING OF AMERICA—AND THE WORLD

This is the story of a sturdy American symbol which has now spread throughout most of the world. The symbol is not the dollar. It is not even Coca-Cola. It is a simple pair of pants called blue jeans, and what the pants symbolize is what Alexis de Tocqueville called "a manly and legitimate passion for equality...." Blue jeans are favored equally by bureaucrats and cowboys; bankers and deadbeats; fashion designers and beer drinkers. They draw no distinctions and recognize no classes; they are merely American. Yet they are sought after almost everywhere in the world—including Russia, where authorities recently broke up a teen-aged gang that was selling them on the black market for two hundred dollars a pair. They have been around for a long time, and it seems likely that they will outlive even the necktie.

This ubiquitous American symbol was the invention of a Bavarian-born Jew.... His name was Levi Strauss.

He was born in Bad Ocheim, Germany, in 1829, and during the European political turmoil of 1848 decided to take his chances in New York, to which his two brothers already had emigrated. Upon arrival, Levi soon found that his two brothers had exaggerated their tales of an easy life in the land of the main chance. They were landowners, they had told him; instead, he found them pushing needles, thread, pots, pans, ribbons, yarn, scissors, and buttons to housewives. For two years he was a lowly peddler, hauling some 180 pounds of sundries door-to-door to eke out a marginal living. When a married sister in San Francisco offered to pay his way West in 1850, he jumped at the opportunity, taking with him bolts of canvas he hoped to sell for tenting.

It was the wrong kind of canvas for that purpose, but while talking with a miner down from the mother lode, he learned that pants—sturdy pants that would stand up to the rigors of the diggings—were almost impossible to find. Opportunity beckoned. On the spot, Strauss measured the man's girth and inseam with a piece of string and, for six dollars in gold dust, had them tailored into a pair of stiff but rugged pants. The miner was delighted with the result, word got around about "those pants of Levi's," and Strauss was in business. The company has been in business ever since.

When Strauss ran out of canvas, he wrote his two brothers to send him more. He received instead a tough, brown cotton cloth made in Nimes, France—called *serge de Nimes*, and swiftly shortening to "denim" (the word "jeans" derives from *Genes*, the French word for Genoa, where a similar cloth was produced). Almost from the first, Strauss had his cloth dyed the distinctive indigo that gave blue jeans their name, but it was not until the 1870's that he added the copper rivets which have long since become a company trademark. The rivets were the idea of a Virginia City, Nevada, tailor, Jacob W. Davis, who added them to pacify a mean-tempered miner called Alkali Ike. Alkali, the story goes, complained that the pockets of his jeans always tore when he stuffed them with ore samples and demanded that Davis do something about it. As a kind of joke, Davis took the pants to a blacksmith and had the pockets riveted; once again, the idea worked so well that word got around: in 1873 Strauss appropriated and patented the gimmick—and hired Davis as a regional manager.

By this time, Strauss had taken both his brothers and his two brother-in-laws into the company and was ready for his third San Francisco store. Over the ensuing years the company prospered locally, and by the time of his death in 1902, Strauss had become a man of prominence in California. For three decades thereafter the business remained profitable though small, with sales largely confined to the working people of the West—cowboys, lumberjacks, railroad workers, and the like. Levi's jeans were first introduced to the East, apparently, during the dude-ranch craze of the 1930's, when vacationing Easterners returned and spread the word about the wonderful pants with rivets. Another boost came in World War II, when blue jeans were declared an essential commodity and were sold only to people engaged in defense work. From a company with fifteen salespeople, two plants, and almost no business east of the Mississippi in 1946, the organization grew in thirty years to include a sales force of more than twenty-two thousand, with fifty plants and offices in thirty-five countries. Each year, more than 250,000,000 items of Levi's clothing are sold—including more than 83,000,000 pairs of riveted blue jeans. They have become, through marketing, word of mouth, and demonstrable reliability, the common pants of America. They can be purchased pre-washed, pre-faded, and pre-shrunk for the suitably proletarian look. They adapt themselves to any sort of idiosyncratic use; women slit them off above the inseams and convert them into long skirts, men chop them off above the knees and turn them into something to be worn while challenging the surf. Decorations and ornamentations abound.

The pants have become a tradition, and along the way have acquired a history of their own—so much so that the company has opened a museum in San Francisco. There was, for example, the turn-of-the-century trainman who replaced a faulty coupling with a pair of jeans; the Wyoming man who used jeans as a towrope to haul his car out of a ditch; the Californian who discovered several pairs in an abandoned mine, wore them, then discovered they were sixty-three years old and still as good as new and turned them over to the Smithsonian as a tribute to their toughness. And then there is the particularly terrifying story of the careless construction worker who dangled fifty-two stories above the street until rescued, his sole support the Levi's belt loop through which his rope was hooked.

Today "those pants of Levi's" have gone across the seas—although the company has learned that marketing abroad is an arcane art. The conservative dress jeans favored in northern France do not move well on the Cote d'Azur; Sta-Prest sells well in Switzerland but dies in Scandinavia; button fronts are popular in France, zippers in Britain.

Though Levi Strauss & Co. has since become Levi Strauss International, with all that the corporate name implies, it still retains a suitably fond regard for its beginnings. Through what it calls its "Western Image Program," employing Western magazine advertisements, local radio and television, and the promotion of rodeos, the company still pursues the working people of the West who first inspired Levi Strauss to make pants to fit the world.

CARIN C. QUINN

Questions for Discussion

1. What are the origins of the words *jeans* and *denim*?

2. Why were rivets added to jeans?

3. What are some of the stories told about the toughness of Levi's blue jeans?

4. Have you read or heard any other stories about Levi's or other types of jeans in addition to the ones Quinn relates in her essay?

Writing Assignments

1. Write a summary of approximately 250 words of "The Jeaning of America—and the World." Refer to Chapter 6, "Writing Summaries," if necessary.

2. Write an essay in which you compare and contrast blue jeans and Barbie dolls. How are they alike? How are they different?

WITCHDOCTORS AND THE UNIVERSALITY OF HEALING

Witch doctors and psychiatrists perform essentially the same function in their respective cultures. They are both therapists; both treat patients, using similar techniques; and both get similar results. Recognition of this should not downgrade psychiatrists—rather it should upgrade witchdoctors.

The term "witchdoctor" is Western in origin, imposed on healers of the Third World by 18th and 19th century explorers. The world was simpler then, and the newly discovered cultures were quickly assigned their proper status in the Order of Things. We were white, they were black. We were civilized, they were primitive. We were Christian, they were pagan. We used science, they used magic. We had doctors, they had witchdoctors.

American psychiatrists have much to learn from therapists in other cultures. My own experience observing and working with them includes two years in Ethiopia and briefer periods in Sarawak, Bali, Hong Kong, Colombia, and with Alaskan Indians, Puerto Ricans, and Mexican-Americans in this country. What I learned from these doctor-healers was that I, as a psychiatrist, was using the same mechanisms for curing my patients as they were—and, not surprisingly, I was getting about the same results. The mechanisms can be classified under four categories.

The first is the naming process. A psychiatrist or witchdoctor can work magic by telling a patient what is wrong with him. It conveys to the patient that someone—usually a man of considerable status—understands. And since his problem can be understood, then, implicitly, it can be cured. A psychiatrist who tells an illiterate African that his phobia is related to a fear of failure, or a witchdoctor who tells an American tourist that his phobia is related to possession by an ancestral spirit will be met by equally blank stares. And as therapists they will be equally ineffective. This is a major reason for the failure of most attempts at cross-cultural psychotherapy. Since a shared world-view is necessary for the naming process to be effective, then it is reasonable to expect that the best therapist-patient relationships will be those where both come from the same culture or subculture.

The second healing component used by therapists everywhere is their personality characteristics. An increasing amount of research shows that certain personal qualities of the therapists—accurate empathy, nonpossessive warmth, genuineness—are of crucial importance in producing effective psychotherapy. Clearly, more studies are needed in this area, but if they substantiate the emerging trend, then radical changes in the selection of therapists will be in order. Rather than selecting therapists because they can memorize facts and achieve high grades, we should be selecting them on the basis of their personality. Therapists in other cultures are selected more often for their personality characteristics; the fact that they have not studied biochemistry is not considered important.

The third component of the healing process that appears to be universal is the patients' expectations. Healers all over the world use many ways to raise the expectations of their patients. The first way is the trip itself to the healer. It is a common observation that the farther a person goes to be healed, the greater are the chances that he will be healed. This is called the pilgrimage. Thus, sick people in Topeka go to the Leahy Clinic in Boston. The resulting therapeutic effects of the trip are exactly the same as have been operating for centuries at Delphi or Lourdes. The next way to raise patients' expectations is the building used for the healing. The more impressive it is, the greater will be the patients' expectations. This has been called the edifice complex. Therapists in different cultures use certain paraphernalia to increase patient expectations. In Western cultures nonpsychiatric healers have their stethoscope and psychotherapists are supposed to have their couch. Therapists in other cultures have their counterpart trademark, often a special drum, mask, or amulet. Another aspect of patients' expectations rests upon the therapist's training. Some sort of training program is found for healers in almost all cultures. Blackfoot Indians, for example, had to complete a seven-year period of training in order to qualify as medicine men.

Finally, the same techniques of therapy are used by healers all over the world. Let me provide a few examples: Drugs are one of the techniques of Western therapy of which we are most proud. However, drugs are used by healers in other cultures as well. Rauwulfia root, for example, which was introduced into Western psychiatry in the 1950s as resperine, a major tranquilizer, has been used in India for centuries as a tranquilizer, and has also been in wide use in West Africa for many years. Another example is shock therapy. When electric shock therapy was introduced by Cerletti in the 1930s, he was not aware that it had been used in some cultures for up to 4000 years. The technique of applying electric eels to the head of a patient is referred to in writings of Aristotle, Pliny, and Plutarch.

What kind of results do therapists in other cultures—witchdoctors—achieve? A Canadian psychiatrist, Dr. Raymond Prince, spent 17 months studying 46 Nigerian witchdoctors, and judged that the therapeutic results were about equal to those obtained in North American clinics and hospitals.

It would appear, then, that psychiatrists have much to learn from witchdoctors. We can see the components of our own therapy system in relief. We can learn why we are effective—or not effective. And we can learn to be less ethnocentric and arrogant about our own therapy and more tolerant of others. If we can learn all this from witchdoctors, then we will have learned much.

EDWIN FULLER TORREY,
THE MIND GAME: WITCHDOCTORS AND PSYCHIATRISTS

Questions for Discussion

1. In "Witchdoctors and the Universality of Healing," Torrey compares psychiatrists and other professionals to witchdoctors. List the points he makes. What method of organization does he use?

2. What is Torrey's thesis in this essay? Do you agree with it? Why or why not?

Writing Assignments

1. Write a summary of approximately 250 words of "Witchdoctors and the Universality of Healing." Refer to Chapter 6, "Writing Summaries," if necessary.

2. Write an essay in which you make a comparison similar to the one made by Torrey. For example, football players and boxers are often referred to as "gladiators," and working mothers are called "superwomen." Follow the pattern of Torrey's essay; that is, establish the characteristics of the profession and show how it fits the analogy you have chosen.

UNIT II

Sentence Structure

SENTENCE STRUCTURE problems abound in the first drafts of many writers, and editing poorly constructed sentences is an important step in the revision process.

If your teacher makes comments such as the following on your papers, then sentence structure is a problem in your writing.

- faulty subject-verb agreement
- fragments
- comma splices
- run-together sentences
- repeated subjects or double subjects
- double comparatives or double superlatives
- double (or multiple) negatives
- faulty parallelisms
- dangling modifiers

You need to learn how to recognize and revise these specific weaknesses in your early drafts so they do not appear in your final draft. Unit II deals with each of these sentence structure problems.

Chapter 8, "Subjects and Verbs," explains how to recognize subjects and verbs. It also explains the rules of subject-verb agreement and provides practices dealing with each rule, in addition to a review practice.

Chapter 9, "Sentence Boundaries," discusses the nature of the complete sentence and defines and exemplifies complete and incomplete (fragmented) sentences. It also explains the different types of fragments and provides practices dealing with each type, in addition to a review practice.

Chapter 10, "Clause Boundaries," defines types of clauses and presents methods of combining clauses. It explains comma splices and run-together sentences and provides practices on each. A discussion of the various methods of revising comma splices and run-together sentences is provided, in addition to information about choosing the best revision. Review practices are also provided.

Chapter 11, "The Forbidden Doubles," explains double subjects, double comparatives and superlatives, and double (or multiple) negatives. It provides practices on each of these forbidden doubles and a review practice.

Chapter 12, "Unbalanced and Illogical Structures," discusses the concepts of sentence balance and sentence logic. Faulty parallelism and dangling modifiers are explained. Practices on unbalanced and illogical structures are provided, as is a review practice.

CHAPTER 8
Subjects and Verbs

8.1 INTRODUCTION

Writers of English do not need to have any explicit knowledge of grammar in order to construct grammatical English sentences, but they do need some understanding of grammatical concepts when they have inadvertently constructed an ungrammatical sentence and need to correct it.

If, for example, your teacher writes comments like "faulty subject-verb agreement," "fragment," "comma splice," or "run-together sentence" on your papers, you need to have some information about grammar to correct those errors. The most essential concepts are those of **subject** and **verb**.

A subject and a verb are necessary in every complete English sentence. In speech, often one or the other—or even both—may be omitted. Occasionally, such omissions are permissible in writing; for example, when dialogue is used:

"Been to town lately?"

"Yes."

"Seen Joe?"

"Not since last Tuesday."

In the kind of writing college students are ordinarily expected to do and the kind of writing expected in most professional jobs, omission of subjects or verbs is seldom acceptable. Every sentence should have both a subject and a verb. (Subjects are underlined once and verbs are underlined twice in the following examples.)

Abraham Lincoln was President of the United States during the Civil War.

The manager promised the customer quick shipment of his order.

Obviously, there is more to each of the preceding sentences than just a subject and a verb, but they form the basic elements of the sentence.

8.2 RECOGNIZING SUBJECTS

Subjects are usually nouns, proper nouns, or pronouns.

Nouns are the names of persons, places, or things.

person — boy
place — city
thing — book

Proper nouns are the names of specific persons, places, or things.

person — Joe Brown
place — El Paso
book   — *Gone with the Wind*

Pronouns sometimes take the place of nouns; often the following pronouns are subjects of sentences.

I   you   he   she   it   we   they

8.3 RECOGNIZING VERBS

Verbs usually express action or indicate a state of being. In normal sentence order, the verb follows the subject. As the following examples illustrate, verbs often consist of more than one word.

The boy <u>walks</u> fast.   (one word)

The boy <u>is walking</u> fast.   (two words)

The boy <u>has walked</u> fast.   (two words)

The boy <u>should have walked</u> fast.   (three words)

==There are many such combinations available in English; usually they consist of a verb ending with *-ed* or *-ing* and one or more helping verbs.== You do not need to learn all of the possible variations, but you do need to know the pattern. Some common helping verbs are listed here.

am, is, are   shall, should
was, were   will, would
been, being   may, might
have, has, had   must
do, does, did   ought
can, could

Sometimes the word following *am, is, are, was, were, been,* or *being* is not an *-ed* or *-ing* form of a verb but is instead a **noun** or an **adjective** (a describing word).

           verb
The boy is walking.

           noun
The boy is his son.

           adjective
The boy is tall.

When the word following *am, is, are, was, were, been, being* is a noun or an adjective, it is not considered part of the verb and should not be indicated as such.

PRACTICE

Following are paragraphs of several simple sentences with different kinds of subjects and verbs. Copy the paragraphs; in each sentence, underline the subject once and the verb twice. Remember to double underline all parts of the verb, but do not double underline words that are not part of the verb.

The boy is walking. (Double underline the *-ing* word after *is*.)

The boy is tall. (Do not double underline the adjective *tall* after *is*.)

Last summer our family went to the Ozarks for a vacation.
                                                              1
We drove over a thousand miles to get there. The trip required
 2   3
two full days of driving.

We stayed at a very nice lodge next to a lake. The lodge
  4   5
was quite old. It had been built during the nineteenth century.
      6

The lounge had a huge fireplace in it. Our second-floor rooms overlooked the lake. A gentle breeze kept our rooms cool and comfortable.

My father fished in the lake every day. He caught very few fish. My brother hiked in the surrounding woods several times. He enjoyed their quiet beauty very much. I swam in the lodge pool every afternoon. The water was very pleasant. Mother played tennis every day. She improved her game considerably.

We ate dinner in the lodge dining room every evening. The food was always excellent. After dinner we went for a walk in the village. We shopped for gifts for friends and relatives. We also bought dozens of souvenirs for ourselves.

Our vacation was over much too soon. Our car was filled with packages on our return trip. Next summer we may return to the same place for our vacation.

8.4 BASIC PATTERN OF SUBJECT-VERB AGREEMENT

One of the conventions of English is that the subject and the verb are supposed to "agree" in person and number.

	SINGULAR	PLURAL
First person	I walk	We walk
Second person	You walk	You walk
Third person	He walks	They walk
	She walks	
	It walks	

As you can see, there is no difference in verb form for five of the six; however, the verb form is different in the third person singular, requiring an *-s* at the end.

The basic pattern of **subject-verb agreement** in English is that singular nouns do not end in *-s*, but third person singular verbs do.

The boy walks.

Conversely, most plural nouns end in -s, but plural verbs do not.

The boys walk.

With some English verbs, the difference between the singular and the plural form is more than an -s.

SINGULAR	PLURAL
The boy ha*s*	The boys ha*ve*
The boy do*es*	The boys do

Note that the basic pattern is still maintained: that is, singular verbs end in -s, but plural verbs do not.

Sometimes subject-verb agreement is a problem for writers, particularly writers who tend to omit word endings in their speech and who then transfer that habit to their writing. If they omit -s endings in their speech, their writing may be characterized by an absence of proper subject-verb agreement. Since writers who omit word endings in their speech and in their writing are often unaware that they do so, the problem of subject-verb agreement may be a difficult one for them to overcome.

If you have a tendency to omit words endings, first you must recognize that you do so; then you must check your writing carefully for omitted word endings and add them where they are required.

PRACTICE

Copy the following paragraphs. In each sentence, underline the subject once, then insert the appropriate verb form, and underline the verb twice. The word in parentheses is the base form of the verb (the form without the third person singular -s ending). If the verb form in parentheses is correct, use it; if it is not, change it to the correct form. If you have a tendency to omit word endings, be especially careful with this practice. Do not omit word endings where they are needed, but do not add them where they are not required.

My sister (have) been taking philosophy this semester. Her
¹
best friend (have) been taking the course too. They (enjoy) the
² ³

class very much. The professor (encourage) the students to participate in the class. Each student (have) a chance to ask questions and to make comments.

According to my sister, the professor (lecture) very well. The students (like) the class very much. They (enjoy) the lectures and the class discussion. They do not (like) the professor's exams, however. He (give) essay exams.

My sister (study) very hard before each exam. Her friend (do) not study so hard. Often she (make) a higher grade than my sister on the exams. Of course, she (write) very well. She (think) fast too.

My sister usually (know) the material better than her friend. She (have) prepared herself for the exam more thoroughly. Unfortunately, she (panic) on exams. She never (do) as well as she should.

After each philosophy exam, the students (sigh) with relief.

8.5 PRESENT TENSE OF THE VERB *to be*

The verb *to be* poses some special problems of subject-verb agreement. Following are the **present tense** forms of the verb *to be*:

	SINGULAR	PLURAL
First person	I am	We are
Second person	You are	You are
Third person	He is	They are
	She is	
	It is	

In addition to maintaining the distinction between third person singular and plural, there is also a distinction made between first person singular and plural.

SUBJECTS AND VERBS 119

Sometimes writers omit these distinctions in their speech and then transfer this habit to their writing, either using the form *be* or omitting the verb completely.

STANDARD WRITTEN ENGLISH FORM	OTHER FORMS
I am walking	I walking
	I be walking
You are walking	You walking
	You be walking
He is walking	He walking
	He be walking
We are walking	We walking
	We be walking
They are walking	They walking
	They be walking

PRACTICE

Copy the following paragraphs. In each sentence, underline the subject once, then insert the appropriate present tense form (*am, is, are*) of the verb *to be*, and underline the verb twice. If you tend to omit some of these distinctions in your speech, be especially careful to select the Standard Written English form.

I _____ taking history this semester. The course
   1
_____ very difficult for me. The class _____ held in a
   2   3
large lecture hall. Over three hundred students _____ in
                                                     4
the class.

The class _____ entirely lecture. Lecture classes
             5
_____ always hard for me. I _____ not a good note
   6   7
taker.

Our next big exam _____ this Friday. I _____
                       8   9
studying hard. A good grade on that exam _____ very im-
                                              10
portant to me.

PAST TENSE OF THE VERB *to be*

The **past tense** forms of the verb *to be* pose fewer problems of subject-verb agreement than do the present tense forms, but they too may sometimes be a source of difficulty for writers. Following are the past tense forms of the verb *to be*:

	SINGULAR	PLURAL
First person	I was	We were
Second person	You were	You were
Third person	He was	They were
	She was	
	It was	

Note that the form *were* is used in four of the six listed; the form *was* is used only in first person singular and third person singular.

PRACTICE

Copy the following paragraphs. In each sentence, underline the subject once, then insert the appropriate past tense form (*was, were*) of the verb *to be*, and underline the verb twice.

A family reunion _____1 held last weekend. Our house _____2 packed with relatives. Several cousins _____3 sleeping on the floor in my room. Their sleeping bags _____4 covering every inch of space.

My favorite aunt _____5 not at the reunion. She _____6 in the hospital at the time. We _____7 all sorry she could not be with us. Fortunately, her condition _____8 not serious.

Sunday a big picnic _____9 held at the park. Tables _____10 covered with food. We _____11 lucky that the weather _____12 pleasant. A good time _____13 enjoyed by everyone.

SUBJECTS AND VERBS

 8.7 SENTENCES WITH MORE THAN ONE SUBJECT

If a sentence has more than one subject and the subjects are joined by the word *and*, a plural verb is usually required. If the subjects are joined by *or* or *nor*, the convention in written English is that the subject closest to the verb determines whether the verb is singular or plural. The various patterns are shown in the following examples.

The <u>boy</u> *and* the <u>girl</u> <u><u>walk</u></u>.   (plural verb)

Neither the <u>boy</u> *nor* the <u>girl</u> <u><u>walks</u></u>.   (singular verb)

Either the <u>boys</u> *or* the <u>girls</u> <u><u>walk</u></u>.   (plural verb)

The <u>boy</u> *or* the <u>girls</u> <u><u>walk</u></u>.   (plural verb)

The <u>boys</u> *or* the <u>girl</u> <u><u>walks</u></u>.   (singular verb)

PRACTICE

Copy the following paragraphs. In each sentence, underline the subjects once, then insert the appropriate verb form, and underline the verb twice. All of the sentences contain more than one subject, but some of them need singular verbs and others need plural verbs. In each sentence, the word in parentheses is the base form of the verb (the form without the third person singular -*s* ending). If the verb form in parentheses is correct, use it; if it is not, change it to the Standard Written English form. If the verb *be* is in parentheses, use *am*, *is*, or *are*.

My brothers and my sister (be) planning a surprise anniver-
                              1
sary party for our parents. Neither my father nor my mother
(know) about their plans.
  2
Neither my brothers nor my sister (have) breathed a word
to them. My uncle and my aunts (have) been invited to the
                                 4
party. Neither my aunts nor my uncle (have) told my parents
                                      5
anything.

Either my brothers or my sister (plan) to trick our parents
                                 6

into leaving the house the day of the party. Then my uncle and my aunts (be)⁷ going to bring the decorations. Either Aunt Ella or Aunt Sara (be)⁸ going to bake a special cake. Uncle Harry or my older brother Joe (be)⁹ going to provide the liquid refreshments. Then my brothers, my sister, my aunts, my uncle, and I (intend)¹⁰ to decorate the house.

8.8 RECOGNIZING PREPOSITIONAL PHRASES

Occasionally, writers make errors in subject-verb agreement because of **prepositional phrases**. There is a natural tendency in English to treat the noun or pronoun immediately preceding the verb as the subject of the sentence and to make the verb agree with that noun or pronoun. In many cases, this noun or pronoun **is** the subject of the sentence; however, there are also a good many instances when that noun or pronoun is actually the object of a preposition. The object in a prepositional phrase does **not** function as the subject of the sentence. To ensure correct subject-verb agreement when prepositional phrases precede the verb, you must determine the true subject of the sentence. To determine the true subject of a sentence, you need to be able to recognize prepositional phrases so that their objects can be eliminated from consideration as possible subjects.

Prepositional phrases are an integral part of the English language. Fortunately, they follow a consistent pattern that you should find easy to recognize with a little practice. The basic structure of the prepositional phrase consists of two parts: the **preposition** and the **object**. Table 1 lists some common English prepositions.

The **object** of the preposition is usually either a **noun** or a **pronoun**. Following are some examples of prepositional phrases with pronouns as objects. (*P* stands for preposition and *O* stands for object).

P	O	P	O
to	us	for	him
to	you	for	her
to	them	for	it

TABLE 1
COMMON ENGLISH PREPOSITIONS

about	behind	except	through
above	below	for	to
across	beneath	from	toward
after	beside(s)	in	under
against	between	inside	until
along	beyond	into	up
among	by	of	upon
around	despite	off	with
at	down	on	within
before	during	over	without

The structure of prepositional phrases with nouns as objects is often more complex than those with pronouns as objects because many nouns are preceded by **noun markers**. The most common noun markers are the articles *a, an,* and *the.* In addition to noun markers, nouns are often preceded by one or more **modifying words**. This pattern is illustrated in the prepositional phrases that follow (*P* stands for preposition, *NM* stands for noun marker, *MOD* stands for modifier, and *O* stands for object).

```
P    NM   MOD  O
to   the  tall boy

P     NM   MOD   MOD  O
from  the  very  tall boy

P    NM   MOD   MOD   MOD     MOD         O
for  the  very  tall  strong  red-haired  boy
```

Theoretically, an infinite number of modifying words may precede the noun; in practice, two or three such words are ordinarily the limit.

Prepositional phrases are used to convey a variety of kinds of information. One of their most common uses is to provide location information.

above the chair   in the chair
behind the chair   on the chair
below the chair   under the chair
beside the chair   upon the chair

Prepositional phrases are also used to provide time information.

   after the meeting during the meeting
   before the meeting until the meeting

They also provide other kinds of information about relationships.

   for the store of the store
   from the store with the store

Prepositional phrases containing the word *of* are often a particular source of difficulty because they are frequently used to modify the subject of the sentence.

   One *of* the boys Most *of* the boys
   A few *of* the boys All *of* the boys
   Some *of* the boys Each *of* the boys
   Many *of* the boys Every one *of* the boys

This construction is often employed with pronouns, as in the following examples:

   One *of* us One *of* them
   A few *of* us A few *of* them
   Some *of* us Some *of* them
   Many *of* us Many *of* them
   Most *of* us Most *of* them
   All *of* us All *of* them
   Each *of* us Each *of* them
   Every one *of* us Every one *of* them

In the preceding examples, the object of the prepositional phrase is plural, but the word that the prepositional phrase is modifying may be singular. In such instances, if that word is the subject of the sentence, then it is the word with which the verb must agree. In the following examples, the prepositional phrases are crossed out to indicate that they play no part in determining the verb form.

  <u>One</u> ~~of the boys~~ <u>walks</u>. (singular)

  <u>Each</u> ~~of the boys~~ <u>walks</u>. (singular)

  Every <u>one</u> ~~of the boys~~ <u>walks</u>. (singular)

SUBJECTS AND VERBS

A few ~~of the boys~~ walk.   (plural)

Some ~~of the boys~~ walk.   (plural)

Many ~~of the boys~~ walk.   (plural)

Most ~~of the boys~~ walk.   (plural)

All ~~of the boys~~ walk.   (plural)

PRACTICE

Copy the following paragraphs, inserting the appropriate verb forms. To determine the subject(s) in each sentence, first eliminate the prepositional phrases from consideration by crossing them out. Then underline the subject once, insert the verb form that agrees with the underlined subject, and underline verb twice. The word in parentheses is the base form of the verb (the form without the third person singular -s ending). If the verb form in parentheses is correct, use it; if it is not, change it to the appropriate form. If the verb be is in parentheses, use am, is, or are.

Some of my friends (be)¹ taking history this semester. A few of them (be)² having problems with the course, but one of them (have)³ failed every exam. Several of us (have)⁴ tried to help him. One of his problems (be)⁵ that he does not read the assignments on a regular basis, so each of the exams (have)⁶ found him woefully unprepared.

Most of us (have)⁷ concluded that he is going to fail the course unless he changes his ways. One of the better students (have)⁸ offered to tutor him. All of us (hope)⁹ he passes the course, but every one of the group (know)¹⁰ that he probably will fail.

8.9 SUBJECTS AFTER VERBS

In most English sentences, the subject **precedes** the verb. The verb does not always follow the subject **immediately** as the sentences in section 8.8 illustrate. Prepositional phrases may come between the subject and the verb as may other parenthetical and/or modifying words, phrases, or clauses. In the majority of English sentences, however, the order is subject-verb. Since this pattern is so overwhelmingly dominant, sentences that are exceptions (sentences where the subject follows the verb) sometimes cause problems in subject-verb agreement for writers.

Probably the most common sentence pattern where the subject **follows** the verb occurs when the sentence begins with the word *there*.

There were several people standing on the corner.

There is not the subject of the sentence; *people* is. Since *people* is a plural subject, the plural verb *were* is required.

Particularly in spoken language, people often begin sentences with "There *was* . . ." or "There *is* . . ." without regard for the subject following the verb. Consequently, written sentences like "There *was* several people standing on the corner" may sound correct.

If you are in the habit of beginning sentences with "There *was* . . ." or "There *is* . . .", you may find that reordering the sentence so that the subject **precedes** the verb will help you to determine whether the singular or the plural form of the verb should be used. For example, "There *was* several people standing on the corner" might sound all right to you, but when the sentence is reordered to "Several people *was* standing there on the corner," you can hear that the subject is plural, so you know that the verb is plural too.

In addition to sentences beginning with *there*, other kinds of sentences may also place verbs before subjects. Sentences beginning with *here* operate in much the same way as sentences beginning with *there*.

Here is the street where I live.

Here are several pastries for you to choose from.

Sentences may also begin with prepositional phrases, followed by the verb and then the subject.

At one end of the table was a pot of coffee.

In the middle were several trays of sandwiches for the guests.

SUBJECTS AND VERBS

In questions, the verb often precedes the subject.

Is the teacher here?

Are you ready for the exam?

PRACTICE

Copy the following paragraphs. In each sentence, underline the subject once, then insert the appropriate verb form, and underline the verb twice. Since the subject follows the verb in these sentences, you may find that reordering each sentence so that the subject precedes the verb will help you to determine the correct answer. Note that the paragraphs are written in the past tense, so the correct verb will be either *was* or *were*.

There _____ several students standing in the hallway.
              1
Here, on the near side, _____ two or three dozen students.
                          2
On the far side, there _____ many more. Down at the end
                         3
of the hallway at a table _____ one student worker process-
                             4
ing their registration forms.

Among those waiting _____ several students who had
                       5
become impatient. There _____ a good many irritated re-
                           6
marks being made. Rising from the crowd _____ an angry
                                           7
chorus of complaints. As the students neared the table, there

_____ a certain amount of pushing and shoving.
   8

On the student worker's face _____ an expression of
                                9
anxiety. Ahead of him _____ hours of dealing with angry
                         10
students. There _____ little doubt that he wished himself
                  11
elsewhere. He seemed to be asking himself, "_____ I crazy
                                                 12
to agree to do this job?"

8.10 REVIEW ON SUBJECTS AND VERBS

Copy the following paragraphs. In each sentence, underline the subject(s) once, then insert the appropriate verb form(s), and underline the verb(s) twice. The word in parentheses is the base form of the verb (the form without the third person singular -*s* ending). If the verb form in parentheses is correct, use it; if it is not, change it to the Standard Written English form. If the verb *be* is in parentheses, use *am, is,* or *are*.

My sister (have)¹ been taking philosophy this semester, and her best friend (have)² been taking the class too. They (enjoy)³ the class very much because the professor (encourage)⁴ the students to participate in class. The class (be)⁵ small, only 20 students, so each student (have)⁶ a chance to ask questions and to make comments.

On the other hand, I (be)⁷ taking history this semester, and I (be)⁸ not enjoying the class at all. It (meet)⁹ at 7:00 in the morning in a large lecture hall, and there (be)¹⁰ over three hundred students in the class. The class (be)¹¹ entirely lecture, and lecture classes always (be)¹² hard for me because I (be)¹³ not a good note taker. To make things even worse, the professor (lecture)¹⁴ in a dull, boring monotone, and I nearly (fall)¹⁵ asleep every class period. Each time I ask myself, "(Be)¹⁶ I going to stay awake today?"

Some of my friends (be)¹⁷ also taking the class this semester, and one of them (have)¹⁸ failed every exam. Several of us (have)¹⁹ tried to help him, but one of his problems (be)²⁰ that he (do)²¹ not read the assignments on a regular basis, so each of the exams (have)²² found him woefully unprepared. He also (cut)²³ class half the time because he (hate)²⁴ to get up so early.

Most of us (have)²⁵ concluded that there (be)²⁶ two options available to him: either he (change)²⁷ his approach or he (fail)²⁸ the class and (take)²⁹ it again next semester. There (be)³⁰ no other choice available since the college (require)³¹ the course.

CHAPTER 9 Sentence Boundaries

9.1 INTRODUCTION

One important convention of written English is that sentences be **complete**, and writers need a good sense of sentence boundaries to ensure that they do not violate this convention.

If your papers are often marked with comments referring to **sentence fragments** (commonly abbreviated "frag"), then you have problems with sentence boundaries that you need to overcome to produce satisfactory writing.

In this chapter, we deal with common types of sentence fragments individually in order of their frequency of occurrence.

9.2 DEPENDENT CLAUSE SENTENCE FRAGMENTS

Although sentence fragments are sometimes a serious problem for writers, they are often not difficult to correct. The most common type of fragment is the **dependent clause** punctuated like an **independent clause**. To recognize such fragments, you must learn to recognize the differences between the two types of clauses.

Every complete English sentence must contain an independent clause. The following are examples of independent clauses:

My sister and I arrived at the party late.

The host and hostess promptly supplied us with food and drink.

Both of us relaxed and spent a pleasant evening.

The guests began to leave.

Note that each of the preceding examples contains at least one subject and at least one complete verb and that each independent clause can be written as a separate sentence (beginning with a capital letter and ending with a period).

However, such complete sentences can be made into incomplete sentences by adding a word at the beginning of the independent clause that makes it a dependent clause. Although it may seem illogical that the addition of a word can change a complete sentence into an incomplete sentence, grammatically that is not the case.

Consider the following independent clauses.

> We had a flat tire.
>
> We finally arrived an hour late.
>
> Neither of us had eaten anything since lunch.
>
> We satisfied our ravenous appetites.
>
> The evening was a pleasant one.

Now look at the same clauses with one word added at the beginning.

> *Because* we had a flat tire.
>
> *When* we finally arrived an hour late.
>
> *Since* neither of us had eaten anything since lunch.
>
> *After* we satisfied our ravenous appetites.
>
> *Although* the evening was a pleasant one.

As you can see, these examples can no longer be considered complete sentences, or independent clauses, because each is now dependent on some information not presented within the sentence boundaries. Consequently, all of them are fragments.

Each of the fragments can be corrected easily by adding an independent clause that completes the sentence by providing the necessary information.

> Because we had a flat tire, *my sister and I arrived at the party some time after it had started.*
>
> When we finally arrived an hour late, *everyone was quite relieved.*
>
> After we satisfied our ravenous appetites, *both of us relaxed and spent a pleasant evening talking with friends.*

Although the evening was a pleasant one, *we were both relieved when we finally arrived home without any further mishaps.*

In most cases, the independent clause does not really need to be "added" because it is already present, either immediately preceding or immediately following the dependent clause. When the dependent clause is punctuated like an independent clause—as a complete sentence beginning with a capital letter and ending with a period—it is commonly labeled a **fragment**.

There are several words and phrases whose presence at the beginning of a clause signals that the clause is dependent. These are called **subordinating conjunctions**. When a subordinating conjunction appears at the beginning of a clause, then the clause is dependent and cannot be punctuated as a complete sentence. Table 2 lists some of the most common subordinating conjunctions.

TABLE 2
COMMON SUBORDINATING CONJUNCTIONS

WORDS	
after	so
although	though
as	unless
because	until
before	when
if	where
since	while

PHRASES	
as if	even though
as long as	in order that
as soon as	so that

PRACTICE A

The following paragraph contains both independent and dependent clauses punctuated as complete sentences. Remember that both independent and dependent clauses have a subject and a complete verb, but only the dependent clause has a subordinating conjunction at the beginning of the clause. Underline the subjects once and the verbs twice, and circle the subordinating conjunctions.

Then label each independent clause SEN for complete sentence and each dependent clause FRAG for fragment.

Because we had a flat tire, My sister and I arrived at the party some time after it had started. My sister has a reputation for being a fanatic about punctuality, So everyone was worried when we were not there at eight o'clock. When we finally arrived an hour late, Everyone was quite relieved. The host and hostess promptly supplied us with food and drink, While they listened to our explanation. Since neither of us had eaten anything since lunch, We were both starved. After we satisfied our ravenous appetites. Both of us relaxed and spent a pleasant evening talking with friends. The guests began to leave, As midnight approached. Because we had arrived late. We stayed late. The other guests had already departed. When we finally left. Even though the evening was a pleasant one. We were both relieved when we finally arrived home without any further mishaps.

PRACTICE B

Rewrite the preceding paragraph, showing correct sentence boundaries. The easiest way to correct the paragraph is simply to eliminate the sentence boundary errors (the extra capital letters and periods).

In some cases, additional punctuation is needed. If the dependent clause comes at the beginning of the entire sentence, preceding the independent clause, a comma should go after the dependent clause.

When we finally arrived an hour late, everyone was quite relieved.

On the other hand, if the dependent clause goes at the end of the sentence, following the independent clause, no comma is necessary in most cases.

The host and hostess promptly supplied us with food and drink while they listened to our explanation.

9.3 MORE DEPENDENT CLAUSE SENTENCE FRAGMENTS

Another type of dependent clause may sometimes cause sentence fragments. Such sentence fragments commonly begin with one of the **relative pronouns**: *who, which,* or *that.* In such clauses, the relative pronoun frequently serves as the subject of the clause.

My sister, who is a fanatic about punctuality, never arrives late.

Notice that this dependent clause is embedded within the independent clause.

My sister never arrives late.   (independent)

Who is a fanatic about punctuality.   (dependent)

When such a dependent clause is punctuated like a sentence, the remainder of the complete sentence is commonly also a fragment.

              FRAG
My sister, who is a fanatic about punctuality.

  FRAG
Never arrives late.

PRACTICE A

Following is a rewritten version of the paragraph in Practice A of Section 9.2. In this version, relative pronouns rather than subordinating conjunctions signal dependent clauses punctuated as sentences. In contrast to the earlier paragraph, the remainder of the sentence may also be a fragment. Circle the relative pronouns to help you recognize the sentence fragments. Label the incomplete sentences, or fragments, FRAG and the complete sentences SEN. Note that two or more sentence fragments may occur consecutively in this practice.

Because we had a flat tire, my sister and I arrived at the
      1
party some time after it had started. My sister, who is a fanatic
                                2

about punctuality. Never arrives anywhere late. Consequently, everyone was worried when we were not there at eight o'clock. Which was the time indicated on the invitation. When we finally arrived an hour late, everyone was quite relieved. Our host and hostess, who listened to our explanation. Promptly supplied us with food and drink. We were both starved since neither of us had eaten anything since lunch. Which had been eight hours earlier. After we satisfied our ravenous appetites, both of us relaxed and spent a pleasant evening talking with old friends. Who expressed concern about our late arrival. The guests began to leave as midnight approached. Because we had arrived late, we stayed late. When we finally left, the other guests that had arrived before us. Had already departed. The evening was a pleasant one. Which we discussed as we drove home. We were both relieved when we finally arrived home without any further mishaps.

PRACTICE B

Rewrite the preceding paragraph, showing correct sentence boundaries. The easiest way to correct the paragraph is simply to eliminate the sentence boundary errors (the extra capital letters and periods).

In some cases, additional punctuation is needed. If the clause is not essential to the meaning of the sentence, it should be set off from the rest of the sentence by commas.

My sister, who is a fanatic about punctuality, never arrives anywhere late.

On the other hand, if the clause is essential to the meaning of the sentence, commas are not needed.

When we finally left, the other guests that had arrived before us had already departed.

Generally speaking, clauses beginning with *which* should be set off by commas, but clauses beginning with *that* do not need commas. Clauses beginning with *who* require commas when they refer to a specific person, as in "My sister, who is a fanatic about punctuality, never arrives anywhere late." If the person is not specified, then commas are not required, as in "She is a woman who never arrives late."

Note: The pronouns *who*, *which*, and *that* have functions other than as relative pronouns. In those other functions, they may appear at the beginning of a complete sentence. For example, *who* and *which* can be interrogative pronouns.

Who is going to the party?

Which car do you like best?

The word *that* may also appear at the beginning of a complete sentence.

That shade of blue is my favorite color.

As you can see, these independent clauses can stand by themselves and thus are different from the dependent clauses begun by the relative pronouns *who, which,* and *that.*

9.4　PHRASE FRAGMENTS

Phrases can also be sentence fragments. In some cases, these phrases may contain either a subject or a verb—but not both a subject and a complete verb. In other cases, neither a subject nor a verb will be present. Following are examples of fragments that are phrases punctuated as sentences.

Because of a flat tire.

At the approach of midnight.

Despite the pleasant evening.

Hearing our explanation.

Being a fanatic about punctuality.

The time indicated on the invitation.

Our ravenous appetites satisfied.

PRACTICE A

Following is yet another version of the paragraph in Sections 9.2 and 9.3. In this version, the fragments are phrases punctuated as sentences. Label these phrases FRAG; label the complete sentences SEN. Note that two or more sentence fragments may occur consecutively in this practice.

Because of a flat tire,¹ My² sister and I arrived at the party some time after it had started. Being³ a fanatic about punctuality. My⁴ sister never arrives anywhere late. Consequently, everyone was worried when we were not there at eight o'clock,⁵ The⁶ time indicated on the invitation. Everyone was quite relieved.⁷ At⁸ our arrival an hour late. The host and hostess,⁹ hearing our explanation, Promptly¹⁰ supplied us with food and drink. Having eaten nothing since lunch.¹¹ Eight¹² hours ago. We¹³ were both starved. Our ravenous appetites satisfied.¹⁴ Both¹⁵ of us relaxed and spent a pleasant evening. Talking¹⁶ with friends. At the approach of midnight,¹⁷ The¹⁸ guests began to leave. We stayed late.¹⁹ Because²⁰ of our late arrival. Seeing²¹ that the other guests had already departed, We²² finally left. Despite²³ the pleasant evening. We²⁴ were both relieved when we finally arrived home. Without²⁵ any further mishaps.

PRACTICE B

Rewrite the preceding paragraph, showing correct sentence boundaries. The easiest way to correct the paragraph is simply to eliminate the sentence boundary errors (the extra capital letters and periods).

In some cases, additional punctuation is needed. Usually, commas are needed after introductory phrases or around parenthetical phrases (interrupting phrases). However, commas are not needed when the phrase comes at the end of the sentence, unless the phrase is an **appositive** (a renaming or identifying phrase). For example, "The time indicated on the invitation" is an appositive phrase.

9.5 REVIEW ON SENTENCE BOUNDARIES

1. The following paragraph is another version of the same paragraph in Sections 9.2, 9.3, and 9.4. This version contains all three types of sentence fragments. Label the incomplete sentences, or fragments, FRAG and the complete sentences SEN. Note that two or more sentence fragments may occur consecutively in this review practice.

Because we had a flat tire.¹ My sister and I arrived at the party² some time after it started. My sister, who is a fanatic about punctuality.³ Never arrives anywhere late.⁴ Consequently, everyone was worried when we were not there at eight o'clock.⁵ Which was the time indicated on the invitation.⁶ When we finally arrived an hour late.⁷ Everyone was quite relieved.⁸ Our host and hostess promptly supplied us with food and drink.⁹ While they listened to our explanation.¹⁰ Having eaten nothing since lunch.¹¹ Eight hours ago.¹² We were both starved.¹³ Our ravenous appetites satisfied.¹⁴ Both of us relaxed and spent a pleasant evening.¹⁵ Talking with friends.¹⁶ Who expressed concern about our late arrival.¹⁷ As midnight approached.¹⁸ The guests began to leave.¹⁹ We stayed late.²⁰ Because of our late arrival.²¹ The other guests had already departed.²² When we finally left.²³ Despite the pleasant evening.²⁴ We were both relieved when we finally arrived home.²⁵ Without any further mishaps.²⁶

2. Rewrite the preceding paragraph, showing correct sentence boundaries. The easiest way to correct the paragraph is simply to eliminate the sentence boundary errors (the extra capital letters and periods). In some cases, additional punctuation is needed.

CHAPTER 10
Clause Boundaries

10.1 INTRODUCTION

Problems with clause boundaries are, at the same time, similar to and different from problems with sentence boundaries. In both cases, writers have a weak sense of the boundaries of the English sentence and its primary structures; in both cases, they lack a sure sense of precisely where marks of punctuation belong and how strong a signal those marks should convey. Lacking this sure sense, these writers may have problems with both sentence boundaries and clause boundaries.

There are differences, however, and some writers consistently have problems with sentence boundaries but not clause boundaries, and other writers just as consistently have problems with clause boundaries but not sentence boundaries.

The major difference is that writers who have problems with sentence boundaries consistently do one or both of the following:

1. They signal boundaries that do not exist. Separating a prepositional phrase from the sentence where it belongs when no punctuation is needed is an example of signaling a boundary that does not exist.

The game was cancelled. Because of the weather.

The sentence should read:

The game was cancelled because of bad weather.

2. They indicate boundaries inappropriately with too strong a signal. Separating a dependent clause at the beginning of a sentence from the independent clause following, using a sentence sig-

nal (a period and a capital letter) when only a comma is needed, is an example.

Because the game was cancelled. We went to a movie instead.

The sentence should read:

Because the game was cancelled, we went to a movie instead.

Conversely, writers who have problems with clause boundaries do exactly the opposite:

1. They do not signal boundaries where they exist. This absence of boundary signals is usually called the **run-together sentence**.

2. They signal boundaries with too weak a mark of punctuation. This too-weak signal is commonly labeled the **comma splice**.

If your teacher makes these comments on your papers, then clause boundaries are a problem in your writing.

In this chapter, we discuss comma splices first, since they are a less difficult problem. Writers who have problems with comma splices do recognize the presence of the clause boundaries, even though they do not signal them correctly. We then discuss run-together sentences. These are a more difficult problem because such sentences provide the reader with no signal at all. Finally, we discuss in detail the various methods of revising comma splices and run-together sentences, and suggestions for revision strategies are given.

10.2 COMMA SPLICES

A **comma splice** is defined as two independent clauses joined only by a comma. The comma is not considered a strong enough signal to indicate this relationship. In the English sentence, the convention is that two independent clauses must be separated in one of four ways:

1. by a period and a capital letter,
2. by a comma and a short (two or three letters) coordinating conjunction: *and, but, or, nor, for, so, yet,*

3. by a semicolon alone,
4. by a semicolon preceding a longer (four letters or more) transitional conjunction: *therefore, however, meanwhile, nevertheless, consequently, moreover, then, thus.*

Following is an example of two independent clauses punctuated as a comma splice and then punctuated in the four acceptable ways.

The history exam was an easy one, most of the students failed.   (comma splice)

The history exam was an easy one. *M*ost of the students failed.   (period and capital letter)

The history exam was an easy one, *but* most of the students failed.   (comma and coordinating conjunction)

The history exam was an easy one; most of the students failed.   (semicolon alone)

The history exam was an easy one; *however,* most of the students failed.   (semicolon and transitional conjunction)

It is also possible to correct this sentence by making one clause subordinate to the other.

Although the history exam was an easy one, most of the students failed.   (one subordinate clause, one independent clause)

Although there is a relationship of meaning between the two independent clauses in the preceding example of a comma splice, there is no **grammatical** relationship. In the most common type of comma splice, there is a grammatical relationship between the two clauses. Frequently, the second clause contains a pronoun that refers to a noun in the first clause or, vaguely, to the entire clause itself. Following is an example of two independent clauses that are grammatically related. They are first punctuated as a comma splice and then in the four acceptable ways. The last example is rewritten with one clause subordinated to the other.

My brother plays tennis, he enjoys the game very much.   (comma splice)

My brother plays tennis. *He* enjoys the game very much. (period and capital letter)

My brother plays tennis, *and* he enjoys the game very much. (comma and coordinating conjunction)

My brother plays tennis; he enjoys the game very much. (semicolon alone)

My brother plays tennis; *moreover,* he enjoys the game very much. (semicolon and transitional conjunction)

My brother plays tennis *because* he enjoys the game very much. (one independent clause, one subordinate clause)

Another type of comma splice occurs when two independent clauses are joined together by a transitional conjunction that is preceded by a comma rather than a semicolon.

Reading mystery novels is one of my sister's favorite leisure activities, *however,* she has been so busy this semester that she hasn't had much time to read. (comma splice)

The easiest way to correct a comma splice like this one is to replace the comma with a semicolon.

Reading mystery novels is one of my sister's favorite leisure activities; *however,* she has been so busy this semester that she hasn't had much time to read. (semicolon and transitional conjunction)

PRACTICE A

Following are paragraphs containing several comma splices. Rewrite the paragraphs, correcting the comma splices by separating independent clauses in one of the four acceptable ways: (1) period and capital letter, (2) comma and coordinating conjunction, (3) semicolon alone, or (4) semicolon and transitional conjunction. Making one clause subordinate to the other is also an acceptable correction. Do not rely completely on one approach; use as many as you can, choosing the most appropriate correction for each sentence.

The car wouldn't start, it also had a flat tire. My brother
¹   ²
called the service station, there wasn't any answer. It was Sun-
                                                        ³
day afternoon, therefore, the service station was closed.

He decided to try to fix the flat himself, he opened the
                                        ⁴
trunk of the car. The spare tire was flat, there wasn't any jack in
                                ⁵
the trunk. He couldn't try to jump start the car either, there
           ⁶
weren't any battery cables in the trunk.

My brother decided to spend a quiet day at home, he really
                                              ⁷
didn't have any other choice. He sat down in his favorite chair
                              ⁸
to watch TV, however, something was the matter with the picture tube. Then he decided to call up a friend of his, no one
                                              ⁹
answered the telephone. Finally he decided to read a book,
                                    ¹⁰
later in the afternoon he took a nap.

PRACTICE B

The following is an exaggerated example of comma splice problems; the entire paragraph is a series of comma splices. Rewrite the paragraph, indicating clause boundaries appropriately. Use a variety of approaches to correct the paragraph.

My little sister is learning to play the drums, she enjoys practicing very much, she takes lessons twice a week, she practices for hours every day, the noise is driving the rest of the family crazy, no one wants to discourage her, her drum teacher says she has talent, next year she is going to try out for the band.

10.3 RUN-TOGETHER SENTENCES

The second type of clause boundary problem is the **run-together sentence**. In some respects, the run-together sentence is a more serious problem than the comma splice since the comma splice does signal clause boundaries, even if inadequately. In the run-together sentence, however, two independent clauses are joined together without any punctuation. Because there is no signal to indicate clause boundaries in the run-together sentence, such sentences are quite confusing to readers.

Run-together sentences can be corrected in the same four ways as comma splices:

1. by a period and a capital letter,
2. by a comma preceding a coordinating conjunction,
3. by a semicolon alone,
4. by a semicolon preceding a transitional conjunction.

They can also be corrected by making one clause subordinate to the other.

Following is an example of a run-together sentence. The four acceptable punctuation corrections are then shown; last is a rewritten version in which one clause is subordinated to the other.

The movie was very exciting *it* was over too soon. (run-together)

The movie was very exciting. *It* was over too soon. (period and capital letter)

The movie was very exciting, *but* it was over too soon. (comma and coordinating conjunction)

The movie was very exciting; it was over too soon. (semicolon alone)

The movie was very exciting; *however,* it was over too soon. (semicolon and transitional conjunction)

Because the movie was very exciting, it was over too soon. (one subordinate clause, one independent clause)

PRACTICE A

Following are paragraphs containing several run-together sentences. Rewrite the paragraphs, correcting the run-together sentences by separating independent clauses in one of the four acceptable ways: (1) period and capital letter, (2) comma and coordinating conjunction, (3) semicolon alone, or (4) semicolon and transitional conjunction. Making one clause subordinate to the other is also an acceptable correction. Do not rely completely on one approach; use as many as you can, choosing the most appropriate correction for each sentence.

My mother has gone back to school to get a degree every-¹ one in the family has pitched in to help out around the house. Every week each person is assigned a set of household duties² the assignments originally were supposed to change each week.

Changing assignments sounded like a good idea it didn't³ work out so well in practice. My brother is very good at yard work⁴ he's a terrible cook. My father is an excellent cook he⁵ hates yard work. The family could tolerate my father's yard work⁶ they couldn't stomach my brother's cooking.

After a few weeks the family made the decision the idea of⁷ alternating work assignments had to be dropped. Now my brother does the yard work every week⁸ my father does the cooking. The yard always looks wonderful⁹ dinner always tastes great. My brother is thinking of becoming a landscape artist my¹⁰ father is planning to write a cookbook.

[margin annotation at item 3: ; however,]

PRACTICE B

The following paragraph is a series of run-together sentences. Rewrite the paragraph, indicating clause bondaries appropriately. Use a variety of approaches to correct the paragraph.

My mother has gone back to school to get a degree she's decided to become a nurse last year my father was seriously ill he had to spend several days in the hospital she felt so helpless she was also impressed by the competence and the professionalism of the nursing staff that's when she decided to become a nurse.

10.4 REVISING COMMA SPLICES AND RUN-TOGETHER SENTENCES

As noted in the earlier discussions of comma splices and run-together sentences in Sections 10.2 and 10.3, there are several ways to correct such problems. Following is an explanation of the different methods and the advantages and disadvantages of each method. The same principles apply in revising both comma splices and run-together sentences.

Revision Method One (separate sentences)

The easiest way to correct comma splices and run-together sentences is to separate the two or more clauses into two or more separate sentences. Since this method is so easy, writers may be tempted to employ it too often. The result, however, is an excessive number of very short sentences and, consequently, an extremely monotonous effect. Following is a revision of the first paragraph of Practice A in Section 10.2 that relies too heavily on this approach.

The car wouldn't start. It also had a flat tire. My brother called the service station. There wasn't any answer. It was Sunday afternoon. Therefore, the service station was closed.

Revision Method Two (compound sentences)

Combining the clauses of the comma splice or run-together sentence into a **compound sentence** is a second method, one most writers use quite frequently. There are three approaches to making the compound sentence:

1. semicolon alone,
2. comma and coordinating conjunction,
3. semicolon and transitional conjunction.

Semicolon Alone. Since this approach is also quite easy to use, writers may be tempted to rely on it too much. Following is a revision using only this method. Again, the effect is quite monotonous.

He decided to try to fix the flat himself; he opened the trunk of the car. The spare tire was flat; there wasn't any jack in the trunk. He couldn't try to jump start the car either; there weren't any battery cables in the trunk.

Comma and Coordinating Conjunction. Writers frequently use this type of compound sentence, joining clauses together with a comma followed by a short conjunction: *and, but, or, nor, for, so, yet.* Although this type of compound can also become monotonous if used too frequently, a more common problem here is the choice of conjunction, specifically overuse of the conjunction *and*. Following is a revision that relies too much on *and*.

> The car wouldn't start, *and* it also had a flat tire. My brother called the service station, *and* there wasn't any answer. It was Sunday afternoon, *and* the service station was closed.

Semicolon and Transitional Conjunction. Using this method, writers can add variety to their writing, joining the two clauses together with a semicolon and a transitional conjunction (for example, *however, therefore, moreover, nevertheless*). Like the other approaches, this one can become monotonous if overused. Further, conjunctions such as *nevertheless* and *moreover* are rather formal and, in some cases, may be inappropriate. Following is a revision that uses these conjunctions excessively and inappropriately.

> *Note:* When these longer conjunctions are used, the semicolon—not the comma—must be used. Otherwise, the sentence is a comma splice.

> He decided to try to fix the flat himself; *therefore,* he opened the trunk of the car. The spare tire was flat; *moreover,* there wasn't any jack in the trunk. He couldn't try to jump start the car either; *furthermore,* there weren't any battery cables in the trunk.

Revision Method Three (complex sentences)

Writers tend to overlook this method of revising comma splices and run-together sentences, but it is often the best choice. When writers use this method, they make one clause subordinate to the other; the subordinate clause may be the first clause in the sentence or it may come later. The word at the beginning of the subordinate clause may be a subordinating conjunction (Table 2 lists common subordinating conjunctions) or a relative pronoun (*who, which, that*). Following is a revision using this approach.

> My brother decided to spend a quiet day at home, *since* he really didn't have any other choice. *When* he sat down in his favorite chair to watch TV, something was the matter with the picture tube. Then he decided to call up a friend of his, *who* did

not answer the telephone. *Although* he had decided to read a book, later in the afternoon he took a nap.

10.5 CHOOSING THE BEST METHOD OF REVISION

When revising comma splices and run-together sentences, the writer must decide which method of revision is best: separate sentences, compound sentences, or complex sentences.

For example, writers should use compound sentences when the information given in the two independent clauses seems of equal weight and importance.

The car wouldn't start, *and* it also had a flat tire.

On the other hand, writers should use complex sentences when the information in one clause seems subordinate to the information in the other clause.

My brother couldn't try to jump start the car either *because* there weren't any battery cables in the trunk.

The major point in this sentence is that he couldn't jump start the car; the clause beginning with *because* explains why.

10.6 CHOOSING THE BEST CONNECTIVE

In addition to choosing the best revision method, writers must also choose the best connective when revising comma splices and run-together sentences. The "best" connective is the word or phrase that conveys the relationship between the information presented in the separate clauses in the most accurate, the most precise, and the most appropriate fashion.

In compound sentences joined by a comma and a short coordinating conjunction, *and* is the most common choice.

The car wouldn't start, *and* it also had a flat tire.

Here *and* seems appropriate because the information presented in the second independent clause ("it also had a flat tire") seems to be an addition to the information presented in the first independent clause ("The car wouldn't start").

If the information in the second clause does not seem to be in addition to that presented in the first clause, *and* may not be the best choice.

> My brother called the service station, *but* there wasn't any answer.

In this compound sentence, *but* is preferable to *and*. When someone makes a call, an answer is expected; the absence of an answer is more of a contradiction than an addition, so *but* is a better choice than *and*.

Another option here would be the following:

> He tried to call the service station; *however,* there wasn't any answer.

The two clauses are presented here as equal, but they are joined by a semicolon and *however*—a conjunction like *but* that carries with it the idea of contradiction. Since these two clauses are rather short and simple and the subject matter is informal, the "comma + *but*" connection seems preferable to the more formal "semicolon + *however*" connection.

In complex sentences, choosing the best connective is also important. The two sentences that follow provide the same basic information, but they give quite different impressions.

> *Because* my mother has gone back to school to get a degree, everyone in the family has pitched in to help out around the house.

> *Although* my mother has gone back to school to get a degree, everyone in the family has pitched in to help out around the house.

The first sentence suggests that the family has "pitched in" willingly; the second implies that they are doing so grudgingly.

Following are two tables that list commonly used connecting words and phrases. Table 3 classifies them according to type and Table 4 according to meaning.

TABLE 3
TYPES OF CONNECTIVES

COORDINATING CONJUNCTIONS[a]	TRANSITIONAL CONJUNCTIONS
and	however
but	therefore
or	meanwhile
nor	nevertheless
for	consequently
so	moreover
yet	then
	thus
PHRASES	
in addition	SUBORDINATING
for example	CONJUNCTIONS
of course	See Table 2.
in the mean time	
on the other hand	
as a result	
in other words	
in conclusion	

[a] The initial letters of these words spell the word *fanboys* (*for, and, nor, but, or, yet, so*), a useful memory device.

TABLE 4
MEANINGS OF CONNECTIVES

ADDITION	COMPARISON
and	similarly
also	likewise
again	in the same way
moreover	in the same manner
furthermore	
in addition	CONCESSION
	(to an opposing viewpoint)
CONTRAST	although
but	though
yet	even though
nor	
however	ILLUSTRATION
nevertheless	for example
on the other hand	for instance
	thus

(continued)

TABLE 4 *(continued)*

REASON	TIME
because	then
for	when
since	after
	occasionally
RESTRICTION	frequently
if	meanwhile
unless	immediately
	eventually
RESULT	in the mean time
so	
thus	
therefore	
consequently	
as a result	

10.7 REVIEW ON CLAUSE BOUNDARIES

Revise the practices in Sections 10.2 and 10.3 for the best method of connection: separate sentences, compound sentences, or complex sentences. In addition to using the best method of connection, also choose the best (the most accurate, the most precise, the most appropriate) connecting words or phrases. For greater variety, try to use words and phrases given in Tables 2, 3, and 4 that you do not ordinarily use.

CHAPTER 11

The Forbidden Doubles

11.1 INTRODUCTION

For many writers, one of the most puzzling aspects of the English language is that sometimes agreement is required and other times it is forbidden. As noted in Chapter 8, subjects and verbs are expected to agree (for example, a third person singular subject such as *the boy* requires a third person singular verb such as *walks: the boy walks*). As noted later in Chapter 15, agreement is also a requirement of correct pronoun usage.

In contrast, there are some circumstances that require a grammatical signal to be given **once** and **only once**. For this reason, the following are forbidden in English: double subjects, double comparatives and superlatives, and double negatives. One interesting aspect of these forbidden doubles is that several hundred years ago, all were regarded as acceptable and, in some instances, required usage. Although they have long been banned from Standard Written English, these older traditions live on in many oral dialects, and speakers of those dialects often maintain such practices in their writing. In addition, many foreign languages accept, or require, these doubles.

Because these doubles are so prevalent in oral dialects of English and in other languages, sometimes writers employ them even though they are considered inappropriate in Standard Written English. Although these concepts are relatively easy to understand, writers who are in the habit of using the forbidden doubles often have a certain amount of difficulty breaking long-established habits.

To avoid using the forbidden doubles in your own writing, first you must learn how to recognize double subjects, double comparatives and superlatives, and double negatives. Then you need to determine if you use these doubles in your oral or written language. Finally, you need to learn how to revise them.

11.2 DOUBLE SUBJECTS

A **double subject** consists of a noun followed by a pronoun, each of which has the same referent.

noun pronoun
John he lost his history book.

noun pronoun
Betty she was late to English class.

noun pronoun
The team they lost the basketball game.

Although the pronoun ordinarily follows the noun immediately, sometimes a few words intervene.

noun pronoun
The people walking down the street they stopped in front of the furniture store.

noun pronoun
The man in the red shirt he was wearing a cowboy hat.

PRACTICE

Copy the following paragraphs, eliminating the double subjects. You may choose to delete either the noun or the following pronoun; use your judgment about which is the better choice.

The school it stood there, surrounded by a tall chain-link fence. People walking down the sidewalk they stopped to watch the children playing before and after school and during recess. When the bell it rang, hordes of children they rushed onto the playground. Some children they raced to the merry-go-round while others they ran to the swings, and still others they rushed to the teeter-totters. Their shouts and cries and laughter they could be heard for some distance.

Two older boys they began to argue about whose turn it was on one of the swings. The shorter boy he hit the taller one in the stomach, and then the taller one he punched the other in the mouth. Then the two of them fell to the ground, rolling over and over, wrestling in the dust. Some of the younger children they ran to where the teachers they were standing and talking. The teachers they stopped their conversation and rushed to where the fight it was taking place.

By this time the fight it had lasted for several minutes and the boys they were beginning to get tired. Their clothes they were all dusty and their shirts they were torn and ripped. The shorter boy he had a bloody nose and the blood it had dripped on his shirt and on the taller boy's shirt too. The taller boy he had the beginnings of a black eye.

The boys they were so engrossed in their fight that neither one of them he heard the teachers approaching. The teachers they began shouting to the boys to stop fighting, but the boys they seemed not to hear or to care. Soon the principal she came running to where the fight it was taking place, and the assistant principal he was right behind her. The principal she directed the assistant principal to help her break up the fight. The principal she shouted "Now," and grabbed the shorter boy and pulled him away from the taller boy. The assistant principal he grabbed for the taller boy, but the taller boy he was furious that the principals they were interrupting the fight. Without thinking,

the boy he turned and hit the assistant principal in the stomach.
The assistant principal he had the wind knocked out of him,[22]
and the boy he stood there stunned at what he had done.

Both boys they were marched off the playground to the[23]
principal's office. The boys they spent several uncomfortable[24]
minutes while the prinicipal and the assistant principal they lectured them about fighting on the playground.

The principal she called the boys' parents, and the parents[25]
they came down to the school. Finally, all of them they agreed[26]
on a suitable punishment for the two boys. By the time every-[27]
thing was finished, the boys they both wished that they had
never seen a swing, and the two of them they decided that their
next fight it would take place in the park or somewhere else—
not on the school playground during recess where adults they
could interfere.

11.3 DOUBLE COMPARATIVES AND SUPERLATIVES

Another type of forbidden double is the **double comparative** or **double superlative**. In Standard Written English, comparisons can be made using either *-er/-est* or *more/most*, as shown here:

POSITIVE	COMPARATIVE	SUPERLATIVE
pretty	prettier	prettiest
	or	*or*
beautiful	more beautiful	most beautiful

Since both types of comparisons are possible, it is also possible, although considered unacceptable in Standard Written English, for both of them to be used at the same time. The result is the double comparative or the double superlative.

DOUBLE COMPARATIVE	DOUBLE SUPERLATIVE
more prettier	most prettiest
more beautifuller	most beautifullest

Because the tendency is to use the *-er/-est* pattern with shorter words and the *more/most* pattern with longer words, *more prettier* and *most prettiest* are more likely to be used than *more beautifuller* and *most beautifullest*.

Pretty and *beautiful* are words whose comparative and superlative forms are **regular**; that is, they are created by adding *-er* or *-est* at the end of the word or placing *more* or *most* before the word. However, some words use **irregular** comparatives and superlatives, and these may be somewhat more susceptible to forbidden doubling because of their irregular patterns. The most common irregulars are listed here:

POSITIVE	COMPARATIVE	SUPERLATIVE
good	better	best
bad	worse	worst

Constructions like *bestest, worstest,* and *mostest* and *more better, more worse/worser,* or *more/most worst* are examples of forbidden irregular double comparatives and superlatives.

PRACTICE

Copy the following paragraphs, eliminating the double comparatives and superlatives. You may choose to eliminate either the *-er/-est* form or the *more/most* form. Use your judgment about which is the better choice. Consult a dictionary if necessary.

The three brothers were very close in age—seventeen, eighteen, and nineteen—and throughout their lives they had competed to see who had the mostest of anything and who was the bestest at any endeavor.

When they were more younger, the most oldest boy had the most greatest advantage over his two more younger brothers, and the most youngest one was always the most unlikeliest to win. But as the brothers grew more older, the most youngest grew the most tallest and the most fastest. By the time they were all in high school, the most youngest was more taller than his two more older brothers.

In addition to being more taller, he was also more heavier,
more stronger, and more better coordinated. In fact, he was the
bestest athlete in the entire school. He was also a more better
student than his more older brothers, who were two of the
worstest students in school, and he was the most handsomest
of the three.

The most oldest brother, John, was dating Susan, the most
prettiest girl in the school. Some people said she was the most
beautifullest girl who had ever gone to that school. She was also
one of the most popularest.

Although Susan was dating John, she actually was more in-
teresteder in James, the most youngest brother. She had noticed
that he was more taller, more stronger, and more handsomer
than his brothers. He was also a more better athlete, a more
smarter student, and one of the most popularest boys in school.
Susan thought that James would be a more successfuller man
than John, more richer, and a more better provider, and probably a more better husband and father.

James too was most attractedest to Susan, but he felt more
anxiouser about competing with his brother for a girl than he
had ever felt about their more earlier rivalries. After John
graduated from high school, he enlisted in the Navy, and Susan
and James began to get more friendlier than ever. Eventually
they became engaged and married.

As it happened, Susan could not have been more wronger.
James turned out to be one of the worstest husbands imagin-
able. The most successfullest of the three brothers was Jason,
the middle brother, who turned out to be more intelligenter
and more ambitiouser than anyone had ever realized. He in-

vented a more efficienter barbecue grill and within a few years was the most wealthiest man in town.

 DOUBLE (OR MULTIPLE) NEGATIVES

The most complicated type of forbidden double is the **double (or multiple) negative**. Double subjects usually occur together and double comparatives and superlatives always occur together (that is, one word follows the other), but double negatives can be scattered throughout a sentence. Unlike double subjects and double comparatives and superlatives, negatives can occur more than twice (for that reason, they are often called "multiple" negatives). However, the double negative is probably more commonly found than the multiple negative. Theoretically, it is possible to write a sentence like the following, with negation occurring at every conceivable place in the sentence.

Nobody didn't never tell nothing to no one nowhere.

In practice, the most common form of double negative consists of a negated verb, with another negated word following.

He didn't tell no one about what he had seen.
He didn't know nothing about car repair.
He didn't never answer my question.

There is one kind of double negative that is regarded as grammatically acceptable: the not un construction. Ordinarily, this construction is used when the speaker or writer wants to avoid making a positive statement.

He is not unkind.
She is not unattractive.

Although such constructions are grammatically acceptable, many authorities on style view them somewhat negatively, so they should be used sparingly—if at all.

PRACTICE

Copy the following paragraphs, eliminating the double/multiple negatives. Usually, there is more than one way to correct each sentence. Use your judgment, choosing the correction that sounds best to you.

One of the things that Rick liked best about college, particularly compared to high school, was that most of his professors didn't never take roll.¹ In the big lecture classes, there wasn't no attempt² at all to keep track of which students attended lectures regularly and which students never made no effort to come to class. Since Rick's history class met at 7:30 in the morning and Rick hadn't never liked³ getting up early, he didn't attend none of the lectures after the first week or so of class.

For a while he set his alarm clock faithfully every day so it would go off at 6:30 so he could get to class, but he couldn't never seem⁴ to get himself out of bed. He would turn off the alarm and go back to sleep, not waking up for no more than⁵ a second or two.

For four weeks he never attended none of his history lectures.⁶ Since the professor had handed out a syllabus during the first class period, Rick didn't worry none⁷ about the class. The syllabus listed the chapters to read in the book and the dates of the midterm and final exams, so Rick figured he wasn't missing nothing⁸ by not attending class. He didn't need to do nothing⁹ except read the book.

Of course, Rick didn't have no copy¹⁰ of the book because it was rather expensive, and when he was at the bookstore, he had decided instead to buy a warm-up suit in the school colors. By the time he had paid for the warm-up suit, some posters for¹¹ his room, and some new tapes, he didn't have no extra money for the history book. Still, he figured there wasn't no hurry;[12] there wasn't no exam scheduled till midterm, and that was the middle of October. Besides there weren't no used books available[13] at the beginning of the semester.

Rick meant to go to the bookstore around the first of October,[14] but he just didn't seem to have no time nor no money to spare. Finally,[15] about the 10th of October, he stopped by the bookstore, but no history books were on none of the shelves. When Rick asked the clerk, she told him there wouldn't be no[16] more books coming in for several weeks because the publisher didn't have none in stock.

Rick didn't worry none though; he was sure he could borrow[17] a book from a friend. None of his friends wouldn't lend[18] him theirs, however, because they hadn't been studying neither, and the first exam was going to cover several hundred pages. Finally Rick managed to make an arrangement with one of the[19] nerds in the dorm who had been attending the lectures and reading assignments. The nerd didn't have no charity because[20] Rick had made fun of him several times. He wouldn't never let[21] Rick have the book except late at night after he had finished studying. Then Rick had to pay him $1.00 an hour to rent the[22] book, and he wasn't allowed to make no marks on none of the pages.

By the time the history exam came, Rick hadn't read no[23] more than half of the assigned chapters, but he figured he could guess his way through the exam. After all he hadn't flunked none of his history exams in high school and lots of[24] times he hadn't read no more than a few assignments.

On the day of the exam, Rick didn't feel none of the anxiety
²⁵
some of the other students did. As he walked in the door, a
                                                        ²⁶
teaching assistant handed him a slip of paper. Rick didn't look
                                                      ²⁷
at it none—just tucked it in his pocket. He sat down and waited
                                                 ²⁸
for someone to pass out exams, but no one handed out nothing. Finally, he looked at the piece of paper he had put in his
       ²⁹
pocket; it was titled "Midterm Exam for American History 101,"
and the exam consisted of one sentence: "Write an essay in
which you discuss thoroughly the causes and the effects of the
Civil War." No one hadn't told Rick that the history professor
            ³⁰
who didn't never take attendance also didn't never give nothing
except essay exams.

11.5 REVIEW ON THE FORBIDDEN DOUBLES

Copy the following paragraphs, eliminating the forbidden doubles. More than one revision may be correct; use your judgment, choosing the correction that sounds best to you.

There wasn't nobody who was a more better teacher and a
             ¹
more nicer person than Mrs. Crawford, my eighth grade history
teacher. Mrs. Crawford she was the bestest teacher I have ever
                            ²
had. Nobody couldn't have taught history and made it more in-
      ³
terestinger than she did.

Mrs. Crawford she didn't teach history by having her stu-
              ⁴
dents not do nothing except memorize important dates and famous names. She talked about the people, the most famousest
                   ⁵
ones and the ones nobody don't never hear nothing about. I
                                                       ⁶
hadn't never realized how the more ordinarier people lived during the more earlier periods of American history.

Mrs. Crawford she was always winning awards for being the bestest teacher, but the other teachers weren't jealous of her none. The teachers they knew that nobody never worked harder than Mrs. Crawford. Mrs. Crawford she helped out the other teachers whenever they needed it. She was truly one of the most nicest people I have ever known.

CHAPTER 12 Unbalanced and Illogical Structures

12.1 INTRODUCTION

One of the characteristics of well-written Standard English is that it flows smoothly. Experienced writers avoid jarring the reader with unbalanced or illogical structures. A poet may want the reader to notice the language of a poem, but a report writer wants the reader to pay attention to the substance of the text—not to its language. Although a few readers—composition teachers and editors, for example—will notice the language of a well-written text, most readers notice the language only when it is not well written. When the language of the text jars the ear or the mind, readers find themselves momentarily sidetracked from the substance of the text. Careful readers then must backtrack, sorting out the knots and tangles of the text. When this sort of backtracking is necessary, the reader has to do the writer's work, and the reader's reaction is one that many people have when they must do someone else's work: irritation. Less careful readers may skip the troublesome sections, but in that case, they may not fully understand the import of the text.

Whether the readers of a writer's text are careful or careless, both the writer and the text suffer a loss of credibility when readers find themselves backtracking or skipping portions of the text. Writers who want to retain credibility with their readers must revise their text, sorting out the knots and tangles for their readers.

In this chapter, we deal with two kinds of structures that may irritate or puzzle readers: unbalanced structures and illogical structures. Such structures may be found in the writing of both inexperienced **and** experienced writers. The difference between the two is that they are rarely found in the final text of experienced writers because they know how to recognize and revise such structures. In contrast, less experienced writers may not recognize such structures—or if they do, they may not know how to revise them. The presence of unbalanced or illogical structures in the text of less experienced writers is not—as some might think—a wholly negative sign. It simply suggests that these writers are working with structures that they do not yet have under control.

If your writing contains unbalanced and illogical structures, first you must learn how to recognize them and then how to revise them. With practice, you can learn how to control these structures.

12.2 UNBALANCED STRUCTURES

One characteristic of good writing is that structures are balanced. Balanced structures are commonly referred to as **parallel**; when structures are unbalanced, there is **faulty parallelism**.

Whenever writers combine two or more units, the possibility of unbalanced structures exists. One reason for this is that writers can say the same thing in several different ways.

> John likes *going* to the movies. (*-ing* word functioning as a noun, referred to as a "gerund")
>
> John likes *to go* to the movies. (*to* in front of the verb, referred to as an "infinitive")
>
> John likes *the movies*. (a noun preceded by *the*)
>
> The fact is *that John likes going to the movies*. (a *that* clause)

Since all of these structures convey approximately the same idea, it is not surprising that sometimes they would be combined in the same sentence.

> This summer John plans *to swim, going to the movies,* and *that a trip to Disney World in Florida is possible.*

With a sentence like the one preceding, the writer is like a juggler attempting to juggle a cup, a saucer, and a platter. He or she may be able to juggle three cups, three saucers, or three platters, but not three different objects. The size and the shape of the objects are different; so too are the size and the shape of unbalanced structures.

For a sentence to be balanced, or parallel, all of the structures must be alike. Various methods of revision are possible, some of which are listed here:

John likes swimm*ing*, go*ing* to movies, and visit*ing* Disney World. (*-ing* constructions)

John likes *to* attend movies, *to* go swimming, and *to* visit Disney World. (*to* constructions)

John likes the *swimming pool, movies,* and *Disney World.* (nouns)

This summer, John plans *that* he will swim every day, *that* he will go to the movies weekly, and *that* he will travel to Disney World in Florida in August. (*that* clauses)

Although all of these revisions are possible, some are better in one type of situation, while others may be better in another. You should experiment with different types of revisions to determine which is appropriate in each situation. You might want to consider which of the preceding revisions sounds better to you and why.

PRACTICE

Copy the following paragraphs, eliminating unbalanced structures. In many cases, more than one revision is possible; use the one that sounds best to you, but do not rely completely on one method of revision.

Every morning at the breakfast table during my vacation, I
¹
looked out of the window, watched the sights, and listening to the sounds. Orange-breasted robins marched through the yard,
²
a pair of blue jays that shrieked and swirled in the air, and a pair of cardinals on the fence. The robins are the solid citizens, the
³
blue jays handsome hooligans, and the cardinals aristocratically aloof. In the bird world, males are gaudy, sporting fancy plum-
⁴
age and colors that are eye-catching. For the males, every day is
⁵
Easter parade, but for the females, each day domestic duties.

In addition to the marching robins, the blue jays that
⁶

UNBALANCED AND ILLOGICAL STRUCTURES   165

shriek, and the cardinals that sit on the fence, there are squirrels playing in the trees and rabbits that hop through the yard. One squirrel runs down the tree and sitting up on his hind legs.⁷ Sometimes the squirrels dart across the street, to climb the trees across the way, and then darting back.⁸ One curious and perhaps he is hungry rabbit approaches a low-blooming rosebush.⁹ Since the owners of the house have not planted lettuce and carrots, only rose bushes and tulips, he takes a bite out of the rose and then hopping away.¹⁰

Every morning I drink my coffee, reading the newspaper, and that I enjoy watching the pastoral scene that greets me.¹¹

12.3 ILLOGICAL STRUCTURES

There are various kinds of illogical constructions, but one of the most prevalent is the **dangling modifier**. A modifier is a word, phrase, or clause that modifies another word in the sentence. The term "modify" means that the word, phrase, or clause describes, explains, or comments on the modified word. For example, in the sentence "The *tall* boy stood up," the word *tall* modifies *boy* since it describes him.

This sort of modification is simple and rarely causes problems for writers, but when the sentence is more complicated, confusion can develop easily, as the following sentence illustrates.

Driving down the street, the accident occurred suddenly

This sentence sounds as if the accident had been driving down the street. The term "dangling" is used because there is no word in the sentence that the phrase *driving down the street* can logically modify; thus, this construction is illogical.

Dangling modifiers often can be found in sentences where the actors who performed the action described have been removed. In the preceding sentence, for example, **someone** must have been driving down the street, but **who**? The sentence does not give that information. The simplest way to correct the sentence is to put a person (or people) into the sentence—in other words, to answer the question, "Who drove down the street?"

> As *I* was driving down the street, an accident occurred. (Turn the phrase into a dependent clause, and make the person the subject of that clause.)
>
> An accident occurred as *I* was driving down the street. (Put the main clause first; then change the phrase to a dependent clause and add a person as the subject.)
>
> *I* was driving down the street when an accident occurred. (Turn the dangling modifier into the main clause, adding a person as the subject; put the main clause first.)
>
> When the accident occurred, *I* was driving down the street. (Turn the dangling modifier into the main clause, adding a person as the subject; put the main clause last.)

Passive constructions also lead to dangling modifiers, as the following sentence illustrates.

> Driving down the street, an accident was seen.

Again, the sentence contains no reference to people; nothing answers the question "Who?" The simplest way to revise the sentence is to put a person (or people) into the sentence, thus answering the questions "Who drove down the street?" and "Who saw the accident?"

> Driving down the street, *I* saw an accident.

Another construction that gives rise to dangling modifiers is the **dummy** subject. Common dummy subjects are *there* and *it*; they are found in subject position but do not function as subjects.

> Driving down the street, *there* was an accident.
>
> Driving down the street, *it* looked like there had been an accident.

One common—but unsuccessful—revision for the dangling modifier is to shift the modifier from the beginning of the sentence to the end. As the following examples illustrate, this method of revision does not correct the dangling modifier.

An accident occurred driving down the street.

An accident was seen driving down the street.

It seemed there had been an accident driving down the street.

Shifting a modifier to the end of the sentence may, however, be helpful as an intermediate stage. The fact that the modifier is dangling may be more obvious, as it is in the preceding sentences, when the modifier is placed at the end.

PRACTICE

Copy the following paragraph, eliminating dangling modifiers. In many cases, more than one revision is possible; use the one that sounds best to you, but do not rely completely on one method of revision. You may want to reorder some sentences for variety.

Planning a party, decisions had to be made about date, location, theme, food, and drink. Wanting to have enough time for the preparations and cleaning up, it seemed a good idea to have the party on Saturday night. Having decided on the night, the location had to be chosen next. Disagreeing for a while, a local park was the final choice. Unable to choose a theme, the party would have none. Not wanting to cook, there would be cold sandwiches, potato chips, and other snacks. For quenching everyone's thirst, there would be available cold drinks of every kind.

12.4 REVIEW ON UNBALANCED AND ILLOGICAL STRUCTURES

Copy the following paragraphs, eliminating the unbalanced and illogical structures. In many cases, more than one revision is possible; use the one that sounds best to you, but do not rely completely on one method of revision. You may want to reorder some sentences for variety.

Graduating from high school, the decision is made by many young people to go on to school. Some go to the university, others to four-year colleges, and there are some who attend community colleges.

Community colleges offer vocational programs in addition to the traditional first two years of college curriculum and vocational schools that also provide such training. Enrolling in vocational training, auto repair, to program computers, and how to prepare income tax returns might be studied. Licensed practical nurses are trained at community colleges as are aides who help teachers.

There are several advantages to community colleges: low tuition, usually there are no large lecture classes, getting a degree in two years, and that there may be a well-paying job ready for the graduate.

Opting for the university, the choice is made by some despite higher tuition, in the freshman year large lecture classes with hundreds of students, and the fact that it takes four years to earn a degree. They do so for various reasons: status and getting a professional job, for example.

In addition to offering degree plans, community colleges and universities frequently offer noncredit courses for people interested in certain subjects or thinking they would like to know more about something. Lasting a few weeks or sometimes continuing throughout the full term, many students enroll in these classes, where they may learn about calligraphy, how to make ceramics, and of the study of the Bible.

Choosing between watching television and to learn something new, or that they can explore interesting subjects, the television set is turned off by many people and going back to school.

UNIT III
Word Form

WRITERS use hundreds, perhaps thousands, of words in a piece of text, and theoretically every word presents an opportunity for an error in word form. In practice, most writers have a few problems with word form, and some writers consistently make errors of this type.

Despite the thousands of words in the English language, the number of common patterns of word form is, fortunately, a limited one. If you have problems with word form, you do not have to learn each word separately, but you do need to learn the basic patterns and to recognize which patterns create problems for you.

Unit III includes chapters on the following topics: Chapter 13, "Nouns"; Chapter 14, "Verbs"; Chapter 15, "Pronouns"; and Chapter 16, "Adjectives and Adverbs." Each chapter explains the patterns characteristic of the type of word under discussion and provides practices dealing with each pattern. Chapter 17, "Homonyms and Near-Homonyms", presents information on these frequent sources of word form problems. A practice is provided on each set of homonyms and near-homonyms.

Because word form problems tend to be highly individual, Unit III is organized so that you can focus on the words and word patterns that create difficulty for you. You need first to learn how to "troubleshoot" your word form problems. A "troubleshooter" is someone who locates and eliminates problems. You need to learn how to locate and eliminate your individual word form problems. To do so, follow these procedures:

1. If your teacher marks a word form problem on your paper—and it should be a word "form" problem, not a word "choice" problem—then refer to the Word Index at the back of the book.
2. The Word Index lists in alphabetical order words that frequently create usage problems for writers. Find the word form problem; the Word Index directs you to the page of the text where that specific word is discussed.
3. In many cases, the word belongs to a particular subcategory, and you should note the other words in the subcategory; perhaps they too cause you word form problems.
4. Read the explanation. If, after reading the explanation, you can correct the word form problem, do so. Make the change—even if it is on a final graded draft—so you will have a record of the problem and the revision.
5. If you are unable to correct the word form problem at this point, do the practice that follows the explanation. You should also do the practice if you consistently have the same word form problems.
6. If, after reading the explanation and doing the practice, you are still unable to correct the word form problem, then consult your teacher or a tutor for further assistance.
7. Make a notebook list of your word form problems. Divide your list into the following: nouns, verbs, pronouns, adjectives and adverbs, homonyms and near-homonyms.
8. Copy the sentence (or portion of the sentence) containing the word form error onto the appropriate list. (If the Word Index directed you to the chapter on Pronouns, then the word form error belongs in the pronouns section of your notebook list.)
9. Correct the word form error by drawing a line through the incorrect form and putting the correct form above it:

    me
    Between you and ~~I~~
10. If the word marked on your paper is not in the Word Index, then it is probably a regular noun, a regular verb, or a regular

adjective or adverb. Your dictionary will list the appropriate word form.

11. The dictionary will also tell you the word's part of speech. If the word is a noun, then you should go to the section on Regular Nouns for an explanation of the problem.
12. As you proceed through the term, you may notice that certain words and certain patterns are persistent problems for you and that you need to edit for them in the early drafts of your papers so that they do not appear in the final draft.

If you follow these procedures consistently, by the end of the term, you should be able to locate and eliminate problems in word form in early drafts of your writing fairly easily and consistently. You will have become an effective word form "troubleshooter."

CHAPTER

13 Nouns

13.1 INTRODUCTION

The traditional definition of **noun** is "the name of a person, place, or thing." Nouns may be either common nouns or proper nouns. The following are **common nouns**.

    boy   person
    lake   place
   book thing

A **proper noun** is the name of a particular person, place, or thing.

   Jack Allen   person
   Lake Tahoe   place
   Gone with the Wind thing (book)

Another way to define nouns is to say that these words usually can be preceded by a **noun marker**, such as *a, an,* or *the.*

   a boy
   an apple
   a tree

Note 1: Abstractions such as *liberty* and *justice* are also nouns, but they are usually not preceded by noun markers: "with *liberty* and *justice* for all."

Note 2: Proper nouns are rarely preceded by noun markers: "*The* Jack Allen I went to high school with would never have done what the grown man has done."

One of the primary characteristics of the English noun is that speakers and writers of English are required to indicate number. A noun is either singular (one) or plural (more than one). With few exceptions, the overwhelming majority of English nouns use different forms for the singular and the plural. Most English nouns form their plurals in a fairly systematic way, but there are a good many common English nouns whose forms do not follow the usual pattern. Nouns following the system more or less consistently are called **regular nouns**, and those not doing so are referred to as **irregular nouns**.

In this chapter, regular English noun plurals are explained first, then variations on the regular pattern are discussed, and finally irregular English noun plurals are described. Practices are provided for all of these. As you do the practices, you should notice patterns that relate to your writing. Some practices should be very easy, others more difficult. If you then look at your writing, you should see the same patterns appear.

Note: An asterisk appears by italicized forms that should **not** be used.

13.2 REGULAR NOUN PLURALS

In Standard Written English, the plural of many nouns is formed simply by adding -s.

SINGULAR	PLURAL
one dog	two dogs
one cat	two cats
one horse	two horses

The pronunciation of the final sound in the plural forms of these words may vary somewhat, but the -s form is consistently used in written English.

Most regular nouns are made plural by adding -s, but -es is added to those regular nouns whose singular form ends in *ch, sh, s, x,* or *z.*

SINGULAR	PLURAL
church	churches
bush	bushes
dress	dresses
box	boxes
quiz	quizzes

There are two kinds of usage problems that can occur with regular English noun plurals: simplification and overcorrection.

Simplification

Simplification occurs when writers omit the final -*s* in their spoken and written English, using the same form for both singular and plural nouns.

	AVOID
SINGULAR	SIMPLIFIED PLURAL (*omitted -s*)
one boy	two *boy**
one cat	two *cat**
one horse	two *horse**

Overcorrection

Overcorrection occurs when writers begin to add -*s* to nouns and sometimes place -*s* signals inappropriately on singular nouns.

	AVOID
SINGULAR	OVERCORRECTED SINGULAR (*unnecessary -s*)
a dog	a *dogs**
a cat	a *cats**
a horse	a *horses**

Table 5 lists the Standard Written English singular and plural forms for regular nouns, which should be used, and the simplified and overcorrected forms, which should be avoided.

TABLE 5
REGULAR NOUN PLURALS: SWE FORMS AND OTHERS

SINGULAR	REGULAR PLURAL	AVOID	
		SIMPLIFIED PLURAL (-s omitted)	OVERCORRECTED SINGULAR (unnecessary -s)
one dog	two dogs	two *dog**	one *dogs**
one cat	two cats	two *cat**	one *cats**
one horse	two horses	two *horse**	one *horses**
one dress	two dresses	two *dress**	one *dresses**

PRACTICE

Copy the following paragraphs, inserting the appropriate Standard Written English noun forms. When the noun is singular, use the base form in parentheses. When the noun is plural, add *-s* or *-es* according to the base form of the noun. If the noun ends in *ch, sh, s, x,* or *z*, add *-es*.

Recently several (store)¹ at a local (mall)² sponsored a (contest)³ for local (artist)⁴. (Dozen)⁵ of local (artist)⁶ entered, including (painter)⁷, (watercolorist)⁸, and (sculptor)⁹. There were (painting)¹⁰ and (watercolor)¹¹ of all (size)¹² and of numerous (subject)¹³. The (sculpture)¹⁴ were equally varied, being made of (wood)¹⁵, (marble)¹⁶, (iron)¹⁷, (steel)¹⁸, and (bronze)¹⁹. Some of the (work)²⁰ of (art)²¹ were abstract, but (other)²² were representational; there were (picture)²³ of rose (bush)²⁴, country (church)²⁵, and (girl)²⁶ in pretty (dress)²⁷.

The entries were displayed in the (mall)²⁸ for two (week)²⁹ before they were judged. A few of the (judge)³⁰ were (instructor)³¹ from a nearby university, several came from the five (branch)³² of the local community (college)³³, and some were (teacher)³⁴ from various elementary and high (school)³⁵ in the (area)³⁶.

First, second, and third (prize)³⁷ were given in several categories. The various (winner)³⁸ sported bright (ribbon)³⁹ and (rosette)⁴⁰ in blue, red, and gold. Each first place (winner)⁴¹ was then eligible for the grand (prize)⁴² for the best entry of all.

A splendid oil (painting)⁴³ of an Indian (chief)⁴⁴ from a local (tribe)⁴⁵ won the grand (prize)⁴⁶. The (Indian)⁴⁷ was dressed in a ceremonial (outfit)⁴⁸, but he was wearing bifocal (glass)⁴⁹ and had a digital (watch)⁵⁰ on his left (wrist)⁵¹. The (title)⁵² of the (painting)⁵³ was "Yesterday and Today."

The (winner)⁵⁴, a retired postal (worker)⁵⁵, was obviously

thrilled. (Article) about him appeared in both of our local
56
(newspaper). He received an engraved sterling silver (bowl)
57   58
etched with many elaborate (design). Several of the (store) also
59   60
had donated (gift) of various (kind), and one (article) showed a
61   62   63
(picture) of the (winner) surrounded by (box) of many (shape)
64   65   66   67
and (size). One (prize) was an expensive gold (watch) donated
68   69   70
by a jewelry (store) at the (mall). When the (winner) had re-
71   72   73
cently retired, some of his (friend) had given him a gold (watch)
74   75
to celebrate his (retirement). Both (newspaper) had a (picture)
76   77   78
of the gentleman wearing his two gold (watch), one on either
79
(wrist).
80

13.3 VARIATIONS ON THE REGULAR PATTERN

Some nouns form their plurals according to the regular pattern, but with significant variations. The most common of these are discussed in this section.

Nouns Ending in *y*

Singular nouns ending in *y* may form their plurals in two different ways: by adding *-s* to the singular form or by changing the *y* to an *i* and adding *-es*.

y Preceded by a Vowel

When the singular form ends in *y* preceded by a vowel, the plural is formed by adding *-s*.

SINGULAR	PLURAL
day	days
boy	boys
key	keys

y Preceded by a Consonant

When the noun ends in *y* preceded by a consonant, then the *y* is changed to *i* and *-es* is added.

SINGULAR	PLURAL
baby	babies
sky	skies
fly	flies
enemy	enemies
liberty	liberties
army	armies

PRACTICE

Copy the following paragraphs, inserting the appropriate Standard Written English noun forms. When the noun is singular, use the base form in parentheses. When the noun is plural, add an -s to the base form if the y is preceded by a vowel; if the y is preceded by a consonant, change the y to i and add -es.

Many (country)¹ today find it necessary to have (spy)² who try to protect the secrets of their own (country)³ while trying to discover the secrets of other (country)⁴, both (ally)⁵ and (enemy)⁶. Sometimes (country)⁷ who consider the United States to be an (enemy)⁸ will send young people who are still (boy)⁹ or girls on long-term underground assignments as (spy)¹⁰. We too send (spy)¹¹ to (country)¹² we regard as our (enemy)¹³ to find out about their (way)¹⁴.

Military organizations are often the objects of these efforts; the air forces, (army)¹⁵, and (navy)¹⁶ of the (country)¹⁷ of the world have learned defenses against their (enemy)¹⁸, but no organization is invulnerable to (stupidity)¹⁹ of various kinds. A set of (key)²⁰ may be left lying out carelessly where someone can make impressions of them. Secret documents may be found lying on (tray)²¹ of papers. Stuffed (toy)²² may be carried in full of electronic gear.

If and when the (spy)²³ are caught, the newspapers fill their pages with (story)²⁴ about them. Politicians make speeches about

the dangers to our many (liberty). One columnist will find (ray)
of sunshine, no matter what happens, while another will announce that our (enemy) are making (monkey) of us.

For weeks and sometimes months, (story) about trials, (attorney), judges, and (jury) will fill the newspapers, television, and radio. Then, mysteriously, (spy) may be exchanged, and in a few weeks or months the (story) are forgotten, and the (worry) about (country) that seem to be our (enemy) are not remembered until the next set of (story) about (spy).

Nouns Ending in *o*

Singular nouns ending in *o* may form their plurals by adding *-s* or *-es*. Many of these nouns may use either plural form.

SINGULAR	PLURAL WITH -s	PLURAL WITH -es
mosquito	mosquitos	mosquitoes
buffalo	buffalos	buffaloes
domino	dominos	dominoes
zero	zeros	zeroes

However, there are several common nouns that must always end with *-s*, never with *-es*; the most frequently used of these are listed here:

SINGULAR	PLURAL WITH -s
auto	autos
ego	egos
lasso	lassos
patio	patios
photo	photos
radio	radios
studio	studios
cello	cellos
combo	combos
duo	duos
piano	pianos
solo	solos
sopranos	sopranos

There are also a few nouns ending in *o* whose plurals must always end in *-es*. Four of the most frequently used are listed here:

SINGULAR	PLURAL WITH *-es*
echo	echoes
hero	heroes
potato	potatoes
tomato	tomatoes

Note: These words can be remembered by making a nonsense word from their first letters: PETH—*p* for *potato*, *e* for *echo*, *t* for *tomato*, and *h* for *hero*. The nonsense sentence, "The *heroes* heard *echoes* of *potatoes* and *tomatoes*," can also be used as a memory device.

PRACTICE

Copy the following paragraphs, inserting the appropriate Standard Written English noun forms. If the noun is singular, use the base form in parentheses. When the noun is plural, the simplest method is to add *-s* to any plural noun ending in *o*, unless the noun is one of the PETH words.

In recording (studio)¹ around the country, artists gather to create music that is heard on (radio)² and (stereo)³ around the world. Although singers often sing (solos)⁴, most other musicians play in groups—in huge orchestras, small jazz (combos)⁵, or even smaller (duo)⁶. One finds (cello)⁷ and (piano)⁸ in orchestras, but (soprano)⁹ may sing opera or jazz.

We hear the (echo)¹⁰ of their music around us daily, on car (radio)¹¹, in backyard (patio)¹², and sometimes in the songs we sing to ourselves. The autographs, the (photo)¹³, and the adulation sometimes create monstrous (ego)¹⁴.

Some performers begin to perceive themselves as (hero)¹⁵ or geniuses, automatically entitled to the trappings of wealth such as jewels and expensive (auto)¹⁶. The starving young performer who considered a cheeseburger, a salad with (tomato)17, and a large order of French fried (potato)18 to be a feast becomes a different person, insisting on gourmet food and expensive wines.

Nouns Ending in *f*

Some singular nouns ending in *f* follow the regular pattern; that is, they form their plural by adding -*s*.

SINGULAR	PLURAL
safe	safes
chief	chiefs
dwarf	dwarfs

Other common nouns ending in *f* follow a variant pattern; in this group of nouns, the singular base noun undergoes a change in the final consonant (from *f* to *v*) and -*es* is added (for example, *himself*, but *themselves*).

SINGULAR	PLURAL
elf	elves
self	selves
shelf	shelves
calf	calves
half	halves
leaf	leaves
thief	thieves
life	lives
knife	knives
wife	wives
wolf	wolves

PRACTICE

Copy the following paragraphs, inserting the appropriate Standard Written English noun forms. When the noun is singular, use the base form in parentheses. When the noun is plural, change the *f* to *v*, and add -*es* when that form is correct. Otherwise, add -*s* to indicate the plural form.

Most of us no doubt think that the day of cattle (thief) is long gone, and stories about their (life) can be found only on book (shelf) filled with western stories about daring cowboys, packs of marauding (wolf), and tribes of Indian warriors led by cunning war (chief). We would probably find (ourself) astonished to discover that cattle (thief) still exist today.

When a local farmer went to feed his herd of (calf), he discovered that the (calf) (themself) were no longer there. (Thief) had stolen the (calf) during the night. When the (sheriff) arrived, he noticed that the (thief) had driven their trucks through an area filled with poison ivy (leaf) and then had walked several feet, crushing the (leaf) as they went.

Quietly, the (sheriff) alerted area doctors and hospitals and asked them to inform him of cases of poison ivy where their patients appeared to have walked through the (leaf) for several feet. He also asked pharmacists to remove poison ivy remedies from their (shelf) and to inform him if they (themself) noticed any circumstances that seemed suspicious.

A few days later the farmer (himself) was standing in line at a local pharmacy and overheard someone asking the pharmacist for an ointment that would work against poison ivy. The speaker said he didn't know how it had happened, but somehow he and his brother had evidently walked through some poison ivy (leaf). Quickly the farmer left the store and called the (sheriff); a few minutes later the pharmacist (himself) called.

When the (sheriff) arrived, the farmer had the license plates of the truck that the poison ivy sufferer had driven away in; he had also noticed poison ivy (leaf) caught on the underside of the truck. Shortly afterward, the (sheriff) had the truck owner's address. When he went to arrest the (thief), their (wife) tried to hide them. Then both of them pulled (knife) on him and tried to escape. Soon they found (themself) arrested, and the (calf) were found and returned to the farmer.

 IRREGULAR NOUN PLURALS

In addition to regular noun plurals and their variations, there are also nouns that follow **irregular** patterns. Usually, these are small groups of words whose plural forms are indicated by internal changes within the noun rather than by the addition of *-s* or *-es* at the end.

There are various subcategories of irregular noun plurals. Each subcategory is a small group of words, but at least some of those words are quite frequently used. In the following discussion, these subcategories of irregular noun plurals are referred to as **"classes."** Each class is numbered and an example of a typical member of the class is given in parentheses. There are three kinds of usage problems that can occur with irregular noun plurals: simplification, regularization, and overcorrection.

Simplification

Simplification occurs when writers use the unchanged singular form for both singular and plural.

	AVOID
SINGULAR	SIMPLIFIED (no change)
one man	two *man**

Regularization

Regularization occurs when writers attempt to form the plural by adding the regular plural *-s* to the singular base.

	AVOID
SINGULAR	REGULARIZED PLURAL (*-s* added to base)
one man	two *mans**

Overcorrection

Overcorrection occurs when writers add *-s* to the irregular plural, thus making the plural signal twice.

	AVOID
SINGULAR	OVERCORRECTED PLURAL *(-s added to irregular)*
one man	two *mens**

In this instance, writers correctly use the irregular plural *men*, but then incorrectly add the regular plural signal *-s* to the end of the word.

Class 1 Irregular Nouns *(man–men)*

One common but troublesome subcategory is the *man–men* class. In this class, the plural is indicated not by adding an *-s* or *-es* but by changing the vowel within the singular base from *a* to *e*. Related to *man–men* and often found in the same context is *child–children*. In this case, the plural of *child* is formed by adding *-ren* to the singular. Table 6 lists the Standard Written English singular and plural forms, which should be used, and the simplified, regularized, and overcorrected forms, which should be avoided.

TABLE 6
CLASS 1 IRREGULAR NOUNS: SWE FORMS AND OTHERS

		AVOID		
SINGULAR	IRREGULAR PLURAL	SIMPLIFIED PLURAL *(no change)*	REGULARIZED PLURAL *(-s added to base)*	OVERCORRECTED PLURAL *(-s added to irregular)*
one man	two men	two *man**	two *mans**	two *mens**
one woman	two women	two *woman**	two *womans**	two *womens**
one child	two children	two *child**	two *childs**	two *childrens**

PRACTICE

Copy the following paragraphs, inserting the appropriate Standard Written English noun forms. When the noun is singular, use the base form shown in parentheses. When the noun is plural, change the base form from *man* to *men*, from *woman* to *women*, from *child* to *children*.

The working roles for (man)₁ and (woman)₂ have changed in American society during the centuries. In colonial America, most (man)₃ and (woman)₄ lived on their own farms and worked there. The (man)₅ of the family, the father and the older sons, worked in the fields and hunted, while the (woman)₆ in the family, the mother and the older daughters, worked in and around the house and took care of the younger (child)₇.

During the Industrial Revolution in the nineteenth century, more and more (man)₈ went to work in factories. An unmarried (woman)₉ might work in a factory, particularly a clothing factory, but a married (woman)₁₀ usually remained at home, cooking, cleaning, and caring for (child)₁₁.

To a considerable extent, the situation remained the same in the first part of the twentieth century, but in both World War I and World War II, when millions of (man)₁₂ were in uniform, their jobs in industry were taken by (woman)₁₃. In war time, many (woman)₁₄ delayed marriage and (child)₁₅. If a (woman)₁₆ already had (child)₁₇, usually family members would take care of the (child)₁₈ while the (woman)₁₉ worked. However, after each war concluded, the (man)₂₀ would return to his factory job, and the (woman)₂₁ would return to the home.

Now, in the latter part of the twentieth century, most (woman)₂₂ expect to work, and most (man)₂₃ expect them to work. The majority of families find that two paychecks, one from the (man)₂₄ and one from the (woman)₂₅, are necessary to support a family with two or more (child)₂₆.

Unfortunately, statistics show that (woman)₂₇ receive only 60

percent of the salary received by (man). Other statistics show
that in families where a (man) and a (woman) are both working,
the average (woman) works approximately 40 hours a week on
household duties such as cooking, cleaning, and taking care of
(child), but the average (man) spends only 10 hours or so a
week engaged in such tasks.

The statistics indicate that, although both (man) and
(woman) today are working outside the home, the average
(woman) makes less money than the average (man), and the
average (woman) also spends many more hours doing household duties than the average (man). The figures also suggest
that ideas of the proper roles for (man) and (woman) are very
resistant to change. In many families, these numbers translate
into disagreements between an individual (man) and an individual (woman) about money and household duties.

Class 2 Irregular Nouns *(tooth–teeth)*

Related to the *man–men* class is the *tooth–teeth* class. In this case, the vowels *oo* in the singular form are changed to *ee* in the plural form. Table 7 lists the Standard Written English singular and plural forms, which should be used, and the simplified, regularized, and overcorrected forms, which should be avoided.

TABLE 7
CLASS 2 IRREGULAR NOUNS: SWE FORMS AND OTHERS

		AVOID		
SINGULAR	IRREGULAR PLURAL	SIMPLIFIED PLURAL (no change)	REGULARIZED PLURAL (-s added to base)	OVERCORRECTED PLURAL (-s added to irregular)
one tooth	two teeth	two *tooth**	two *tooths**	two *teeths**
one foot	two feet	two *foot**	two *foots**	two *feets**
one goose	two geese	two *goose**	two *gooses**	two *geeses**

PRACTICE

Copy the following paragraphs, inserting the appropriate Standard Written English noun forms. When the noun is singular, use the base form shown in parentheses. When the noun is plural, change the base form to show the appropriate plural, from *tooth* to *teeth*, from *foot* to *feet*, from *goose* to *geese*.

Last weekend my cousin took her little boy to a park where ducks and (goose)₁ swim in a pool, waddle around on shore, and beg food from park visitors. Because her (foot)₂ were tired, she sat down on a park bench to rest.

Her little boy, who wanted to play with the ducks and (goose)₃, wandered too close to a huge, bad-tempered, gray (goose)₄. The (goose)₅ flapped his wings and hissed loudly at the child, who quickly decided to run back to his mother for protection.

In his hurry to reach the bench where his mother was sitting, he caught his right (foot)₆ on a protruding tree root, tripped, and fell. When my cousin heard his cry, she jumped to her (foot)₇ and raced to where he was lying on the ground with a huge gray (goose)₈ hissing at him and flapping his wings.

As soon as she arrived, the (goose)₉ strutted off to where the rest of the flock of (goose)₁₀ were standing. Her son was lying on the ground crying, clutching his right (foot)₁₁ with one hand and holding his other hand to his mouth. When she looked in his mouth, she saw that his (tooth)₁₂ were covered with blood.

Alarmed, she rushed him to an emergency dental clinic, thinking that some of his (tooth)₁₃ might have been severely damaged. She was greatly relieved to hear that not a single (tooth)₁₄ had been injured; he had only bitten his tongue when he had fallen. Then, she took him to a hospital emergency room to have his injured right (foot) examined, but that proved to be only a slightly sprained right ankle.[15]

That evening, after she had put her son to bed, she remarked to her husband that the next time she wanted to amuse her son and rest her (foot) at the same time, she intended to take him to a movie because the cost of the medical and dental bills from the visit to the free park had been enough to pay for several movies.[16]

Class 3 Irregular Nouns *(mouse–mice)*

Another subcategory related to the *man–men* class and the *tooth–teeth* class is the *mouse–mice* class. In this subcategory, as in the other two, the plural form is indicated by a change in the vowel, from *ou* to *i*. In this case, however, the final consonant preceding the final *e* also is changed from an *s* to a *c*. In the singular base, the spelling is *mouse*; in the plural, the spelling is *mice*. Table 8 lists the Standard Written English singular and plural forms, which should be used, and the simplified, regularized, and overcorrected forms, which should be avoided.

TABLE 8
CLASS 3 IRREGULAR NOUNS: SWE FORMS AND OTHERS

		AVOID		
SINGULAR	IRREGULAR PLURAL	SIMPLIFIED PLURAL (no change)	REGULARIZED PLURAL (-s added to base)	OVERCORRECTED PLURAL (-s added to irregular)
one mouse	two mice	two *mouse**	two *mouses**	two *mices**
one louse	two lice	two *louse**	two *louses**	two *lices**

PRACTICE

Copy the following paragraphs, inserting the appropriate Standard Written English noun forms. When the singular form is needed, use the base form shown in the parentheses. When the plural form is needed, change the base form from *mouse* to *mice* or from *louse* to *lice*.

Two common pests are (mouse)₁ and (louse)₂. Although many people are afraid of (mouse)₃, an occasional (mouse)₄ is not a serious problem. Often attempts to get rid of (mouse)₅ can create more problems than their presence. One should be particularly careful of (mouse)₆ poison, especially if there are pets or small children in the house. In order to get rid of (mouse)₇, perhaps the old-fashioned (mouse)₈ trap, placed where children and pets cannot reach it, is the best solution.

(Louse)₉ are also ordinarily rather harmless, but children who share combs can spread head (louse)₁₀ because each (louse)₁₁ is so small that no one notices it move from head to comb to head. Getting rid of (louse)₁₂ can be rather difficult; special shampoos are required and then everything in the house, including bedding and furniture, must be cleaned very carefully to ensure that not a single (louse)₁₃ remains.

It is probably easier to eliminate (mouse)₁₄ from a house than (louse)₁₅, since the sight of one (mouse)₁₆ does not necessarily mean that there are dozens of (mouse)₁₇ hiding away, but the sight of one (louse)₁₈ may indicate the presence of thousands more (louse)₁₉.

Class 4 Irregular Nouns *(deer–deer)*

Some English nouns are the same in both the singular and the plural; these are referred to as **zero plurals**. Some common examples are listed in Table 9; the table lists the Standard Written English singular and plural forms, which should be used, and the regularized forms, which should be avoided.

There are also several other words that can form their plurals in the regular pattern, adding *-s*, or can be equally correct in the zero plural form. Some of these are listed in Table 10.

TABLE 9
CLASS 4 IRREGULAR NOUNS: SWE FORMS AND OTHERS

		AVOID
SINGULAR	ZERO PLURAL	REGULARIZED PLURAL
deer	deer	*deers**
sheep	sheep	*sheeps**
moose	moose	*mooses**
species	species	*specieses**
Chinese	Chinese	*Chineses**
Japanese	Japanese	*Japaneses**

TABLE 10
CLASS 4 IRREGULAR NOUNS: ZERO AND REGULAR PLURALS

SINGULAR	ZERO PLURAL	REGULAR PLURAL
bear	bear	bears
fish	fish	fishes
bass	bass	basses
perch	perch	perches
trout	trout	trouts

PRACTICE

Copy the following paragraphs, inserting the appropriate Standard Written English noun forms. In addition to the zero plurals, some other more common plurals are included. Use the base form in parentheses when the zero plural is the correct form. When other plural forms are required, make the necessary changes to the base form.

Two (group)¹ from the Orient came recently to visit our city zoo. There were several (Japanese)² in one group, and a small number of (Chinese)³ in the other. The two (group)⁴ of (Oriental)⁵ were much more interested in the native American (species)⁶ than in the more exotic (animal)⁷.

Ignoring the various (family) of (lion), (tiger), and other exotic (species), they concentrated on the (sheep), (deer), (moose), and (elk). They were equally interested in the grizzly (bear). The aquarium, with (dozen) of (kind) of (fish) also fascinated them, particularly native American sport (fish) such as (bass), (perch), and (trout).

13.5 POSSESSIVE NOUNS

Possessive nouns are indicated by the presence of an apostrophe (for example, the *boy*'s *book*). We call these constructions "possessive," but they may be used to indicate other kinds of relationships. For example, Alzheimer's disease does not belong to a man named Alzheimer; rather, it was named after Dr. Alois Alzheimer, a German physician who first discovered the disease.

Often writers have no problem recognizing possessive nouns and knowing that an apostrophe is required, but sometimes the placement of the apostrophe is a more difficult problem. The location of the apostrophe depends on whether the writer is using a regular singular possessive noun, a regular plural possessive noun, or an irregular plural possessive noun.

Singular Possessive Nouns

A singular noun is made possessive by adding *'s* after the noun. Table 11 provides examples of singular nouns and their possessive forms.

TABLE 11
SINGULAR POSSESSIVE NOUNS

SINGULAR	POSSESSIVE
boy	boy's
dog	dog's
cat	cat's
horse	horse's
watch	watch's
lady	lady's

PRACTICE

Copy the following paragraphs, inserting the appropriate noun forms. Many of the singular nouns are possessive, but some are not. Add *'s* to those that should be possessive; do not add *'s* to those that should not be possessive.

My cousin (Josie)¹ two children, Connie and Rick, went to visit their (father)² Aunt Madeline, who has a reputation for being a bit of an (eccentric)³. In fact, Aunt (Madeline)⁴ nickname is Aunt Mad.

Like many elderly ladies, Aunt (Mad)⁵ favorite companions are the animals with which she has filled her (house)⁶. Her (dog)⁷ name is Winston Churchill, her (cat)⁸ name is Jackie O, and her (bird)⁹ name is Bubbles. Aunt (Mad)¹⁰ claim is that each (animal)¹¹ name is appropriate because of the (owner)¹² appearance and disposition.

Certainly it is true that Winston (Churchill)¹³ appearance does remind one of the famous British Prime Minister, since he is a rather overweight (bulldog)¹⁴. (Jackie O)¹⁵ appearance also seems appropriate since she is a sleek, well-groomed, elegant (cat)¹⁶; Aunt (Mad)¹⁷ final touch has been the rhinestone (collar)¹⁸. To (Connie)¹⁹ questions about the (canary)²⁰ name, Bubbles, Aunt (Mad)²¹ response was that the (canary)²² real name was Beverly Sills, after the retired opera (singer)²³. Beverly Sills, the (singer)²⁴, is blond and is known for having a "bubbly" disposition; according to Aunt (Mad)²⁵ logic, her (canary)²⁶ yellow feathers and happy chirping make Bubbles the appropriate (name)²⁷.

After a (week)²⁸ visit, Connie and Rick returned home. Although their parents were not surprised to hear about Winston (Churchill)²⁹ rheumatism and (Jackie O)³⁰ latest litter of kittens, they had not heard before of the (canary)³¹ nickname, Bubbles. At (Rick)³² sug-

gestion that their new (puppy) name should be Prince Charles
                          33
because of his rather large ears, each (parent) response was,
                                              34
"Oh, no!"

Regular Plural Possessive Nouns

When a regular plural noun is possessive, only an apostrophe is added. The regular noun is made plural by adding the *s*. Since the *s* is already there, only an apostrophe is added after the *s*; for example, *the two boys' coats*. In this example, *the two boys* (a regular plural noun) ends in *s*; the possessive refers to their *coats*, so an apostrophe is added after the *s*. Table 12 lists examples of regular plural possessive nouns.

TABLE 12
REGULAR PLURAL POSSESSIVE NOUNS

SINGULAR	PLURAL	PLURAL POSSESSIVE
cat	cats	cats'
dog	dogs	dogs'
horse	horses	horses'
watch	watches	watches'
lady	ladies	ladies'

PRACTICE

Copy the following paragraphs, inserting the appropriate noun forms. All of the nouns in parentheses are plural, but not all of them are possessive. If the plural noun is possessive, add an apostrophe after the *s*; if the noun is not possessive, do not add an apostrophe.

The Turner (Brothers) Farms are owned by two (brothers)
                    1   2
whose family has owned land in the area for several (generations).
                                                          3
The (brothers) (wives) are also from local (families). The two
       4   5   6
(families) (farms) are each devoted to different agricultural
    7   8
(specialties).
     9
The older brother raises (cows) and (pigs), and the (cows)
                            10   11   12

barn and the (pigs) pen are the largest (buildings) on his farm. The
                                13   14
younger brother raises (horses) and (dogs); the (horses) (pastures)
                         15   16   17   18
surround the farmhouse, making a pleasant scene, while the
(dogs) (runs) are located inconspicuously behind the house.
 19   20

In the spring, the (farms) are filled with the (sights) and
                     21   22
(sounds) of young (animals). The (mares) (foals) and the (cows)
  23   24   25   26   27
(calves) stand in the (pastures) with their (mothers). The (sows)
  28   29   30   31
litters squeal boisterously, and the (puppies) yapping fills the air.
                                        32

The (brothers) (days) and (nights) are often occupied with
    33   34   35
the birth and care of the young (animals), while their (wives) time
                                  36   37
is occupied with planting spring (gardens). The (animals) fertility
                                   38   39
and the (plants) abundance feed the (brothers) (families) and the
         40   41   42
(families) of many others.
  43

Irregular Plural Possessive Nouns

Irregular plural noun possessives are constructed in the same way as regular singular noun possessives.

the *boy's* coat (referring to a coat belonging to one boy)

Table 13 lists examples of irregular plural possessive nouns. Since their plural forms do not end in *s*, it is necessary to add *'s* to indicate the possessive relationship.

TABLE 13
IRREGULAR PLURAL POSSESSIVE NOUNS

SINGULAR	PLURAL	PLURAL POSSESSIVE
man	men	men's
woman	women	women's
child	children	children's
goose	geese	geese's
mouse	mice	mice's
deer	deer	deer's

PRACTICE

Copy the following paragraphs, inserting the appropriate plural possessive forms. Not all of the plural possessives required are irregular. If a regular plural possessive is needed, insert the appropriate form.

Doug Scott and George Lehman were partners in a company that manufactured (men), (women), and (children) shoes. Doug
                                  1   2   3
was in charge of the (men) shoe department, while George
                      4
supervised the (women) department. In the (children) department,
                 5   6
Doug supervised the production of (boys) shoes, and George
                                    7
did the same for the production of (girls) shoes.
                                     8

The two (men) wives were also good friends, both teaching at
          9
the same private (girls) school, belonging to some of the same
                   10
(women) clubs, and sharing the supervision of many of their
  11
(children) activities.
   12

Sometimes the two families went on outings together to places such as the (children) zoo. The zoo did not display exotic
                                       13
animal exhibits, with lions, tigers, elephants, and giraffes. Instead, there were small herds of moose and deer. The children were fascinated by the two (moose) great antlers and by the several
                                    14
(deer) graceful leaps.
  15

The zoo also had small flocks of ducks and geese. The noise of all the (ducks) quacking and the (geese) hissing also interested
         16   17
the children. Another section contained several types of rodents, including hamsters and mice. Three (hamsters) cages and four
                                                  18
(mice) cages occupied this small section of the zoo.
  19

CHAPTER 14 Verbs

14.1 INTRODUCTION

For many writers, the English verb offers a greater variety of pitfalls than any other part of speech. Most writers have problems with at least a few verbs; some writers have problems with many verbs. The verb is complicated for various reasons:

First, there is a minimum of four different forms for most verbs and five for others; each of these forms has specific places where it should be used and others where it should not be used.

Second, subject-verb agreement must always be maintained (see Chapter 8).

Third, many commonly used verbs do not follow a regular pattern, and their use must be learned one by one.

Fourth, there is a rather elaborate set of terminology used in discussing verbs. An explanation of verb terminology is given later in the chapter so that you and your teacher will have a common frame of reference. As you do the practices, the verb concepts and terms will become increasingly familiar to you.

Some of the practices in this chapter should be very easy for you, while others will be more difficult. If you look at your writing, you should be able to see somewhat the same patterns of verb usage problems.

14.2 TROUBLESHOOTING VERBS

Follow the general procedures outlined in the introduction to Unit III. Because of the number and complexity of English verbs, the following procedures may also be required.

1. Consult the Word Index for the page number of the in-text discussion of the verb form problem.

2. Turn to the page in the text where discussion of the verb form problem begins.
3. Consult Table A of the section, which lists the principal parts of the verb.
4. Then consult Table B, which provides examples of the Standard Written English forms in brief sentences.
5. Correct the verb form error.
6. If you are unable to make the correction, do the practice provided in that section of the text.
7. Check the completed practice against Table C, which shows examples of verb forms to avoid; an asterisk appears by italicized forms that should **not** be used. Correct the practice if you have used any of those forms.
8. If you are still unable to correct the verb form error, consult your teacher or a tutor for further assistance.

14.3 REGULAR VERBS

Most of the time writers have relatively little difficulty with completely regular verbs. **Regular verbs** are verbs that use the same form in both past tense and past participle, usually created by adding *-ed* to the base form of the verb.

BASE	PAST	PAST PARTICIPLE
walk	walked	had walked

There are two usage issues with regular verbs: when to add *-s* and when to add *-ed*.

When to Add *-s*

In Standard Written English, *-s* is added only to third person singular, present tense verbs. All other present tense verbs use the base form.

	SINGULAR	PLURAL
First person	I walk.	We walk.
Second person	You walk.	You walk.
Third person	He walks.	They walk.
	She walks.	
	It walks.	

The two most common usage problems are simplification and overcorrection.

Simplification

Sometimes writers who have a tendency to omit word endings may omit the *-s* ending on the third person singular verb. When they do so, they are engaging in **simplification**; that is, they are relying entirely on the base form rather than making the appropriate modifications to the form that are required in Standard Written English.

	AVOID
STANDARD WRITTEN ENGLISH	SIMPLIFIED FORM (omitted *-s*)
He *walks* to the store.	He *walk** to the store.

Overcorrection

Overcorrection occurs when writers, realizing that they need to add *-s*, but not yet having mastery of the system, overcompensate and add *-s* endings where they are not appropriate.

	AVOID
STANDARD WRITTEN ENGLISH	OVERCORRECTED FORM (unnecessary *-s*)
They walk.	They *walks*.*

Another reason for this overcorrection may be that writers know that *-s* is required on most plural nouns and consequently assume that *-s* is also required on plural verbs. Constructions like this are usually considered errors in subject-verb agreement (see Chapter 8), but another explanation is that the distinctions of English verb form have not been observed.

Nevertheless, the third person singular verb form is quite consistent, and once writers master the basic pattern, it can be applied in many situations. Thus, one very simple pattern is replaced by a more complicated but still very regular pattern.

PRACTICE

Copy the following paragraphs, inserting appropriate Standard Written English verb forms. When the verb in parentheses needs an -*s* because the subject is in the third person singular, add an -*s*. If the verb ends in *y*, change the *y* to *i* and add -*es*. Not all verbs in parentheses are third person singular; those that are not should remain unchanged.

A college basketball arena during a championship game (seem)¹ to be a bubbling cauldron of tension and excitement. A player (dribble)² the ball down the floor, going for the basket, and (jump)³ high in the air as he (try)⁴ to get the ball in the basket. Another player (surge)⁵ forward, (throw)⁶ an arm high into the air, and (deflect)⁷ the ball from the basket. The ball (shoot)⁸ over the players' heads and each player (rush)⁹ to grab the loose ball.

The referees (run)¹⁰ up and down the side, trying to follow the swift tumultuous action on the floor. One referee (spy)¹¹ a player fouling another and (blow)¹² shrilly on his whistle. The players (line)¹³ up in front of the basket as the fouled player (try)¹⁴ for a free throw. The crowd (hold)¹⁵ its breath as the ball (fly)¹⁶ through the air towards its goal and (groan)¹⁷ when it (hit)¹⁸ the backboard aimlessly. A second time the player (shoot)¹⁹ for a free throw; his face (show)²⁰ the tension and strain of the moment. Again the ball (fly)²¹ through the air, but this time, it (swish)²² through the hoop. The crowd (roar)²³ its approval; a second later the buzzer (sound)²⁴ the end of the game.

The home team (win)²⁵ by one point, and the player who threw the final point (find)²⁶ himself surrounded by the other players on the team. They all (shout)²⁷ joyfully and (pound)²⁸ him on the back. He (walk)²⁹ off the floor while the crowd (cheer)³⁰. The coach (smile)³¹ and (shake)³² his hand.

Afterward a reporter (ask)³³ him how he felt when he heard

the sound of the buzzer, and he (answer)[34] with a smile while a photographer (shoot)[35] his picture. The next day the local newspaper (carry)[36] a story about the game. A headline (trumpet)[37] the score, and the front page (carry)[38] a picture of the smiling basketball player. On such a glorious note, the season (end)[39], and the player (go)[40] back to classes and exams.

When to Add *-ed*

The *-ed* ending is added to the base form of the verb to form the past tense and past participle of the regular verb.

PAST TENSE   PAST PARTICIPLE
He walked.   I have walked.
                   He has walked.
                   He had walked.

In addition to being used in perfect verbs (those with the auxiliary *have/has/had*), the past participle is also used in combination with forms of *be* to form the passive.

He *was asked* to give a speech.

The past participle can also be used as an adjective.

He had a *satisfied* expression on his face.

The two most common usage problems are simplification and overcorrection.

Simplification

Sometimes writers who have a tendency to omit word endings may omit the *-ed* ending on the past tense and the past participle of the regular verb. When they omit these endings, they are engaging in **simplification**; that is, they are relying on the base form rather than making the appropriate modifications to the form that are required in Standard Written English.

	AVOID
STANDARD WRITTEN ENGLISH	SIMPLIFIED FORM (omitted -ed)
He *walked*.	He *walk**.
He *had walked*.	He had *walk**.
He was *asked* to give a speech.	He was *ask** to give a speech.
He had a *satisfied* expression on his face.	He had a *satisfy** expression on his face.

Some verbs seem to be particularly susceptible to this kind of simplification.

	AVOID
STANDARD WRITTEN ENGLISH	SIMPLIFIED FORM (omitted -ed)
He *used* to write letters.	He *use** to write letters.
He was *supposed* to be at the meeting.	He was *suppose** to be at the meeting.
He was *surprised*.	He was *surprise**.

Overcorrection

Overcorrection occurs when writers, realizing that *-ed* endings are needed but not yet having mastery of the system, overcompensate and add them where they are inappropriate; for example, with dummy and modal auxiliary verbs.

Dummy Auxiliary. The forms of the dummy auxiliary *do* (*do, does, did*) are used in questions, in negatives, and in emphatic statements. Following are some examples of Standard Written English forms and their overcorrections.

	AVOID
STANDARD WRITTEN ENGLISH	OVERCORRECTED FORM (unnecessary -ed)
Did he *walk*? (question)	*Did* he *walked**?
He *did* not *walk*. (negative)	He *did* not *walked**.
He *did walk*. (emphatic)	He *did walked**.

The unnecessary adding of *-ed* seems to occur more frequently in combination with *did* than with *do* and *does*. Presumably, *did walked* is, in a sense, simply a double signal of the past tense, both on the auxiliary and on the main verb.

Modal Auxiliaries. The same principle operates when the modal auxiliaries are used; that is, -ed should not be added to the base form of the main verb. Following are some examples of Standard Written English forms and their overcorrections.

STANDARD WRITTEN ENGLISH	AVOID OVERCORRECTED FORM (unnecessary -ed)
He *shall walk*.	He *shall walked**.
He *should walk*.	He *should walked**.
He *will walk*.	He *will walked**.
He *would walk*.	He *would walked**.
He *may walk*.	He *may walked**.
He *might walk*.	He *might walked**.
He *can walk*.	He *can walked**.
He *could walk*.	He *could walked**.

The unnecessary adding of *-ed* to forms of the main verb seems to occur more often with the past modals (*should, would, might, could*) than with the present modals (*shall, will, may, can*). Again, the past tense seems to be signaled twice, on the modal auxiliary and on the main verb itself.

Nevertheless, the past tense and past participle of regular verbs are quite consistent, and once writers master the basic pattern, it can be applied in many situations. Thus, one very simple pattern is replaced by a more complicated but still fairly regular pattern.

PRACTICE A

Copy the following paragraphs, inserting appropriate Standard Written English verb forms. When either the past tense or the past participle is used, add *-ed* to the verb in parentheses; do not add *-ed* when it is not appropriate. If the verb ends in *y*, change the *y* to *i* and add *-ed*.

After the basketball player (walk) off the floor at the end of the championship season, he (return) to his classes and the usual occupations of students: reading assignments, taking exams, and writing papers. At the end of the semester he (graduate)³ with a degree in business. He (hope)⁴ for a chance at the pros and (wait)⁵ patiently through the draft. Finally, on the last round, a team (draft)⁶ him. The player (attend)⁷ the team's summer camp, but he did not (make)⁸ the cut. Later, he (return)⁹ to the university and (enter)¹⁰ a graduate degree program in business, and his old coach (offer)¹¹ him a part-time job as his assistant. In some ways, the old routine (return)¹², and he (attend)¹³ his classes—reading assignments, taking exams, and writing papers. His afternoons were (occupy)¹⁴ with helping young men who (continue)¹⁵ to (play)¹⁶ the game he himself had (play)¹⁷ so well and (love)¹⁸ so much.

Finally, he (receive)¹⁹ his master's degree and was (offer)²⁰ a job at a local bank. His years as a player and as an assistant coach had (cause)²¹ him to be a highly recognizable figure in the community, so the bank had him (picture)²² in advertisements in the paper. So many customers began to (ask)²³ for him that the bank (decide)²⁴ to feature him in its television commercials. The advertising department (suggest)²⁵ that the commercials with him should (appear)²⁶ during the local sportscast. Everyone (agree)²⁷ that this was a good idea, and soon the commercials (appear)²⁸ regularly every evening at 6:20.

More and more customers (ask)²⁹ to speak to the young man in the commercial and were (add)³⁰ daily to the bank's account. At the end of the year, the former basketball player had (cause)³¹ more new accounts to be (add)³² than anyone else at the bank. The president of the bank (single)³³ him out for praise at the end-of-the-year banquet, and he also (receive)³⁴ a large bonus and a good raise.

PRACTICE B

Copy the following paragraphs, inserting appropriate Standard Written English verb forms. When either the past tense or the past participle is used, add *-ed* to the verb in parentheses; do not add *-ed* when it is not appropriate. If the verb ends in *y*, change the *y* to *i* and add *-ed*.

After he had (work)¹ at the bank for several years, he (start)² dating an attractive young teacher who (work)³ at the local high school that he had (attend)⁴. After they had (date)⁵ for several months, they (decide)⁶ that they would (marry)⁷ that summer. The wedding was (plan)⁸ for June, so they could take a honeymoon vacation.

After they had (marry)⁹ and (return)¹⁰ from their honeymoon, they (return)¹¹ to work to the good-natured joking of their colleagues and friends. They had both (resolve)¹² that neither one would be (embarrass)¹³ by the joking. They knew that their friends' joking was (suppose)¹⁴ to be an expression of friendship, and they had become (use)¹⁵ to the teasing during their engagement.

Finally, after a few weeks had (pass)¹⁶, and the kidding had (die)¹⁷ down, they began to (feel)¹⁸ comfortable as a married couple. Before long it (seem)¹⁹ to them that they had always been (marry)²⁰ to each other and could not (imagine)²¹ how they could have (live)²² without each other.

The former basketball player—now a banker—began to (coach)²³ in a local basketball league, and his wife (decide)²⁴ she would (return)²⁵ to school to get her master's degree. They (purchase)²⁶ a house and began to (make)²⁷ plans for a family after the wife (finish)²⁸ her degree.

14.4 VARIATIONS ON THE REGULAR PATTERN

Variant regular verbs are like regular verbs in that the forms for the past tense and the past participle are the same. However, they are different in that their past tense and past participle form is not simply base plus *-ed*.

Typical usage problems with variant regular verbs include simplification, regularization, overcorrection, and misclassification.

Simplification

Simplification of variant regular verbs takes much the same form as with completely regular verbs. The base form is used for third person singular, past tense, and past participle.

	AVOID
STANDARD WRITTEN ENGLISH	SIMPLIFIED FORM
THIRD PERSON SINGULAR	
He *catches* the ball.	He *catch** the ball.
	(omitted -es)
PAST TENSE	
He *caught* the ball.	He *catch** the ball.
	(unchanged verb form)
PAST PARTICIPLE	
He *had caught* the ball.	He had *catch** the ball.
	(unchanged verb form)

Regularization

Regularization occurs when writers do not realize that a variant regular form is required and instead attempt to use the *-ed* form for the past tense and past participle.

	AVOID
STANDARD WRITTEN ENGLISH	REGULARIZED FORM
PAST TENSE	
He *caught* the ball.	He *catched** the ball.
	(-ed added to base form)
PAST PARTICIPLE	
He *had caught* the ball.	He *had catched** the ball.
	(-ed added to base form)

Overcorrection

Overcorrection is similar to that found in the completely regular verbs. It occurs when writers add *-s* to present tense forms other than third person singular. It also occurs when the past tense/past participle form is used with the dummy auxiliary or the modal auxiliary when the base form should be used.

	AVOID
STANDARD WRITTEN ENGLISH	OVERCORRECTED FORM
PRESENT TENSE	
They *catch* the ball.	They *catches** the ball. (unnecessary -es)
DUMMY AUXILIARY	
Did you *catch* the ball?	*Did* you *caught** the ball? (base form needed)
MODAL AUXILIARY	
You *should catch* the ball.	You *should caught** the ball. (base form needed)

Misclassification

Misclassification is considerably less common; it occurs when writers assume that the variant belongs in a different class than it actually does. Perhaps the most common instance of this occurs with the verb *bring*.

	AVOID
STANDARD WRITTEN ENGLISH	MISCLASSIFIED FORM
PAST TENSE	
He *brought* a friend.	He *brang** a friend.
PAST PARTICIPLE	
He *had brought* a friend.	He *had brung** a friend.

In this case, the assumption has been made that the variant regular verb *bring* is actually an irregular verb like *ring* or *sing* (*ring, rang, rung; sing, sang, sung*).

Classes of Variant Regular Verbs

There are several subcategories of variant regular verbs. These subcategories, referred to as "**classes**," are presented in the following discussion. Each class is numbered and a typical member of that class is given in parentheses.

Class 1 Variants (*teach-taught*)

Class 1 variant regular verbs retain the initial consonant (or consonants) of the base form and add *aught* or *ought* to form their past tense and past participle. Table 14A lists the principal parts of common verbs of this class.

TABLE 14A
CLASS 1 VARIANTS: PRINCIPAL PARTS

BASE FORM	PAST TENSE	PAST PARTICIPLE
catch	caught	caught
teach	taught	taught
bring	brought	brought
buy	bought	bought
fight	fought	fought
think	thought	thought
seek	sought	sought

Table 14B illustrates the Standard Written English forms, which should be used. Table 14C illustrates the simplified, regularized, overcorrected, and misclassified forms, which should be avoided.

TABLE 14B
CLASS 1 VARIANTS: STANDARD WRITTEN ENGLISH FORMS

THIRD PERSON SINGULAR He *catches* the ball.	*PAST TENSE* He *caught* the ball.	*DUMMY AUXILIARY* He *did* not *catch* the ball.
THIRD PERSON PLURAL They *catch* the ball.	*PAST PARTICIPLE* He *had caught* the ball.	*MODAL AUXILIARY* He *should catch* the ball.

TABLE 14C
CLASS 1 VARIANTS: FORMS TO AVOID

SIMPLIFIED	
THIRD PERSON SINGULAR He *catch** the ball. *(omitted -s)*	PAST TENSE He *catch** the ball last time. *(unchanged verb form)*
	PAST PARTICIPLE He *had catch** the ball many other times. *(unchanged verb form)*

REGULARIZED	
	PAST TENSE He *catched** the ball. *(-ed added to base form)*
	PAST PARTICIPLE He *had catched** the ball. *(-ed added to base form)*

OVERCORRECTED	
THIRD PERSON PLURAL They *catches** the ball. *(unnecessary -s)*	DUMMY AUXILIARY He *did* not *caught** the ball. *(base form needed)*
	MODAL AUXILIARY He *should caught** the ball. *(base form needed)*

MISCLASSIFIED	
PAST TENSE He *brang** his books. or He *brung** his books.	PAST PARTICIPLE He *had brang** his books. or He *had brung** his books.

PRACTICE

Copy the following paragraphs, inserting appropriate Standard Written English forms of the past tense or past participle. If the verb is neither past tense nor past participle, do not change its form.

Because the second-grade boy (think)¹ he had fallen in love with his teacher, he wanted to (buy)² her a particularly nice Christmas present. Whenever he went shopping with his mother, he (seek)³ the perfect gift for his teacher. He had (think)⁴ of diamonds or emeralds or rubies, but the prices in the jewelry stores (bring)⁵ him to the realization that he could not afford to (buy)⁶ such an expensive gift. Soberly, he reviewed the meager contents of his wallet and (think)⁷ about what he could really afford. Finally, he found what he had (seek)⁸, a lovely brooch in the form of a gold Christmas tree, sparkling with emeralds, rubies, and diamonds, for only $4.95. He suspected that the jewels might not be totally real, but he (fight)⁹ off the idea and convinced himself that she might not notice.

The last day before school was dismissed for the holidays, he (bring)¹⁰ the gift to school. He had hidden it in the pocket of his coat because he (think)¹¹ his classmates might tease him. After the teacher had (teach)¹² the lessons for the day, the children were allowed a small Christmas party. When school was over for the day and the other children had left, he (seek)¹³ out his teacher and (catch)¹⁴ her before she left the schoolroom. He presented her with the gift he had (buy)¹⁵. She seemed surprised that he had (bring)¹⁶ her a special present, but she thanked him warmly. She (think)¹⁷ what a nice little boy he was and (seek)¹⁸ some way to let him know that she was touched by his gift, so she pinned the brooch to her coat collar before she left and gave him a big hug. As he ran home from school, he (fight)¹⁹ to keep his feet on the ground and (think)²⁰ to himself how beautiful she had looked with the sparkling gold Christmas tree on her coat collar.

Class 2 Variants (*keep-kept*)

Class 2 variant regular verbs make a change in the vowel sound (and spelling) of their base and add *t* to form their past tense and past participle. Table 15A lists the principal parts of common verbs of this class.

TABLE 15A
CLASS 2 VARIANTS: PRINCIPAL PARTS

BASE FORM	PAST TENSE	PAST PARTICIPLE
keep	kept	kept
sleep	slept	slept
sweep	swept	swept
weep	wept	wept
feel	felt	felt
kneel	knelt	knelt
deal	dealt[a]	dealt
lose	lost[a]	lost
leave	left[b]	left

Note: [a]Pronunciation of the vowel sound changes, but the spelling does not.
[b]Pronunciation of the vowel sound and the final consonant changes; so does the spelling.

Table 15B illustrates the Standard Written English forms, which should be used. Table 15C illustrates the simplified, regularized, and overcorrected forms, which should be avoided.

TABLE 15B
CLASS 2 VARIANTS: STANDARD WRITTEN ENGLISH FORMS

THIRD PERSON SINGULAR	PAST TENSE	DUMMY AUXILIARY
He *sleeps* soundly.	He *slept* soundly.	He *did* not *sleep* soundly.
THIRD PERSON PLURAL	PAST PARTICIPLES	MODAL AUXILIARY
They *sleep* soundly.	He *had slept* soundly.	He *should sleep* soundly.

TABLE 15C
CLASS 2 VARIANTS: FORMS TO AVOID

SIMPLIFIED	
THIRD PERSON SINGULAR He *sleep** soundly. *(omitted -s)*	PAST TENSE He *sleep** soundly last night. *(unchanged verb form)*
	PAST PARTICIPLE He *had sleep** soundly the entire week. *(unchanged verb form)*

REGULARIZED	
	PAST TENSE He *sleeped** soundly. *(-ed added to base form)*
	PAST PARTICIPLE He *had sleeped** soundly. *(-ed added to base form)*

OVERCORRECTED	
THIRD PERSON PLURAL They *sleeps** soundly. *(unnecessary -s)*	DUMMY AUXILIARY He *did* not *slept** soundly. *(base form needed)*
	MODAL AUXILIARY He *should slept** soundly. *(base form needed)*

PRACTICE

Copy the following paragraphs, inserting appropriate Standard Written English forms of the past tense or the past participle. If the verb is neither past tense nor past participle, do not change its form.

The young girl was going off to college, and the night before she (leave)¹ she (keep)² a date with the boy she had dated during her last year of high school. They talked about how they (feel)³ about each other and swore their devotion.

After she went in the house, she (feel)⁴ her heart was breaking, and she (kneel)⁵ on the floor of her room and (weep)⁶ for some time. Because she could not (sleep)⁷, she decided to clean her room. She (sweep)⁸ the floor and found in a corner a picture that she thought she had (lose)⁹; it showed the two of them on prom night. She (feel)¹⁰ that she could not (deal)¹¹ with her grief and again she (weep)¹².

She never (sleep)¹³ throughout the entire night and (feel)¹⁴ that fate had (deal)¹⁵ her a cruel blow in separating her from her boyfriend.

The next day her parents drove her to the college she was to attend a few hundred miles from her home town. Because she had (weep)¹⁶ the night away, she (sleep)¹⁷ through much of the trip.

Finally, they arrived; her parents helped her to take her suitcases and her boxes to her dorm room, but soon they (leave)¹⁸ for the long drive home. As they drove away, she (weep)¹⁹ again and (feel)²⁰ that she had (lose)²¹ everyone who cared about her.

But she (feel)²² better the first day of classes when a nice-looking young man sat by her in history class and (keep)²³ her company on the walk back to the dorm. Although she (keep)²⁴ writing to her high school boyfriend, she had (lose)²⁵ some of her feeling for him. She (feel)²⁶ somewhat guilty, and she (deal)²⁷ with her guilt by writing less and less often. Apparently he too had (lose)²⁸ some of his interest in her, because eventually they (leave)²⁹ off writing to each other completely.

Class 3 Variants (*send-sent*)

Class 3 variant regular verbs change the final *d* of the base form to *t* to form their past tense and past participle. Table 16A lists the principal parts of common verbs of this class.

TABLE 16A
CLASS 3 VARIANTS: PRINCIPAL PARTS

BASE FORM	PAST TENSE	PAST PARTICIPLE
build	built	built
lend	lent	lent
send	sent	sent
spend	spent	spent

Table 16B illustrates the Standard Written English forms, which should be used. Table 16C illustrates the simplified, regularized, and overcorrected forms, which should be avoided.

TABLE 16B
CLASS 3 VARIANTS: STANDARD WRITTEN ENGLISH FORMS

THIRD PERSON SINGULAR	PAST TENSE	DUMMY AUXILIARY
He *spends* money freely.	He *spent* money freely.	He *did* not *spend* money freely.
THIRD PERSON PLURAL	PAST PARTICIPLE	MODAL AUXILIARY
They *spend* money freely.	He *has spent* money freely.	He *should spend* more carefully.

TABLE 16C
CLASS 3 VARIANTS: FORMS TO AVOID

SIMPLIFIED	
THIRD PERSON SINGULAR He *spend** money freely. (omitted -s)	PAST TENSE He *spend** money freely. (unchanged verb form)
	PAST PARTICIPLE He *had spend** money freely. (unchanged verb form)

(continued)

TABLE 16C (continued)	
REGULARIZED	
	PAST TENSE He *spended** money freely. (-ed added to base form) *PAST PARTICIPLE* He *had spended** money freely. (-ed added to base form)
OVERCORRECTED	
THIRD PERSON PLURAL They *spends** money freely. *(unnecessary -s)*	*DUMMY AUXILIARY* He *did* not *spent** money freely. *(base form needed)* *MODAL AUXILIARY* He *should spent** more carefully. *(base form needed)*

PRACTICE

Copy the following paragraphs, inserting appropriate Standard Written English forms of the past tense or past participle. If the verb is neither past tense nor past participle, do not change its form.

The young couple decided that they wanted to (build)¹ their own house rather than buying one that had already been (build)². They (send)³ off for blueprints of a house that they had seen pictured in the newspaper. Then they (spend)⁴ several weekends looking for the perfect building lot. Finally, they visited their banker and asked him to (lend)⁵ them the money for the lot and the cost of building the house.

The banker (spend)⁶ some time explaining to them that no money could be (lend)⁷ by the bank until they had (spend)⁸ considerable effort ensuring that the house would be (build)⁹ ac-

cording to city ordinances and that all sorts of financial and other requirements would have to be met before a nickel could be (spend) on such a venture.
                          10

He recommended that they make an appointment with a general contractor who (build) individual houses. He (send)
                                       11   12
them off convinced that the extra fees for the contractor would be money well (spend). It was obvious that the banker would
                           13
not agree to (lend) them the money for the house and the lot
              14
until they had (spend) some time ensuring that the house would
                15
be properly (build).
            16

Class 4 Variants (*feed-fed*)

Class 4 variant regular verbs change the vowel sound of the base to form their past tense and past participle; with one exception, a corresponding change in spelling (from *ee* or *ea* to *e*) takes place. Table 17A lists the principal parts of common verbs of this class.

TABLE 17A
CLASS 4 VARIANTS: PRINCIPAL PARTS

BASE FORM	PAST TENSE	PAST PARTICIPLE
bleed	bled	bled
breed	bred	bred
feed	fed	fed
lead	led	led
meet	met	met
read	read	read[a]

Note: [a]Although the spelling remains the same, the base form and the past tense and past participle are not pronounced the same. The pronunciation of the base form is "*reed*," the pronunciation of the past tense and past participle is "*red*."

Table 17B illustrates the Standard Written English forms, which should be used. Table 17C illustrates the simplified, regularized, and overcorrected forms, which should be avoided.

TABLE 17B
CLASS 4 VARIANTS: STANDARD WRITTEN ENGLISH FORMS

THIRD PERSON SINGULAR He *feeds* his cat daily.	*PAST TENSE* He *fed* his cat yesterday.	*DUMMY AUXILIARY* He *did* not *feed* his cat.
THIRD PERSON PLURAL They *feed* their cat well.	*PAST PARTICIPLE* He *had fed* his cat earlier.	*MODAL AUXILIARY* He *should feed* his cat later.

TABLE 17C
CLASS 4 VARIANTS: FORMS TO AVOID

SIMPLIFIED

THIRD PERSON SINGULAR He *feed** his cat daily. *(omitted -s)*	*PAST TENSE* He *feed** his cat yesterday. *(unchanged verb form)*
	PAST PARTICIPLE He *had feed** his cat earlier. *(unchanged verb form)*

REGULARIZED

	PAST TENSE He *feeded** his cat yesterday. *(-ed added to base form)*
	PAST PARTICIPLE He *had feeded** his cat earlier. *(-ed added to base form)*

OVERCORRECTED

THIRD PERSON PLURAL They *feeds** their cat well. *(unnecessary -s)*	*DUMMY AUXILIARY* He *did* not *fed** his cat. *(base form needed)*
	MODAL AUXILIARY He *should fed** his cat later. *(base form needed)*

PRACTICE

Copy the following paragraphs, inserting appropriate Standard Written English forms of the past tense or past participle. If the verb is neither past tense nor past participle, do not change its form.

When ten-year-old Sarah went to visit her aunt and uncle who owned a farm, she had (read)₁ about farms and had seen pictures of farm animals in her school books, but she had never actually been on a farm. Her aunt and uncle (meet)₂ her at the bus station because the nearest city with an airport was over 100 miles away.

The next day she watched her uncle (feed)₃ the pigs, who rolled over in the mud happily and went to sleep after they had been (feed)₄. She walked to the pasture with her uncle to see the cattle and was somewhat shocked to discover that all the cows were (breed)₅ to one bull who had sired all of the young calves in the pasture.

She was also unaccustomed to the idea that dogs were working animals, since her own was a somewhat pampered and spoiled pet who would not go for a walk unless Sarah put a leash on her and (lead)₆ her. She attempted to do the same with some of the farm dogs, but they wanted no part of being (lead)₇ about on a leash. One had evidently cut itself rather badly on something because its paw (bleed)₈ freely. When Sarah tried to (meet)₉ him with bandages and sympathy, he snarled at her and ran away from where the other dogs were being (feed)₁₀.

After her visit was over, Sarah traveled back to the city where she lived with her parents, who (meet)₁₁ her at the bus station. After that, when Sarah (read)₁₂ in her school books about farms, she knew more than any of the other students and (lead)[13] the class discussion about farm life.

Class 5 Variants (*find-found; swing-swung*)

Class 5 variant regular verbs change the vowel sound and the spelling of the base to form their past tense and past participle. The spelling is *i* in the base form; in the past tense and past participle, it changes to *o, u,* or *ou.* Table 18A lists the principal parts of common verbs of this class.

TABLE 18A
CLASS 5 VARIANTS: PRINCIPAL PARTS

BASE FORM	PAST TENSE	PAST PARTICIPLE
find	found	found
grind	ground	ground
sting	stung	stung
swing	swung	swung
wring	wrung	wrung
strike	struck	struck
win	won	won

Table 18B illustrates the Standard Written English forms, which should be used. Table 18C illustrates the simplified, regularized, and overcorrected forms, which should be avoided.

TABLE 18B
CLASS 5 VARIANTS: STANDARD WRITTEN ENGLISH FORMS

THIRD PERSON SINGULAR	PAST TENSE	DUMMY AUXILIARY
He *swings* a bat.	He *swung* a bat.	He *did* not *swing* a bat.
THIRD PERSON PLURAL	PAST PARTICIPLE	MODAL AUXILIARY
They *swing* a bat.	He *had swung* a bat.	He *should swing* a bat.

TABLE 18C
CLASS 5 VARIANTS: FORMS TO AVOID

SIMPLIFIED

THIRD PERSON SINGULAR He *swing** a bat. *(omitted -s)*	PAST TENSE He *swing** a bat yesterday. *(unchanged verb form)*
	PAST PARTICIPLE He *had swing** a bat many times. *(unchanged verb form)*

REGULARIZED

	PAST TENSE He *swinged** a bat yesterday. *(-ed added to base form)*
	PAST PARTICIPLE He *had swinged** a bat many times. *(-ed added to base form)*

OVERCORRECTED

THIRD PERSON PLURAL They *swings** a bat. *(unnecessary -s)*	DUMMY AUXILIARY He *did* not *swung** a bat. *(base form needed)*
	MODAL AUXILIARY He *should swung** the bat carefully. *(base form needed)*

PRACTICE

Copy the following paragraphs, inserting appropriate Standard Written English forms of the past tense or past participle. If the verb is neither past tense nor past participle, do not change its form.

As the season (grind)[1] itself toward the end, the high school baseball team (find)[2] itself doing unexpectedly well. They had (win)[3] over half their games and they had a chance at first place in their conference.

Finally, it was the last game of the season, the one they had to (win)⁴ to be conference champions.

In the seventh inning, they were ahead 7 to 4, and their pitcher had (strike)⁵ out two batters and walked two. If he could (strike)⁶ out the next batter, the inning would be over. He threw his best pitch, and the batter (swing)⁷ his bat and missed. He missed the second pitch too, but when he (swing)⁸ at the third pitch, the bat did (strike)⁹ the ball and hit it out of the park. The home crowd groaned and (wring)¹⁰ its hands in anguish; the score was 7 to 7.

Now the game was tied, and neither side (find)¹¹ itself able to score in the eighth inning.

In the top of the ninth, the pitcher, who had been (sting)¹² by what had happened in the seventh inning, came up to bat. He (swing)¹³ mightily at the ball, missing two pitches in a row. On the third pitch, his bat (strike)¹⁴ the ball solidly, and he scored a run. Now it was 8 to 7, and the home crowd groaned and (wring)¹⁵ its hands in ecstasy.

In the bottom of the ninth, the pitcher (find)¹⁶ himself facing the opposing team's best batters. Each batter seemed to (swing)¹⁷ at the ball with greater ferocity than the one before, but he managed to (strike)¹⁸ them out, three in a row. After pitching nine innings and scoring the winning run, the pitcher felt that he had almost (win)¹⁹ the game by himself and was delighted when he received the MVP award.

Class 6 Variants (*cut-cut*)

Class 6 variant regular verbs do not change their base to form their past tense and past participle; all three forms are identical.

Table 19A lists the principal parts of common verbs of this class.

TABLE 19A
CLASS 6 VARIANTS: PRINCIPAL PARTS

BASE FORM	PAST TENSE	PAST PARTICIPLE
bet	bet	bet
bid	bid	bid
burst	burst	burst
cut	cut	cut
hit	hit	hit
hurt	hurt	hurt
set	set	set

Table 19B illustrates the Standard Written English forms, which should be used. Table 19C illustrates the simplified, regularized, and overcorrected forms, which should be avoided.

TABLE 19B
CLASS 6 VARIANTS: STANDARD WRITTEN ENGLISH FORMS

THIRD PERSON SINGULAR	PAST TENSE	DUMMY AUXILIARY
He *hurts* himself.	He *hurt* himself.	He *did* not *hurt* himself.
THIRD PERSON PLURAL	PAST PARTICIPLE	MODAL AUXILIARY
They *hurt* themselves.	He *has hurt* himself.	He *could hurt* himself.

TABLE 19C
CLASS 6 VARIANTS: FORMS TO AVOID

SIMPLIFIED
THIRD PERSON SINGULAR
He *hurt** himself.
(omitted -s)

(continued)

TABLE 19C (continued)

REGULARIZED

PAST TENSE
He *hurted** himself yesterday.
(-ed added to base form)

PAST PARTICIPLE
He *had hurted** himself earlier.
(-ed added to base form)

OVERCORRECTED

THIRD PERSON PLURAL	DUMMY AUXILIARY
They *hurts** themselves. *(unnecessary -s)*	He *did* not *hurted** himself. *(base form needed)*
	MODAL AUXILIARY He *could hurted** himself. *(base form needed)*

Variants with No Pattern (*say-said*)

There are several common variant regular verbs that fall into no particular subcategory, since only one verb (or, at most, two) follows that pattern. These verbs must be learned individually. Table 20A lists the principal parts of common verbs of this class.

TABLE 20A
VARIANTS WITH NO PATTERN: PRINCIPAL PARTS

BASE FORM	PAST TENSE	PAST PARTICIPLE
hold	held	held
sell	sold	sold
tell	told	told
make	made	made
say	said	said
sit	sat	sat
stand	stood	stood

Table 20B illustrates the Standard Written English forms, which should be used. Table 20C illustrates the simplified, regularized, and overcorrected forms, which should be avoided.

TABLE 20B
VARIANTS WITH NO PATTERN: STANDARD WRITTEN ENGLISH FORMS

STANDARD WRITTEN ENGLISH FORMS		
THIRD PERSON SINGULAR He *tells* many lies.	PAST TENSE He *told* many lies.	DUMMY AUXILIARY He *did* not *tell* the truth.
THIRD PERSON PLURAL They *tell* many lies.	PAST PARTICIPLE He *had told* many lies.	MODAL AUXILIARY He *should tell* the truth.

TABLE 20C
VARIANTS WITH NO PATTERN: FORMS TO AVOID

SIMPLIFIED	
THIRD PERSON SINGULAR He *tell** many lies. *(omitted -s)*	PAST TENSE He *tell** one yesterday. *(unchanged verb form)*
	PAST PARTICIPLE He *had tell** lies before. *(unchanged verb form)*

REGULARIZED	
	PAST TENSE He *telled** a lie yesterday. *(-ed added to base form)*
	PAST PARTICIPLE He *had telled** lies before. *(-ed added to base form)*

OVERCORRECTED	
THIRD PERSON PLURAL They *tells** many lies. *(unnecessary -s)*	DUMMY AUXILIARY He *did* not *told** the truth. *(base form needed)*
	MODAL AUXILIARY He *should told** the truth. *(base form needed)*

PRACTICE

Copy the following paragraphs, inserting appropriate Standard Written English forms of the past tense or past participle. If the verb is neither past tense nor past participle, do not change its form. Note that this practice includes variants that do not change form in addition to those with no pattern.

Many states are trying to (make)¹ a decision about whether or not to (sell)² lottery tickets. Proponents argue that many people will (bet)³ whether it is legal or not and that the state might as well reap the benefits.

Opponents have (say)⁴ that gambling is immoral and the state should not appear to condone such activities. Some have (tell)⁵ stories of compulsive gamblers who (bet)⁶ so heavily that their families are seriously (hurt)⁷ by their activities.

Both sides (make)⁸ their points and (tell)⁹ their views on the issue, and legislators often have a difficult time trying to (make)¹⁰ a decision after everyone has (say)¹¹ everything there is to (say)¹².

When the economy of a state has been badly (hurt)¹³, however, and the budget is ready to (burst)¹⁴ its bounds, then the issue of to (bet)¹⁵ or not to (bet)¹⁶ is no longer academic. When voters are (tell)¹⁷ that either lottery tickets must be (sell)¹⁸ or taxes must be raised and services must be (cut)¹⁹, some may change their views. Many may (make)²⁰ the decision that letting people (bet)²¹ is not so serious after all. Letting the state (sell)²² lottery tickets to people who want to (bet)²³ may hurt a few compulsive gamblers, but having to raise taxes or to (cut)²⁴ services would (hurt)²⁵ everyone.

14.5 IRREGULAR VERBS

Writers sometimes have problems with commonly used verbs that do not follow the regular pattern. These are called **irregular verbs**. **Regular verbs** form their past tense and past participle by adding *-ed* to the base form. The verb *walk*, which has been used previously to illustrate various forms of the verb, is an example of a regular verb.

PRESENT TENSE
(base form)
walk   I walk to the store today.

PAST TENSE
walked   I walked to the store yesterday.

PAST PARTICIPLE
walked   I have walked to the store many times.

Most English verbs follow this pattern. New verbs and foreign verbs brought into English also follow this pattern.

They *yakked* on the phone for hours

The rustlers *vamoosed* down the canyon.   (from Spanish)

In contrast, irregular verbs use different forms for the past tense and the past participle. Some of our most commonly used verbs are irregular; these verbs must be learned individually or as members of a small group following the same (or similar) pattern.
Many of these irregular verbs follow a pattern like *sing*.

PRESENT TENSE
(base form)
sing   I sing today.

PAST TENSE
sang   I sang yesterday.

PAST PARTICIPLE
sung   I have sung many times.

Others follow a pattern like *drive*.

> *PRESENT*
> *(base form)*
> drive   I drive today.
>
> *PAST*
> drove   I drove yesterday.
>
> *PAST PARTICIPLE*
> driven   I have driven many times.

Various kinds of usage problems can occur with irregular verbs: simplification, regularization, and overcorrection.

Simplification

With irregular verbs, **simplification** may be of two types. The first type of **simplification** follows the same pattern as for regular verbs; that is, the base form of the verb is used for the third person singular, the past tense, and the past participle.

STANDARD WRITTEN ENGLISH	AVOID SIMPLIFIED TO ONE FORM
THIRD PERSON SINGULAR	
He *drives* well.	He *drive** well. *(omitted -s)*
PAST TENSE	
He *drove* several hours yesterday.	He *drive** several hours yesterday. *(unchanged verb form)*
PAST PARTICIPLE	
He *had driven* three days.	He *had drive** three days. *(unchanged verb form)*

Another type of **simplification**, and the more common problem with irregular verbs, occurs when writers adopt one form or the other, either the past tense or the past participle, and use it as both past tense and past participle. In such instances, writers correctly form their third person singular, adding *-s*; their only deviation from Standard Written English is the use of the one form for both past tense and past participle rather than the required two.

With some irregular verbs, the tendency is to choose the past tense form and to use it for both past tense and past participle.

	AVOID
STANDARD WRITTEN ENGLISH	SIMPLIFIED TO TWO FORMS
THIRD PERSON SINGULAR	
He *drives* to the store.	He *drives* to the store.
PAST TENSE	
He *drove* well.	He *drove* well.
PAST PARTICIPLE	
He *had driven* for hours.	He *had drove** for hours. *(past tense used)*

With other verbs, the choice might be either the past tense or the past participle.

	AVOID
STANDARD WRITTEN ENGLISH	SIMPLIFIED TO TWO FORMS
THIRD PERSON SINGULAR	
He *comes* to class on time.	He *comes* to class late every morning.
PAST TENSE	
He *came* to the party late.	He *come** to the party late last night. *(past participle used)*
PAST PARTICIPLE	
He *had come* to the party with friends.	He *had came** to the party with friends. *(past tense used)*

Regularization

Regularizing irregular verbs is also a common problem; that is, the past tense and the past participle are formed in the same manner as regular verbs, with *-ed*.

STANDARD WRITTEN ENGLISH	AVOID REGULARIZED FORM
PAST TENSE	
He *drove* the car yesterday.	He *drived** the car yesterday. *(-ed added to base)*
He *threw* the ball hard.	He *throwed** the ball hard. *(-ed added to base)*
PAST PARTICIPLE	
He *had driven* the car well.	He *had drived** the car well. *(-ed added to base)*
He *had thrown* the ball hard.	He *had throwed** the ball hard. *(-ed added to base)*

Overcorrection

Overcorrection occurs when writers add *-s* to forms of the present tense other than third person singular. It also takes place when the past tense or past participle form is used with the dummy auxiliary or modal auxiliary.

STANDARD WRITTEN ENGLISH	AVOID OVERCORRECTED FORM
PRESENT TENSE	
They *drive* too fast.	They *drives** too fast. *(unnecessary -s)*
DUMMY AUXILIARY	
He *did* not *drive* fast.	He *did* not *drove** fast. *(base form needed)*
MODAL AUXILIARY	
He *should drive* slower.	He *should drove/driven** slower. *(base form needed)*

Classes of Irregular Verbs

There are several subcategories of irregular verbs. The subcategories, referred to as "**classes**," are presented in the following discussion. Each class is numbered and a typical member of that class is given in parentheses.

Class 1 Irregulars (*sing-sang-sung*)

Class 1 irregular verbs use different vowels for the three principal parts: *i* in the base form, *a* in the past tense, and *u* in the past participle. Table 21A lists the principal parts of common verbs of this class.

TABLE 21A
CLASS 1 IRREGULAR VERBS: PRINCIPAL PARTS

BASE FORM	PAST TENSE	PAST PARTICIPLE
sing	sang	sung
ring	rang	rung
spring	sprang	sprung
begin	began	begun
drink	drank	drunk
shrink	shrank	shrunk
sink	sank	sunk
swim	swam	swum

Table 21B illustrates the Standard Written English forms, which should be used. Table 21C illustrates the simplified, regularized, and overcorrected forms, which should be avoided.

TABLE 21B
CLASS 1 IRREGULAR VERBS: STANDARD WRITTEN ENGLISH FORMS

THIRD PERSON SINGULAR	PAST TENSE	DUMMY AUXILIARY
He *rings* the bell.	He *rang* the bell.	He *did* not *ring* the bell.

THIRD PERSON PLURAL	PAST PARTICIPLE	MODAL AUXILIARY
They *ring* the bell.	He *had rung* the bell.	He *should ring* the bell.

TABLE 21C
CLASS 1 IRREGULAR VERBS: FORMS TO AVOID

SIMPLIFIED

THIRD PERSON SINGULAR He *ring** the bell. *(omitted -s)*	PAST TENSE He *ring** the bell yesterday. *(unchanged verb form)* or He *rung** the bell. *(past participle used)*
	PAST PARTICIPLE He *had* already *ring** the bell. *(unchanged verb form)* or He *had* already *rang** the bell. *(past tense used)*

REGULARIZED

	PAST TENSE He *ringed** the bell. *(-ed added to base form)*
	PAST PARTICIPLE He *had ringed** the bell. *(-ed added to base form)*

OVERCORRECTED

THIRD PERSON PLURAL They *rings** the bell. *(unnecessary -s)*	DUMMY AUXILIARY He *did* not *rang/rung** the bell. *(base form needed)*
	MODAL AUXILIARY He *should rang/rung** the bell. *(base form needed)*

PRACTICE

Copy the following paragraphs, inserting the appropriate Standard Written English form of the past tense or past participle for each verb in parentheses. If the verb requires neither past tense nor past participle, do not change its form.

After George had (drink)¹ several cans of beer, he (begin)² to (sing)³ somewhat bawdy songs. Some of his friends joined in and the room (ring)⁴ with loud choruses and raucous laughter. His wife (shrink)⁵ into a corner and pretended that she did not hear the words that he (sing)⁶. Her heart (sink)⁷ at the thought of letting him drive home.

Soon George (spring)⁸ to his feet and announced that he would challenge anyone to (swim)⁹ more laps in the swimming pool outside than he could. Since it was the middle of February, several voices (ring)¹⁰ out in protest at the idea, but others (sing)¹¹ out words of encouragement.

George (drink)¹² another can of beer and (begin)¹³ to walk toward the arcadia door, stumbling as he went. When he reached the pool, he jumped in and promptly (sink)¹⁴ from sight. He came to the surface and (begin)¹⁵ to (sink)¹⁶ again. After he had (sink)¹⁷ for the third time, someone jumped in and (swim)¹⁸ toward him to rescue him. People (spring)¹⁹ to help the two of them as they emerged dripping from the pool.

Furious, George's wife drove her shivering husband home as he continued to (sing)²⁰ bawdy songs. After he had (drink)²¹ some hot coffee, he went to bed. The next day his head (ring)²² and he could not (begin)²³ to (spring)²⁴ out of bed. His wife (sing)²⁵ merrily when she saw how wretched he was. Later she pointed out that his best suit had (shrink)²⁶ as a result of his midnight swim.

Class 2 Irregulars (*drive-drove-driven*)

Class 2 irregular verbs use different vowel sounds, but not always different spellings, in the base form and the past tense. The past participle uses the vowel *i* (pronounced like the *i* in *hit*) and an *-en* ending is added. Table 22A lists the principal parts of common verbs of this class.

TABLE 22A
CLASS 2 IRREGULAR VERBS: PRINCIPAL PARTS

BASE FORM	PAST TENSE	PAST PARTICIPLE
drive	drove	driven
ride	rode	ridden
rise	rose	risen
write	wrote	written
bite	bit	bitten
hide	hid	hidden

Note: Sometimes the final consonant is doubled; other times it is not.

Table 22B illustrates the Standard Written English forms, which should be used. Table 22C illustrates the simplified, regularized, and overcorrected forms, which should be avoided.

TABLE 22B
CLASS 2 IRREGULAR VERBS: STANDARD WRITTEN ENGLISH FORMS

THIRD PERSON SINGULAR	PAST TENSE	DUMMY AUXILIARY
He *drives* the car.	He *drove* the car.	He *did* not *drive* fast.
THIRD PERSON PLURAL	PAST PARTICIPLE	MODAL AUXILIARY
They *drive* too fast.	He *had driven* the car.	He *should drive* slower.

TABLE 22C
CLASS 2 IRREGULAR VERBS: FORMS TO AVOID

SIMPLIFIED	
THIRD PERSON SINGULAR	PAST TENSE
He *drive** the car.	He *drive** the car.
(omitted -s)	(unchanged verb form)

PAST PARTICIPLE
He *had drive** the car.
(unchanged verb form)
or
He *had drove** the car.
(past tense used)

REGULARIZED

PAST TENSE
He *drived** the car.
(-ed added to base form)

PAST PARTICIPLE
He *had drived** the car.
(-ed added to base form)

OVERCORRECTED

THIRD PERSON PLURAL
They *drives** too fast.
(unnecessary -s)

DUMMY AUXILIARY
He *did* not *drove** fast.
(base form needed)

MODAL AUXILIARY
He should *drove** slower.
(base form needed)

PRACTICE

Copy the following paragraphs, inserting the appropriate Standard Written English form of the past tense or past participle for each verb in parentheses. If the verb requires neither past tense nor past participle, do not change its form.

The fishermen had (rise) before dawn to leave on their fishing trip. Then they had (drive) several hundred miles to their destination, a lake (hide) in the wilderness.

While one man (drive), the others (ride) along quietly, napping occasionally to catch up on lost sleep. Finally, they reached a narrow road marked by a sign that had the name of the lake (write) on it and an arrow pointing down the narrow road.

They (drive)⁷ several miles down the rutted, bumpy road until they reached the (hide)⁸ lake, where they unloaded the car and pitched their tents. The next morning they all planned to (rise)⁹ early so they could be fishing at dawn, when the fish were most likely to (bite)¹⁰. After a quick breakfast, they silently rowed their boat toward a good fishing spot where the fish should (bite)¹¹. The first man had barely cast his line in the water when a fish (rise)¹² to the bait. Although the fish was (hide)¹³ under the water, he could tell by the way the line had jerked when the fish had (bite)¹⁴ that it was a big one. After a homeric battle, he landed the huge fish, one certainly to (write)¹⁵ home about.

Throughout the day the fish (bite)¹⁶ eagerly, but none as big as the first one (rise)¹⁷ to the fisherman's bait. Late in the afternoon they caught their limit, so they packed up the car and (drive)¹⁸ home. As they (ride)¹⁹ along, they talked eagerly about the day, the way the fish had (hide)²⁰ beneath the surface, the way they had (rise)²¹ to the bait, the way they had (bite)²² the hook. They all agreed that the trip had been so successful that an article should be (write)²³ about it and published in the local newspaper.

Class 3 Irregulars (*choose-chose-chosen*)

Class 3 irregular verbs change their vowel in the past tense; in the past participle, the vowel of either the base form or the past tense may be used, and an *-en* ending is added. Table 23A lists the principal parts of common verbs of this class.

Table 23B illustrates the Standard Written English forms, which should be used. Table 23C illustrates the simplified, regularized, and overcorrected forms, which should be avoided.

TABLE 23A
CLASS 3 IRREGULAR VERBS: PRINCIPAL PARTS

BASE FORM	PAST TENSE	PAST PARTICIPLE
choose	chose	chosen
freeze	froze	frozen
break	broke	broken
speak	spoke	spoken
take	took	taken
shake	shook	shaken
fall	fell	fallen

TABLE 23B
CLASS 3 IRREGULAR VERBS: STANDARD WRITTEN ENGLISH FORMS

THIRD PERSON SINGULAR	PAST TENSE	DUMMY AUXILIARY
He *chooses* a blue tie.	He *chose* a blue tie.	He *did* not *choose* to run.
THIRD PERSON PLURAL	PAST PARTICIPLE	MODAL AUXILIARY
They *choose* not to play.	He *had chosen* a white shirt.	He *should choose* another profession.

TABLE 23C
CLASS 3 IRREGULAR VERBS: FORMS TO AVOID

SIMPLIFIED	
THIRD PERSON SINGULAR	PAST TENSE
He *choose** a blue tie.	He *choose** a blue tie.
(omitted -s)	*(unchanged verb form)*
	PAST PARTICIPLE
	He *had choose** a blue tie.
	(unchanged verb form)
	or
	He *had chose** a blue tie.
	(past tense used)

(continued)

TABLE 23C (continued)	
REGULARIZED	
PAST TENSE He *choosed** a blue tie. (-ed added to base form) *PAST PARTICIPLE* He *had choosed** a white shirt. (-ed added to base form)	
OVERCORRECTED	
THIRD PERSON PLURAL They *chooses** not to play. *(unnecessary -s)*	*DUMMY AUXILIARY* He *did* not *chose** to run. *(base form needed)* *MODAL AUXILIARY* He *should chose** another profession. *(base form needed)*

PRACTICE

Copy the following paragraphs, inserting the appropriate Standard Written English form of the past tense or past participle for each verb in parentheses. If the verb requires neither past tense nor past participle, do not change its form.

The lake had (freeze)₁ over, and the ice looked safe for skating—with no (break)₂ areas showing. The two brothers did not (speak)₃ to their parents about the ice-skating expedition they wanted to (take)₄ because they knew their parents would forbid them to do so, concerned that the ice might (break)₅ and they might (fall)₆ into the freezing water.

They waited until their parents were busy and then (take)₇ off on their expedition. The younger boy (choose)₈ to stay close

to the edge of the lake, while his more daring older brother skated toward the center of the lake. Suddenly the ice in the center cracked and (break) and the older brother (fall) into the
                                                                                    9   10
freezing water. His younger brother (take) one look and (freeze)
                                                                    11   12
in his tracks. He ran toward the boat shed and (take) an old life
                                                                                           13
preserver lying there, then ran back to the lake and scooted the life preserver across the ice to the spot where his brother had (fall) through the ice. The boy in the freezing water had not
14
(speak) a word since the ice had (break), but he (take) a desper-
 15   16   17
ate lunge at the life preserver and caught it in his (freeze)
                                                                                                  18
hands.

The younger boy, who had tied a rope to the life preserver and had held onto it tightly, (speak) to his brother in a voice
                                                                              19
that (shake) with cold and fear, telling him to hold tight to the
          20
life preserver. Slowly and carefully, he tried to pull his brother out of the water, but the ice around the hole (break) and (fall)
                                                                                                          21   22
into the water whenever his brother tried to pull himself onto it.

At last, after many terrible minutes had passed, his brother found a place where the ice did not (break) because it was still
                                                                                                          23
(freeze) hard. When the younger boy (take) a step toward his
 24   25
brother lying there on the ice, he could barely understand the words (speak) by the trembling lips, but he realized that if he
                   26
(take) too many steps across the ice, it might (break) and (fall)
 27   28   29
under the weight of both of them. Wisely, he (choose) to stay
                                                                                 30
on the side, pulling his brother across the ice with the rope.

When the two (shake) boys reached the house, neither
                                       31
could (speak) from the cold and the fear. Their parents (take)
            32   33
one look at them and knew what had happened. (Shake) by the
                                                                                                 34

thought that they might have lost both their sons that day on the (freeze)³⁵ lake, they (choose)³⁶ not to lecture them. The icy waters of the lake had (speak)³⁷ with a louder voice than any parent could, one that neither boy would ever forget.

Class 4 Irregulars (*wear-wore-worn*)

Class 4 irregular verbs end their base with *-ear*, the past tense with *-ore*, and the past participle with *-orn*. Table 24A lists the principal parts of common verbs of this class.

TABLE 24A
CLASS 4 IRREGULAR VERBS: PRINCIPAL PARTS

BASE FORM	PAST TENSE	PAST PARTICIPLE
bear	bore	born
tear	tore	torn
wear	wore	worn
swear	swore	sworn

Table 24B illustrates the Standard Written English forms, which should be used. Table 24C illustrates the simplified, regularized, and overcorrected forms, which should be avoided.

TABLE 24B
CLASS 4 IRREGULAR VERBS: STANDARD WRITTEN ENGLISH FORMS

THIRD PERSON SINGULAR	PAST TENSE	DUMMY AUXILIARY
She *wears* a new dress.	She *wore* a new dress.	They *did* not *wear* black.
THIRD PERSON PLURAL	PAST PARTICIPLE	MODAL AUXILIARY
They *wear* their best clothes.	She *had worn* a new dress.	He *should wear* his new suit.

TABLE 24C
CLASS 4 IRREGULAR VERBS: FORMS TO AVOID

SIMPLIFIED	
THIRD PERSON SINGULAR She *wear** a new dress. *(omitted -s)*	PAST TENSE She *wear** a new dress. *(unchanged verb form)*
	PAST PARTICIPLE She *had wear** a new dress. *(unchanged verb form)* or She *had wore** a new dress. *(past tense used)*

REGULARIZED	
	PAST TENSE She *weared** a new dress. *(-ed added to base form)*
	PAST PARTICIPLE She *had weared** it before. *(-ed added to base form)*

OVERCORRECTED	
THIRD PERSON PLURAL They *wears** their best clothes. *(unnecessary -s)*	DUMMY AUXILIARY They *did* not *wore** black. *(base form needed)*
	MODAL AUXILIARY He *should wore** his new suit. *(base form needed)*

PRACTICE

Copy the following paragraphs, inserting the appropriate Standard Written English form of the past tense or past participle for each verb in parentheses. If the verb requires neither past tense nor past participle, do not change its form.

Striding through the woods, the hiker (bear)¹ a heavy backpack on her shoulders. The clothes she (wear)² were old but comfortable. Although nothing was (tear)³, the knees of her jeans and the elbows of her shirt were (wear)⁴ thin. She had (swear)⁵ to herself that she was not going to (wear)⁶ clothes that made her look like a picture in *Hikers' Monthly*.

Branches (tear)⁷ at her as she hiked through the ever-thickening foliage, and the backpack she had (bear)⁸ for several hours seemed to grow heavier and heavier. Finally, when she had begun to feel she could (bear)⁹ the burden no longer, she reached a pleasant clearing close to a rushing brook. She (swear)¹⁰ to herself gratefully and (tear)¹¹ the backpack off her shoulders as quickly as she could. Her feet felt (wear)¹² to the bone, so she took off her shoes and socks and thrust her tired feet into the cool, rippling water of the stream.

Class 5 Irregulars (*know-knew-known*)

Class 5 irregular verbs change the vowel in the past tense, and the past participle ends in *-own*. Table 25A lists the principal parts of common verbs of this class.

TABLE 25A
CLASS 5 IRREGULAR VERBS: PRINCIPAL PARTS

BASE FORM	PAST TENSE	PAST PARTICIPLE
blow	blew	blown
grow	grew	grown
know	knew	known
throw	threw	thrown
fly	flew	flown
draw	drew	drawn

Table 25B illustrates the Standard Written English forms, which should be used. Table 25C illustrates the simplified, regularized, and overcorrected forms, which should be avoided.

TABLE 25B
CLASS 5 IRREGULAR VERBS: STANDARD WRITTEN ENGLISH FORMS

THIRD PERSON SINGULAR	*PAST TENSE*	*DUMMY AUXILIARY*
He *knows* the answer.	He *knew* the answer.	He *did* not *know* the answer.
THIRD PERSON PLURAL	*PAST PARTICIPLE*	*MODAL AUXILIARY*
They *know* the answer.	He *had known* the answer.	He *should know* the answer.

TABLE 25C
CLASS 5 IRREGULAR VERBS: FORMS TO AVOID

SIMPLIFIED	
THIRD PERSON SINGULAR	*PAST TENSE*
He *know** the answer.	He *know** the answer.
(omitted -s)	*(unchanged verb form)*
	PAST PARTICIPLE
	He *had know** the answer.
	(unchanged verb form)
	or
	He *had knew** the answer.
	(past tense used)

REGULARIZED
PAST TENSE
He *knowed** the answer.
(-ed added to base form)
PAST PARTICIPLE
He *had knowed** the answer.
(-ed added to base form)

(continued)

TABLE 25C (continued)

OVERCORRECTED

THIRD PERSON PLURAL	DUMMY AUXILIARY
They *knows** the answer. *(unnecessary -s)*	He *did* not *knew** the answer. *(base form needed)*
	MODAL AUXILIARY He *should knew** the answer. *(base form needed)*

PRACTICE

Copy the following paragraphs, inserting the appropriate Standard Written English form of the past tense or past participle for each verb in parentheses. If the verb requires neither past tense nor past participle, do not change its form.

The wind had (blow)₁ for days and nights on end, and the people forced to listen to its unceasing sound steadily (grow)₂ more and more irritable. They (know)₃ that in the spring the wind might (blow)₄ for weeks.

The lawns looked like someone had (throw)₅ garbage on them, and dogs and cats were (draw)₆ to the overturned garbage cans. Newspaper boys carefully (throw)₇ their papers on porches, but the wind grabbed them and (blow)₈ them in every direction.

Some parents took their children to a local park to (fly)₉ their kites, but the wind (blow)₁₀ so hard that the kites were (throw)₁₁ into the trees. The children (grow)₁₂ unhappy about having their kites (blow)₁₃ to shreds and began to cry. Desperately, the parents tried to (draw)₁₄ the children's attention to the swings and other equipment in the park, but they (know)₁₅ there was little chance of success. One small child, who was knocked down by a playful dog, (throw)₁₆ a crying fit right there in the park.

After he had settled down and had (blow)¹⁷ his nose, his mother (know)¹⁸ that it was time to take him home. The other children (grow)¹⁹ restless too, and their parents (draw)²⁰ sighs of relief as the ill-fated kite-flying expedition finally came to its unhappy conclusion.

Irregular Verbs with No Pattern (*go-went-gone*)

Some verbs follow no particular pattern and must be learned individually. Table 26A lists the principal parts of some common verbs with no pattern.

TABLE 26A
IRREGULAR VERBS WITH NO PATTERN: PRINCIPAL PARTS

BASE FORM	PAST TENSE	PAST PARTICIPLE
lie	lay	lain
give	gave	given
come	came	come
eat	ate	eaten
get	got	gotten
see	saw	seen
go	went	gone
run	ran	run

Table 26B illustrates the Standard Written English forms, which should be used. Table 26C illustrates the simplified, regularized and overcorrected forms, which should be avoided.

TABLE 26B
IRREGULAR VERBS WITH NO PATTERN: STANDARD WRITTEN ENGLISH FORMS

THIRD PERSON SINGULAR	PAST TENSE	DUMMY AUXILIARY
He *eats* lunch.	He *ate* lunch.	He *did* not *eat* lunch.
THIRD PERSON PLURAL	PAST PARTICIPLE	MODAL AUXILIARY
They *eat* lunch.	He *had eaten* lunch earlier.	He *should eat* more fruit.

TABLE 26C
IRREGULAR VERBS WITH NO PATTERN: FORMS TO AVOID

SIMPLIFIED

THIRD PERSON SINGULAR	PAST TENSE
He *eat** lunch.	He *eat** lunch earlier.
(omitted -s)	*(unchanged verb form)*
	PAST PARTICIPLE
	He *had* already *eat**.
	(unchanged verb form)
	or
	He *had* already *ate**.
	(past tense used)

REGULARIZED

PAST TENSE
He *eated** lunch.
(-ed added to base form)

PAST PARTICIPLE
He *had eated** lunch.
(-ed added to base form)

OVERCORRECTED

THIRD PERSON PLURAL	DUMMY AUXILIARY
They *eats** lunch.	He *did* not *ate** lunch.
(unnecessary -s)	*(base form needed)*
	MODAL AUXILIARY
	He *should ate** more fruit.
	(base form needed)

PRACTICE

Copy the following paragraphs, inserting the appropriate Standard Written English form of the past tense or past participle of each verb in parentheses. If the verb requires neither past tense nor past participle, do not change its form.

The young lawyer had decided to (run)₁ for office after she had (get)₂ a great deal of encouragement from her friends and

colleagues. Her family (see) what would come, but they too
                      3
(give) her their support.
  4

   One of her support groups decided to (give) a series of
                                            5
small dinner parties so the voters could (get) to know their can-
                                            6
didate better. The guests (come) to a supporter's home for the
                            7
dinner and after everyone had (eat) and was relaxed, the candi-
                                  8
date (give) a speech about her views on the issues.
      9

   Although some listeners who (come) would give the candi-
                                  10
date their full attention, she (see) that a good many others just
                                11
(lie) back in their chairs and (go) to sleep.
 12   13

   After she had (go) to several of these occasions and had
                   14
(eat) her dinner and had (give) her speech, she began to think
 15   16
that this approach was not really the best way to (run) a cam-
                                                    17
paign. People would (come) to the dinner and would (eat) the
                      18   19
free food and then (get) too sleepy to pay attention to the
                    20
speech she (give).
            21
   She asked her supporters to (give) light buffet suppers in-
                                 22
stead, and she (get) them to remove all the chairs from the din-
                 23
ing room. This way people would still (come) to (see) the candi-
                                         24   25
date and after they had (eat) they would be relaxed and recep-
                          26
tive to the speech she would (give). But since they could not
                               27
(lie) back in their chairs and (go) to sleep, they would have to
 28   29
give some attention to the speech she would (give).
                                               30

14.6 VERB TERMINOLOGY

Definition

Verbs are usually defined as words that express action or a state of being.

He *hit* the ball. (action)

He *is* a good batter. (state of being)

(See Chapter 8 for more information about verb recognition.)

Categories

There are three major verb categories: **linking**, **transitive**, and **intransitive**.

Linking Verbs

The **linking verb** links the **subject** with a **subjective complement** following the verb. The most common linking verbs are the forms of *to be (is, am, are, was, were, been)*.

He **is** a good *batter.*

The *batter* **is** *good.*

The **subjective complement** may rename (*batter*) or describe (*good*) the subject.
Other common linking verbs are *feel, taste, smell,* and *appear.*

The *cake* **tastes** *delicious.*

The *playground* **sounds** *noisy.*

Transitive Verbs

Transitive verbs are verbs with a **direct object** that receives the action; in other words, the verb **transfers** the action from the subject (the doer) to the direct object (the receiver). The standard order of sentences using transitive verbs is subject, verb, direct object.

The *batter* **hit** the *ball.*

The *batter* is the doer, *hitting* is the action performed, and the *ball* is the receiver of the action.

Intransitive Verbs

Intransitive verbs are followed neither by a subjective complement nor by a direct object.

Time **flies**.

Sentences that end so abruptly are fairly uncommon in English. Usually, the intransitive verb is followed by a word or several words.

He **walked** *slowly down the street.*

He **walked** *slowly.*

He **walked** *down the street.*

Slowly and *down the street* are neither subjective complements nor direct objects. They do not rename or describe the subject, nor are they receivers of action.

Principal Parts of the Verb

The principal parts of the verb are the base form, the third person singular, the past tense, the past participle, and the present participle.

The Base Form

The **base form** is the simplest form of the verb. It is the form used in the construction known as the **infinitive**, which consists of *to* plus the base form.

TO	+	BASE	=	INFINITIVE
to		walk		to walk
to		drive		to drive
to		go		to go
to		see		to see

This is also the form used in the **present** tense, with the exception of third person singular. (See Chapter 8 for a discussion of subject-verb agreement.)

	SINGULAR	PLURAL
First person	I walk.	We walk.
Second person	You walk.	You walk.
Third person		They walk.

The base form is used with **modal auxiliaries** (*shall-should; will-would; may-might; can-could*).

MODAL	+	BASE	=	MODAL VERB
shall		walk		shall walk
should		walk		should walk
will		walk		will walk
would		walk		would walk
may		walk		may walk
might		walk		might walk
can		walk		can walk
could		walk		could walk

The base form is also used with forms of the **dummy auxiliary** *do*.

DUMMY	+	BASE	=	EMPHATIC/NEGATIVE/QUESTION
do		walk		do walk
does		walk		does walk
did		walk		did walk

Third Person Singular

The third person singular form consists of the base form plus -s.

BASE	+	-s	=	THIRD PERSON SINGULAR
walk		-s		He walks.
drive		-s		She drives.
move		-s		It moves.

Some verbs undergo a somewhat greater change, adding letters or changing their spelling and then ending in -s.

BASE	+	-s AND MORE	=	THIRD PERSON SINGULAR
go		-es		He goes.
do		-es		She does.
have		-s (drop *ve*)		It has.

Past Tense

The **past tense** form is used for what is referred to as the **simple past,** meaning that no auxiliary (or helping) verbs are used. The most common and the simplest kind of past tense consists of the base form plus *-ed*.

BASE	+	-ed	=	PAST TENSE
walk		-ed		He walked.

Past Participle

The **past participle** is the form used when the action being described is in the past, and a form of the auxiliary *have-has-had* is used. For most English verbs, the past tense and the past participle use the same form. These verbs are called **regular** verbs (see Section 14.3).

PAST TENSE	PAST PARTICIPLE
He walked.	They have walked.
	He has walked.
	She had walked.

However, some verbs have two different forms for the past tense and the past participle. These verbs are called **irregular** verbs (see Section 14.5).

PAST TENSE	PAST PARTICIPLE
He went.	He had gone.
He drove.	He had driven.
He sang.	He had sung.

The past participle is also used in what is called the **passive**, which uses a form of the verb *to be* (*is, am, are, was, were, been*).

The dog *was walked* by his master. The past participle can also be used as an **adjective** to describe a noun.

He had a *satisfied* expression on his face.

Present Participle

The **present participle** consists of the base form of the verb plus *-ing*.

BASE	+	-ing	=	PRESENT PARTICIPLE
walk		-ing		walking

The present participle has various uses. It is used in combination with forms of the verb *to be* (*am, is, are, was, were*) to create what are referred to as **progressive** constructions.

FORMS OF to be (present)	+	PRESENT PARTICIPLE	=	PRESENT PROGRESSIVE
am		walking		I am walking.
is		walking		He is walking.
are		walking		They are walking.

FORMS OF to be (past)	+	PRESENT PARTICIPLE	=	PAST PROGRESSIVE
was		walking		She was walking.
were		walking		They were walking.

The present participle can also be used as an **adjective** to describe a noun.

The *sleeping* boy.

Auxiliary Verbs

Auxiliary verbs, also known as **helping verbs**, combine with one of the principal parts of the main verb to create specific verb tenses. There are four major types of auxiliaries: the *have* forms, the *be* forms, the dummy auxiliary (forms of *do*), and the modal auxiliaries.

have Forms

The *have* forms are *have-has-had*. These combine with the past participle to form what are called **perfect** constructions (the word **perfect** in this context simply means "completed").

Present perfect (*have, has*). The **present perfect** forms are used when the action has been completed **before** the present time.

THIRD PERSON SINGULAR	OTHER FORMS
He has walked.	I have walked.
He has spoken.	We have spoken.
He has driven.	You have driven.
He has eaten.	They have eaten.

EXAMPLE:
> Today, he *has walked* two miles, *has driven* to the grocery store, and *has eaten* lunch.

All of these actions were completed before the present moment. This form is also used for **continuing** actions.

> He *has driven* to work every day at 7:30 for the past week.

Past perfect (*had*). The **past perfect** is used when an action has been completed at some point in the past.

> He had walked.
>
> He had driven.
>
> He had eaten.

EXAMPLE:
> By this time yesterday, he *had walked* five miles, *had driven* to the shopping mall, *had walked* around for some time, and *had eaten* a large pizza. (past perfect)
>
> All he *has done* today is sleep. (shifts to present perfect)

be Forms

Progressive. Forms of *be* are used in combination with the present participle (*-ing* form) to create what are called **progressive** constructions. Progressive means that the action is, was, or will be continuing, or progressing.

PRESENT PROGRESSIVE
> He is walking. (The action continues in the present.)

PAST PROGRESSIVE
> He was walking. (The action continued in the past.)

Passive. Forms of *be* are also combined with the past participle to create what is called the **passive**. In passive sentences, the subject of the sentence is not the doer of the action stated in the verb but instead the receiver of that action. Passive sentences contrast with the more commonly used active construction, where the subject of the sentence is the doer of the action. Following are several pairs of sentences that illustrate the difference between the passive and the active.

Note 1: The word **doer** should not be taken too literally. Although the doer may be a person, it might also be an abstraction, such as the term *liberty*, or a nonhuman force like *the weather*.

Note 2: The doer is not always specified in passive sentences, but when it is, it is found in a prepositional phrase beginning with *by*; for example, "He is driven *by ambition*."

ACTIVE	PASSIVE
They *asked* him to make a speech.	He *was asked* to make a speech.
They *gave* him ten minutes to speak.	He *was given* ten minutes to speak.
They *received* him with applause.	He *was received* with applause.
Ambition *drives* him.	He *is driven* by ambition.
His actions *anger* them.	They *are angered* by his actions.
They *asked* him to return.	He *has been asked* to return.

Dummy Auxiliary

The forms of the verb *do* (*do, does, did*) are known as the **dummy auxiliary**. They are so called because they are not used in simple declarative statements, but are added in questions, negatives, or emphatic statements.

Note: A useful memory device is to remember that all of the **dummy** auxiliaries begin with *d*.

DECLARATIVE	DUMMY AUXILIARY
He walked.	*Did* he walk? (Question)
He spoke.	He *did* not speak. (Negative)
He ate.	He *did* eat. (Emphatic)

Note: The base form of the verb is used in these constructions; there is no *-ed* ending added or any other change in the base form of the verb.

Modal Auxiliaries

The **modals** are called that because they are considered to indicate mood or condition; for example, whether something is probable, possible, or necessary. The modals are listed here:

> shall-should   may-might
> will-would   can-could

Following are some examples of modals combined with the main verb.

> He *shall* walk.   He *may* walk.
> He *should* walk.   He *might* walk.
> He *will* walk.   He *can* walk.
> He *would* walk.   He *could* walk.

Note: The base form of the verb is used with modals. There is no *-ed* ending added or any other change to the base form of the verb.

One additional point about modals is that they are usually referred to as **present** or **past**. However, the distinctions being made are not true distinctions of time in many instances. For example, "He *can walk*" means "He is able to walk"; however, "He *could walk*" may be used to mean something like "He is able to walk with a cane if he tries, but he doesn't make any effort." If Joe asks George, "*Will* you lend me ten dollars?" and George answers, "I *will* be glad to lend you ten dollars," then Joe may expect the ten dollars. If, however, George answers, "I *would* be glad to lend you ten dollars," then Joe probably knows as soon as he hears the word *would* not to expect the ten dollars, because the rest of the sentence will probably be something like "I *would* be glad to lend you ten dollars, but I don't get paid until Friday, and as matter of fact, I was just going to ask you if you could lend me fifty cents for the candy machine." Needless to say, Joe should not expect the ten dollars under these circumstances.

Following are some pairs of modals; the parenthetical statement completes what seems implicit in the modal.

I *will call* you this weekend (*I promise*).

I *would call* you this weekend (*but I may be busy*).

I *shall turn* in my English paper on time (*I promise*).

I *should turn* in my English paper on time (*but I probably won't*).

I *may go* to see that movie tonight (*I'm thinking about it*).

I *might go* to see that new movie tonight (*I'm thinking about it but somewhat doubtful*).

Most native English speakers use modals accurately to express distinctions of meaning without being aware that they are doing so. But English modals may be a source of difficulty to speakers of other languages that use equivalents of these words differently.

CHAPTER 15
Pronouns

15.1 INTRODUCTION

Writers often have problems with pronouns—and with good reason—since pronouns are a relatively complex part of speech in the English language. Fortunately, the number of pronouns is limited, and writers can achieve mastery of the pronoun system with practice.

A rather elaborate set of terminology is employed with pronouns, and a discussion of that terminology is presented in this chapter. Do not concern yourself excessively with learning this terminology. It has been provided so that you and your teacher will have a common frame of reference. As you work through the practices in this chapter, pronoun terminology and concepts should become increasingly familiar to you. You will find some of the practices easy and others more difficult. As you do them, you should notice certain patterns; if you look at your writing, somewhat similar patterns of pronoun usage problems should appear.

Two types of pronouns often create usage problems for writers: personal pronouns and reflexive pronouns.

15.2 PERSONAL PRONOUNS

Personal pronouns require different forms according to each of the following: person, number, gender, and function. Table 27 lists the various forms of the personal pronouns. As the table indicates, some pronouns are far more complex than others.

Pronoun Reference

The traditional definition of the **pronoun** is that it takes the place of a noun, and one of the conventions of Standard Written

TABLE 27
PERSONAL PRONOUNS

PERSON	NUMBER		FUNCTION
	SINGULAR	PLURAL	
First	I	we	Subjective
	me	us	Objective
	my, mine	our, ours	Possessive
Second	you	you	Subjective
	you	you	Objective
	your, yours	your, yours	Possessive
Third (gender)	he (masculine) she (feminine) it (neuter)	they	Subjective
	him (masculine) her (feminine) it (neuter)	them	Objective
	his (masculine) her, hers (feminine) it, its (neuter)	their, theirs	Possessive

English is that a pronoun must have an **antecedent**, or **referent**. The pronoun should refer specifically to a noun already named, either in a preceding sentence or in the sentence in which the pronoun occurs. The following paragraph illustrates appropriate pronoun reference. The antecedent of each pronoun is given in parentheses.

John lost *his* (John) wallet at the grocery store, and a clerk found *it* (wallet) lying in the aisle. The clerk called John, telling *him* (John) that *she* (clerk) had found *his* (John) wallet. When John picked *it* (wallet) up, *he* (John) thanked *her* (clerk) and gave *her* (clerk) a ten dollar reward. *She* (clerk) thanked *him* (John) for *it* (reward).

Writers should avoid **vague pronoun reference**—that is, using pronouns without a clear antecedent. The pronouns *which*, *this*, and *it* seem particularly susceptible to vague pronoun reference. In the following sentences, none of these pronouns have specific referents; referents are also missing for other pronouns.

I have been studying for my math exam, but *it's* very difficult for me. I don't really know what *they're* going to ask, *which* makes *it* even more difficult. *They* say that *he* gives hard exams. I'll be so glad when *this* is over with.

Here is the same paragraph revised to show appropriate pronoun reference.

I have been studying for my math exam, but *the subject* is very difficult for me. I don't really know what *the professor* is going to ask. *Not knowing what to review* makes *the studying* even more difficult. *Students* who have taken math from *this professor* in previous semesters say that he gives hard exams. I'll be so glad when *this exam* is over with.

Pronoun Shifting

Another convention of Standard Written English is that writers should avoid unnecessary **pronoun shifting** in person and number.

Shifts in Person

In spoken language, the situation normally indicates whether the speaker is referring to himself or herself (first person), addressing someone else (second person), or speaking about someone else (third person).

I (first person) am telling *you* (second person) that *he* (third person) told *me* (first person) that *you* (second person) had said to *him* (third person) what *I* (first person) asked *you* (second person) not to repeat to *him* (third person) or anyone else.

In written language, however, writers must provide the reader with the context, and pronouns that shift from one person to another can be both confusing and irritating to the reader. The following examples illustrate shifts in person and appropriate revision.

SHIFTING PRONOUN REFERENCE
Do all of the *students* (third person) in the class have *your* (second person) books with *you* (second person)?

REVISION
   Do all of the *students* (third person) in the class have *their* (third person) books with *them* (third person)?

SHIFTING PRONOUN REFERENCE
   Everyone (third person) should check to see if *you* (second person) have left anything in the room.

REVISION
   Everyone (third person) should check to see if *he* or *she* (third person) has left anything in the room.

Shifts in Number

In spoken language, the situation usually makes it clear whether the singular or the plural is needed.

   Although *we* (plural) talked to both of *them* (plural), *I* (singular) spent more time talking to *her* (singular) than *you* (singular) spent talking to *him* (singular).

However, written language requires writers to provide the reader with the context, and shifting pronoun number can be confusing and irritating to the reader. The following examples illustrate shifts in pronoun number and appropriate revision. Note that more than one revision is possible.

SHIFTING PRONOUN NUMBER
   A *student* (singular) should bring *their* (plural) books to class.

REVISION TO SINGULAR
   A *student* (singular) should bring *his* or *her* (singular) books to class.

REVISION TO PLURAL
   Students (plural) should bring *their* (plural) books to class.

SHIFTING PRONOUN NUMBER
   Anyone (singular) wanting to park on campus must have *their* (plural) parking permit.

REVISION TO SINGULAR
   Anyone (singular) wanting to park on campus must have *his* or *her* (singular) parking permit.

REVISION TO PLURAL

Drivers (plural) wanting to park on campus must have *their* (plural) parking permit.

Gender

Gender distinctions in English are required only in the third person singular pronoun, which has masculine, feminine, and neuter forms.

MASCULINE	FEMININE	NEUTER
he	she	it
him	her	its
his	hers	

For the most part, English uses what is referred to as "natural" gender. People and animals that are biologically male are referred to by the **masculine pronouns**. People and animals that are biologically female are referred to by the **feminine pronouns**. The **neuter pronouns** are used to refer to abstractions (for example, *liberty*) and inanimate objects (for example, *tree*, *chair*, *book*).

When the sex of the referent is known, then gender choice is easy, but in some cases, the sex of the referent is unknown. In the past, the custom has been to use the third person singular masculine pronouns (*he*, *him*, *his*) in such instances, but many regard such language as sexist, and writers are urged to avoid sexist language. For example, the following sentence uses sexist language.

Does everyone have *his* books?

Unless the group is entirely male, the use of *his* in this situation is sexist.

Unfortunately, there is no agreed-upon solution to this problem. Probably most people would revise the sentence as follows, even though *everyone* is singular and *their* is plural and the revision violates the rule against shifting number.

Does *everyone* have *their* books?

Another solution is to use both the masculine and the feminine pronouns, but many find this construction awkward, particularly when it occurs repeatedly.

Does everyone have *his* or *her* books, and has everyone given *his* or *her* speech and submitted *his* or *her* paper?

Sometimes the entire sentence can be shifted to the plural, but the plural construction is not always successful. The following sentence does not convey exactly the same meaning as the others.

Do all of the students have *their* books?

In a classroom situation, the sentence can be shifted to second person, but the solution is not practical in writing, which is more often in the third person.

Do all of you have *your* books?

Another approach is to omit the pronoun(s).

Does everyone have books?

Does everyone have the necessary books?

Has everyone given a speech and submitted the assigned paper?

Since there is no single agreed-upon solution to this problem, writers should choose the most appropriate usage according to the specifics of the writing situation.

PRACTICE

Copy the following paragraphs, eliminating vague, shifting, and sexist pronouns; changes in pronoun may require changes in verb form. In some cases, more than one revision is possible.

(They)₁ say that if (one)₂ does not go to college as soon as (they)₃ graduate from high school, then (he)₄ may never again have the opportunity. (One)₅ might get married, (which)₆ could cause (them)₇ to have no chance for college. If (you)₈ have children and other family responsibilities, (they)₉ say proceeding with (his)₁₀ education is very difficult.

(It)₁₁ may be true, but (you)₁₂ can attend college part-time, even if (one)₁₃ is working and (they)₁₄ have children and family responsibilities. (It's)₁₅ not easy, but still (one)₁₆ can do (it)₁₇, if (he)₁₈ really wants to.

Pronoun Function

Distinctions of **pronoun function** can also create usage problems for writers. **Subjective** pronouns are required when pronouns function as subjects or subjective complements, **objective** pronouns are required when pronouns function as objects, and **possessive** pronouns are required when pronouns indicate ownership or similar relationships.

Possessive Pronouns

By and large, possessive pronouns cause relatively little difficulty in oral language, since English speakers ordinarily know when and how to indicate these relationships (for example, *my* book, *our* book; The book is *mine*; The book is *ours*). These forms do occasionally cause some problems in writing, since writers may become confused about the spelling of possessive pronouns.

Because possessive nouns are indicated with an apostrophe (for example, *John's* book), sometimes writers assume that apostrophes are always used to indicate possession. As a result, they may add apostrophes to possessive pronouns, writing sentences such as those that follow. However, apostrophes are **not** used with possessive pronouns. The appropriate Standard Written English forms of possessive pronouns are listed here, in addition to some examples of forms to avoid.

(See Section 17.2A, "The Most Troublesome Homonyms," for an extended discussion of problems with possessive pronouns, in addition to some practice exercises.)

STANDARD WRITTEN ENGLISH	AVOID
That book is *yours*.	That book is *yours'*.
	That book is *your's*.
That book is *his*.	That book is *his'*.
That book is *hers*.	That book is *hers'*.
	That book is *her's*.
That book is *ours*.	That book is *ours'*.
	That book is *our's*.
That book is *theirs*.	That book is *theirs'*.
	That book is *their's*.
The dog wagged *its* tail.	The dog wagged *its'* tail.
	The dog wagged *it's* tail.

Subjective and Objective Forms of Pronouns

Another common usage problem for writers is the appropriate use of the subjective and objective forms of pronouns. Simple sentences, such as "I saw *him* at the store," rarely cause difficulties; adult native speakers of English do not use constructions like "*Me* saw *him* at the store." But writers may have problems when sentences are more complicated.

One source of difficulty is our tendency to think of the part of the sentence preceding the verb as subject territory and the part of the sentence following the verb as object territory. In fact, such is the case in a large percentage of English sentences—but not all. In the sentence "*I* saw *him*," the word preceding the verb is *I*, a subject pronoun in subject territory, and the word following the verb is *him*, an object pronoun in object territory. Thus, our inclinations in this sentence are grammatically accurate.

SUBJECT TERRITORY	VERB	OBJECT TERRITORY
I	saw	him
(subjective)		(objective)

Compound Pronouns. Probably the most common pronoun errors occur when the pronoun is part of a **compound** (for example, *Bill and I, Bill and me*). Sometimes writers avoid using objective forms and substitute subjective forms when they are not appropriate. "I saw *he*" is not very common, but we do occasionally hear or see "I saw Bill and *he*." "*Me* saw him" is also uncommon, but "Bill and *me* saw him" or "*Me* and Bill saw him" is less so.

In terms of etiquette, most adult English speakers regard it as bad manners "to put oneself first" in such constructions. "*Me* and Bill saw him" might be considered impolite by the individual who would say instead "Bill and *me* saw him." The correct form is "Bill and *I* (first person, subjective) saw *him*" (third person, objective).

Object of the Preposition. The compound pronoun as object of the preposition specifically creates usage problems. **Prepositions** are words like *of, with, to,* and *for* (see Table 1 for a list of common prepositions). A preposition followed by a noun or pronoun constitutes a **prepositional phrase**.

PREPOSITION	+	NOUN	=	PREPOSITIONAL PHRASE
of		the team		of the team
with		the group		with the group
to		the store		to the store
for		the school		for the school

PREPOSITION	+	PRONOUN	=	PREPOSITIONAL PHRASE
of		them		of them
with		us		with us
for		me		for me
to		him		to him

Writers rarely make mistakes when there is only one object of the preposition, but when there are two or more objects, and one or more is a pronoun, then usage problems may arise. Sentences such as the following are not uncommon.

That is between *he* and *she*.

Between is a preposition, so the sentence should read:

That is between *him* and *her*.

When prepositional phrases are found in subject territory, the potential for misuse seems to increase dramatically.

Between you and *I*, I don't believe he knows what he's talking about.

The sentence should read:

Between you and *me*, I don't believe he knows what he's talking about.

Pronoun Use After Linking Verbs. Verbs like *saw*, which can take objects, are referred to as **transitive** verbs, but not all English verbs are transitive. For example, the various forms of the **linking** verb *to be* (*is, am, are, was, were, been*) do not take objects. Instead, they take subjective complements; a **subjective complement** refers back to the subject or completes the sentence, and as its name implies, the subject form of the pronoun is used. (See Chapter 14, Section 14.6, for a more complete discussion of transitive and linking verbs.)

That was *he*.

This is *I*.

In oral language, speakers often use objective forms when strict rules of usage requires subjective forms.

That was *him*.

This is *me*.

These constructions are used somewhat less often in writing, but subjective and objective problems of this type do occur.

PRACTICE

Copy the following paragraphs, inserting the appropriate pronouns. The pronoun in parentheses is the subjective form and should be retained if the pronoun functions as a subject or as a subjective complement. If the pronoun functions as a direct object, an indirect object, or an object of the preposition, use the objective form. If the pronoun functions as a possessive, use the possessive form. You may want to consult Table 27 as you do the practice.

(I)₁ brother, (I)₂ sister, and (I)₃ decided to give a surprise anniversary party for (we)₄ parents. (We)₅ parents had been married for twenty-five years so (it)₆ would be a silver anniversary party. Since the anniversary date proper fell on a Monday, (we)₇ decided to move (it)₈ celebration to the preceding Saturday so (we)₉ parents' friends could attend.

All of (we)₁₀ agreed that the celebration would have to be a fairly inexpensive one, since none of (we)₁₁ had very much money. My older brother had recently graduated from college, and (he)₁₂ had just begun (he)₁₃ first professional job; a few years lay ahead of (he)₁₄ before (he)₁₅ would begin to make a large salary.

(I)₁₆ older sister and (I)₁₇ were both attending college, so neither of (we)₁₈ had much money. (We)₁₉ both worked part-time to pay for (we)₂₀ books and tuition, but (we)₂₁ still lived at home with (we)₂₂ parents to cut down on living expenses. (She)₂₃ spoke to (I)₂₄ about putting together the celebration and said, "Just between (you)₂₅ and (I)₂₆, (I)₂₇ don't know how (we)₂₈ can afford to have

an expensive party for (we) folks' anniversary." (I) too was wor-
                                  29   30
ried and responded to (she), "(I) feel the same way and between
                         31   32
(you) and (I), (I) don't know where (I) am even going to get the
 33   34   35   36
money for a decent gift."

(We) younger brother and sister were thrilled about the
 37
party and thought (it) to be a great idea, but (they) had no idea
                   38   39
of (it) cost. When all of (we) met, (they) suggested all sorts of
   40   41   42
expensive ideas, and those of (we) who were older had to shout
                               43
(they) down. (I) older brother, who was earning more money
 44   45
than all of the rest of (we) put together, began to feel that pres-
                        46
sure was being placed on (he) to pay all of the expenses, but (I)
                         47   48
older sister and (I) took (he) aside and after (he) had listened to
                 49   50   51
(she) and (I), (he) began to realize that (we) younger brother
 52   53   54   55
and sister simply did not understand the cost.

Since (I) older sister is the family peacemaker, (she) sug-
      56   57
gested that (we) make out a list of expenses. Each of (we) was
            58   59
detailed to find out the cost of renting a hall, buying champagne,
and meeting other expenses. (We) were all to meet again a week
                             60
later, and each of (we) would present (he) or (she) information
                   61   62   63
to the group.

When (we) met again, (it) was obvious from the expressions
      64   65
on the faces of the younger ones that the prices (they) had dis-
                                                  66
covered had shocked (they) profoundly. (I) had been assigned
                     67   68
the task of finding out how much (it) would cost to rent a hall,
                                  69
and (I) discoveries had shocked (I) equally.
    70   71

As (we) went through (we) list, (it) became apparent that all
   72   73   74
of (we) had underestimated the cost of (we) idea. Since (I) had
   75   76   77
been assigned the task of finding out how much (it) would cost
                                                 78
to rent the hall, (they) asked (I) to go first. (I) discoveries had
                  79   80   81

shocked (I) and when (I) reported (they) to (I) brothers and sis-
                82   83   84   85
ters, (they) too were equally shocked by (they).
       86   87

   By the time (we) had reached the end of the list of ex-
                   88
penses, (it) had become evident to all of (we) that (we) either
        89   90   91
were going to have to give up the idea of an anniversary party
for (we) parents, or (we) were going to have to change (we)
    92   93   94
ideas considerably.

   Once more playing the role of peacemaker, (I) older sister,
                                              95
suggested that (we) consider family resources. Although (we)
                 96   97
backyard was too small for a party and (we) parents would un-
                                        98
doubtedly discover what (we) were doing if (we) tried to set up
                         99   100
a party under (they) noses, there were others in the family who
              101
might be able to help (we) if (we) asked (they).
                      102   103   104

   (We) father's only brother and (he) wife had a large house
    105   106
with a large backyard, and (they) children were all grown up;
                            107
perhaps (they) would let (we) use (they) backyard. Other family
        108   109   110
members might bring food if (we) asked (they), and perhaps
                             111   112
(we) could find enough money for domestic champagne if each
113
of (we) contributed what (he) or (she) could.
   114   115   116

   All of those (we) asked were delighted to offer (they) assis-
                117   118
tance and with all of (we) working together, (we) finally succeeded
                      119   120
in providing (we) parents with a very nice anniversary party.
             121
(They) said (they) were quite surprised and (they) thanked (we)
 122   123   124   125
again and again. (I) mother took (I) older sister and (I) aside and
                 126   127   128
said, "Just between (you) and (I), (I) thought something was
                    129   130 131
going on, but (I) didn't want to spoil the surprise for (you)
              132   133
father." Later (I) saw (I) father take (I) older brother aside and
               134   135   136
say something quietly to (he). (I) saw (he) smile as (he) listened
                         137   138   139   140
to what (he) father was saying.
        141

Soon after that, (he) signalled to (I) sister and (I) to meet
                    142   143   144
(he) in the corner. After a few minutes (we) were able to get
145   146
through the crowd toward (he). When (we) reached where (he)
                         147   148   149
was standing, (he) told (we) what (we) father had said. Then
              150   151   152
(we) told (he) what (we) mother had said. (He), (I) sister, and (I)
153   154   155   156   157   158
all laughed about the conspiracy of silence and (we) all agreed
                                                 159
to keep the information from (we) younger brother and sister,
                             160
since (they) thought the conspiracy had been successful. (We)
      161   162
wanted (they) to think that (they) had successfully pulled off
       163   164
the operation, although (we) suspected that (we) parents had
                        165   166
caught on from what one of (they) had said or done.
                           167

(We) had heard (they) mysteriously shushing each other
168   169
whenever either (we) mother or father had entered the room.
                170
(They) would become suspiciously silent and when (they) had
171   172
been asked what (they) had been up to, each of (they) would
                 173   174
get a smirk on (he) or (she) face and swear, "It wasn't (I)."
               175   176   177

15.3 REFLEXIVE PRONOUNS

Reflexive pronouns consist of a personal pronoun and *self* or *selves*. Here is a list of the reflexive pronouns.

	SINGULAR	PLURAL
First person	myself	ourselves
Second person	yourself	yourselves
Third person	himself (masculine) herself (feminine) itself (neuter)	themselves

Reflexive pronouns are used in situations like the following. Note that, in these sentences, the reference for the reflexive has already appeared prior to the use of the reflexive.

Joe cut *himself* badly when he was shaving.

Although *I* do not like Jim *myself*, I try to be pleasant to him because his wife is a lovely person.

Reflexive pronouns should **not** be used as a substitute for personal pronouns.

John and *myself* did the study.

His wife and *himself* were injured in a serious car wreck.

The use of the reflexive pronoun is inappropriate in such sentences; personal pronouns should be used instead.

John and *I* did the study.

His wife and *he* were injured in a serious car wreck.

Sometimes writers do not form reflexive pronouns correctly, using *hisself* rather than *himself* and *theirselves* rather than *themselves*. This problem occurs because some reflexives are combinations of the possessive form and *-self* or *-selves*, but others are combinations of the objective form and *-self* or *-selves*.

POSSESSIVE +	*-self/-selves*	=	REFLEXIVE PRONOUNS
my	-self		myself
your	-self		yourself
our	-selves		ourselves
your	-selves		yourselves

OBJECTIVE +	*-self/-selves*	=	REFLEXIVE PRONOUNS
him	-self		himself
her	-self		herself
it	-self		itself
them	-selves		themselves

This distinction does not create a problem with *herself* and *itself*. *Her* is also a possessive form, and there is no separate competing form to substitute. Since the possessive form for *it* is *its*, there is also no separate competing form to substitute for *it* + *-self*.

For *himself*, there is a competing form *his*; consequently, *hisself* (*his* + *-self*) is possible. The same is true for *themselves*, where the competing possessive form *their* makes possible *theirselves* (*their* + *-selves*).

Another usage problem that occurs occasionally with the reflexive is the misspelling of the plural reflexive. See Chapter 13, Section 13.3, for a discussion of this usage issue.

PRACTICE

Copy the following paragraphs, inserting reflexive pronouns correctly. The subjective form of the pronoun + *-self* is in parentheses. Choose either the objective or possessive form and combine it with *-self* for singular reflexive pronouns and *-selves* for plural reflexive pronouns.

When they graduate from high school, many young people find (they + -self)¹ in a quandary about their future. Some decide to go to college right away, others decide to delay college for a while, and still others feel vocational school is the appropriate choice; each young person must make the choice about what is right for (he + -self)² or (her + -self)³.

When I graduated from high school, I (I + -self)⁴ had no doubt that going to college right away was the right course for me. However, some of my friends made different choices for (they + -self)⁵.

Katherine, one of my oldest friends, decided (she + -self)⁶ to delay college for at least a year. As she (she + -self)⁷ told me, "Since I don't know what I want for (I + -self)⁸, it seems better to wait until I can make an intelligent decision."

She made the decision by (she + -self)⁹, but when she announced it to her parents they found (they + -self)¹⁰ shocked and horrified by her choice. They had always assumed, without thinking about what Katherine (she + -self)¹¹ wanted, that she would go to college immediately after high school. Katherine (she + self)¹² told me that she and her parents had a good many discussions among (they + -self)¹³ about her decision.

"You should consider what I want for (I + -self)$_{14}$, not what you wanted for (you + -self)$_{15}$," she had told her mother. Her mother had explained that although she had never had the chance (she + -self)$_{16}$ to go to college, she was most concerned by her daughter's refusal of such an opportunity. "Well," said Katherine, "just because you couldn't go to college after you graduated from high school doesn't mean that you could not enroll (your + -self)$_{17}$ now."

Her father listened quietly as his wife and daughter argued and finally decided by (he + -self)$_{18}$ that each one had a point. To Katherine he said, "You make the decision that you feel is right for you (you + -self)$_{19}$. If you want to delay college, I will not object (I + -self)$_{20}$." To his wife he said, "If you have always wanted to go to college, why deny (you + -self)$_{21}$ any longer? Katherine is old enough to take care of (she + -self)$_{22}$. If going to college is what you want for (you + -self)$_{23}$, go ahead and enroll at the community college or the university right here in the city. Many older people are enrolling (they + -self)$_{24}$ in college these days."

At first Katherine's mother demurred, but finally she said, "Yes, I will; it's something I have always wanted for (I + -self)$_{25}$." She turned to Katherine and said, "You must decide (you + -self)$_{26}$ what is right for you and I will decide for (I + -self)$_{27}$ what is right for me."

Katherine's father was quite pleased with (he + -self)$_{28}$. He had felt for some time that it was right that his wife begin to pay more attention to (she + -self)$_{29}$ and her own needs rather than devoting (she + -self)$_{30}$ entirely to Katherine and him.

Between (we + -selves)$_{31}$, Katherine and I agreed that everything had worked out for the best. Katherine (she + -self) was happy with her decision, her mother was delighted by the opportunity to pursue for (she + -self) something she had always wanted, and her father was pleased that he had come up with the solution (he + -self).

Although I had (I + -self) been somewhat upset when Katherine had first told me of her decision, I had by that point accepted the fact that the decision (it + -self) was hers to make—not mine. "You (you + -self) have to make your own choice," I had told her, "just as I made the decision (I + -self) about what was right for me. The choice (it + -self) is not so important as is the right to make the choice. Each person has to choose what is right for (he + -self) or (she + -self)."

CHAPTER 16
Adjectives and Adverbs

16.1 INTRODUCTION

Adjectives and adverbs are modifiers, and writers who use them skillfully can add detail and precision to their writing. Fortunately, adjectives and adverbs create relatively few usage problems for writers.

16.2 ADJECTIVES

Adjectives modify nouns and pronouns. We can recognize them easily because they usually occur in one of the two positions: preceding a noun or following a linking verb such as *to be*.

The *tall* boy walked down the street. (precedes a noun)

John is *tall*. (follows a linking verb)

He is *tall*. (follows a linking verb)

Many adjectives provide sensory information—that is, information concerning the five senses: sight, sound, smell, taste, or touch.

the *blue* dress
the *noisy* radio
the *pungent* herbs
the *sweet* candy
the *coarse* material

Another characteristic of adjectives is that many of them can be modified by **intensifiers**, or **qualifiers**, such as *very, quite, rather, really, fairly,* and *too.*

a *very* pretty dress

a *quite* handsome suit

a *rather* expensive car

a *really* unpleasant color

a *fairly* difficult task

Comparatives and Superlatives

Most adjectives have three degrees: positive, comparative, and superlative. The **comparative** is used when comparing two items; the **superlative** is used comparing three or more items. The comparative forms of an adjective are created either by adding *-er* to the end of the positive form of the adjective or by placing the word *more* before the adjective. The superlative forms are created either by adding *-est* to the end of the positive form of the adjective or by placing the word *most* before the adjective. The general rule is that short adjectives of one or two syllables take the *-er* and *-est* endings, and longer adjectives use *more* and *most.*

POSITIVE	COMPARATIVE	SUPERLATIVE
tall	taller	tallest
beautiful	more beautiful	most beautiful

Double Comparatives and Superlatives

Double comparatives occur when writers use both forms, *more* and *-er,* on the same word. **Double superlatives** occur when both *most* and *-est* are used on the same word.

DOUBLE COMPARATIVE	DOUBLE SUPERLATIVE
more prettier	most prettiest

Neither double comparatives nor double superlatives are regarded as acceptable in Standard Written English. (See Chapter 11, Section 11.3, for further discussion of double comparatives and superlatives.)

Irregular Comparatives and Superlatives

Not all comparatives and superlatives use the *-er, -est* or *more, most* forms. Following is a list of **irregular** comparatives and superlatives.

POSITIVE	IRREGULAR COMPARATIVE	IRREGULAR SUPERLATIVE
good	better	best
bad	worse	worst
far	farther	farthest
far	further	furthest

Note: *Fartherest* and *furtherest* are incorrect forms since they contain both the comparative *-er* and the superlative *-est*.

Absolute Adjectives

Certain adjectives in English are called **absolute**. Ordinarily, these adjectives should not be compared.

ABSOLUTE	ADJECTIVES
unique	dead
perfect	round

Sometimes writers use words like *deader*, but if something is *dead*, logically it cannot be *more dead*. *Unique* is probably the word where this rule is observed the most strictly, since *unique* means "one of a kind," and therefore presumably nothing could be *more unique* or *most unique*.

PRACTICE

Copy the following paragraphs, inserting the appropriate comparative and superlative forms. The positive form is given in parentheses, followed by a + symbol and the abbreviation *comp* or *sup*. If *comp* is given, use the comparative form (*more* in front of the word or *-er* after the word). If *sup* is given, use the superlative form (*most* in front of the word or *-est* after the word). Do not use double comparatives or superlatives. If the adjective is absolute, disregard instructions to use the comparative or superlative; if the adjective is irregular, use the appropriate form.

One of my (old + sup) and (good + sup) friends is my
                          1   2
next door neighbor, Joe. Throughout elementary school, Joe was always the (short + sup) boy in the class. I was always (tall
                                  3
+ comp) than he was until we reached high school. Suddenly,
4

Joe began to grow, and soon he was the (tall + sup)₅ boy in school.

As he grew (tall + comp)₆, he also grew (confident + comp)₇ and (popular + comp)₈. Once he had been the (shy + sup)₉ boy I knew; now he was one of the (assertive + sup)₁₀. In his senior year he began to date the (beautiful + sup)₁₁ girl in school. Everyone remarked that the two of them together were one of the (handsome + sup)₁₂ couples they had ever seen, and some called them the (perfect + sup)₁₃ pair.

Although Joe's new girlfriend was the (pretty + sup)₁₄ girl in school, her personality was one of the (bad + sup)₁₅. Joe kept hoping that she would get (good + comp)₁₆ in this area, but instead she seemed to become (bad + comp)₁₇ and (bad + comp)₁₈. For one thing, she had a terrible temper, and the (angry + comp)₁₉ she became, the (hard + comp)₂₀ she was to deal with. He would try to reason with her, but she was (dead + sup)₂₁ to logic when she became angry.

Finally, they had an argument in which she went (far + comp)₂₂ than she ever had before. In addition to her terrible temper, she was the (jealous + sup)₂₃ girl Joe had ever dated. She had become (convinced + comp)₂₄ and (convinced + comp)₂₅ that Joe was secretly dating another girl.

After the argument, the (bad + sup)₂₆ they ever had, Joe stopped dating her and began to date her (young + comp)₂₇ sister. Although the (old + comp)₂₈ sister was (pretty + comp)₂₉, the (young + comp)₃₀ sister had a (pleasant + comp)₃₁ personality. Joe was (happy + comp)₃₂ than he had been in a long time, and he felt (good + comp)₃₃ about himself than he had for some time.

Count and Mass Nouns

English nouns may be either count nouns or mass nouns. **Count nouns** are things that can be counted, whereas **mass nouns** cannot be counted. Different adjective forms may be required for count nouns and mass nouns.

	POSITIVE	COMPARATIVE	SUPERLATIVE
(count)	many	more	most
(mass)	much	more	most

More and *most* can be used with both count and mass nouns, but *many* is used only with count nouns and *much* only with mass nouns.

> He has *many* good friends. (*Friends* can be counted.)
>
> Did you have *much* luck in Las Vegas? (*Luck* cannot be counted.)
>
> He has attended *many* fine schools. (*Schools* can be counted.)
>
> He has *much* knowledge on that subject. (*Knowledge* cannot be counted.)
>
> He has told *many* lies about his past. (*Lies* can be counted.)
>
> There is *much* truth in what you say. (*Truth* cannot be counted.)

Few and *little* use different forms for the comparative and superlative as well as the positive. *Few*, *fewer*, and *fewest* are used with count nouns; *little*, *less*, and *least* with mass nouns.

	POSITIVE	COMPARATIVE	SUPERLATIVE
(count)	few	fewer	fewest
(mass)	little	less	least

> I have been on a diet, but I lost *fewer* pounds this month than I did last month. (*Pounds* can be counted.)

ADJECTIVES AND ADVERBS

I have been on a diet, but I lost *less* weight this month than I did last month. (*Weight*, in this sense, cannot be counted.)

PRACTICE

Copy the following paragraphs, inserting the appropriate count and mass words. In parentheses the words *many/much* or *few/little* are given; if no + symbol follows these words, choose the appropriate count or mass form. If the word is followed by a + symbol and *comp*, insert the appropriate comparative form. If the word is followed by a + symbol and *sup*, insert the appropriate superlative form.

The "graying of America" is a phenomenon that concerns (many/much)₁ people today. As (many/much + comp)₂ and (many/much + comp)₃ of our population reaches the age of 65, the country faces a variety of problems it has never had to deal with before. Although (many/much + sup)₄ of this population is healthy, serious medical problems represent a major concern. (Few/Little)₅ families can tolerate the expenses of extended illness, and even (few/little + comp)₆ individuals can.

The single elderly woman who must rely entirely on social security is particularly vulnerable because she probably made (few/little + comp)₇ money than her male counterparts and consequently must exist on very (few/little)₈. She must live longer on (few/little + comp)₉ than the male who made (many/much + comp)₁₀ money but lives (few/little + comp)₁₁ years.

Another problem is that (few/little + comp)₁₂ and (few/little + comp)₁₃ working people will be supporting (many/much + comp)₁₄ and (many/much + comp)₁₅ elderly. By the year 2000 it is estimated that the (few/little + sup)₁₆ number of workers will be supporting the highest number of elderly that our society has ever seen. It would not be surprising if at (few/little + sup)$_{17}$ some of them felt resentment. Although there is (few/little)$_{18}$ chance of a war between generations, it seems (many/much + sup)$_{19}$ likely that both groups will begin to feel (many/much + comp)$_{20}$ resentment toward each other.

The growing numbers of elderly will ensure that they will have (many/much + comp)$_{21}$ and (many/much + comp)$_{22}$ political power. Since young people are (few/little + comp)$_{23}$ likely to vote than older people, the shrinking numbers of young people will have even (few/little + comp)$_{24}$ power than they should.

Since our society has never faced this situation before, it is (many/much + sup)$_{25}$ impossible to predict what will happen. One hopes that solutions will be devised that will cause the (few/little + sup)$_{26}$ damage and that affect the (few/little + sup)$_{27}$ number of people adversely.

16.3 ADVERBS

Adverbs are rather difficult to recognize for several reasons: (1) they are highly movable and may be found anywhere in the sentence; (2) they have no specific form that can be relied on; and (3) their usual definition is rather vague. Ordinarily, **adverbs** are said to modify verbs, adjectives, and other adverbs. For the purpose of this discussion, the term **adverb** is used only in reference to words that modify verbs, providing more detailed or precise information than the verb alone. The term **qualifier**, or **intensifier**, is used to refer to words that modify adjectives and adverbs.

Adverbs provide "when," "where," and "how" information.

I have seen him *somewhere*. (location)

He lives *nearby*. (location)

The doctor will see you *now*. (time)

The store opened *late*. (time)

He ran *fast*. (how)

They walked *carefully*. (how)

Many adverbs are formed by adding *-ly* to an adjective, like the word *carefully* in the preceding sentence. Here are some other examples.

She spoke *beautifully*. (adjective *beautiful* + *-ly*)

She smiled *prettily*. (adjective *pretty* + *-ly*)

He behaved *badly*. (adjective *bad* + *-ly*)

He ran *rapidly*. (adjective *rapid* + *-ly*)

However, many adverbs do not end in *-ly* (for example, *yesterday, always, often, upstairs*), and some words that end in *-ly* are not adverbs (for example, *ugly*, adjective; *bully*, noun).

Some words use the same form as adjective and as adverb.

POSITIVE	COMPARATIVE	SUPERLATIVE
early	earlier	earliest
fast	faster	fastest
hard	harder	hardest
late	later	latest
long	longer	longest
low	lower	lowest

These adjectives do not add *-ly* to create adverbs. We would say:

It was a *fast* race. (adjective)

He ran *fast*. (adverb)

We do not say:

He ran *fastly*.

The *-er, -est* forms are used on the preceding adverbs, but most adverbs use the *more, most* forms for comparatives and superlatives.

She spoke *more* beautifully.

She smiled *most* prettily.

One common problem with adverbs is that sometimes writers use adjectives (noun modifiers) when they should use adverbs (verb modifiers).

His *poor* writing hurt his grade. (correct use of adjective)

The fact that he wrote *poorly* hurt his grade. (correct use of adverb)

He wrote *poor* and that hurt his grade. (incorrect use of adjective, adverb needed)

One set of words frequently causes problems: *good/bad*. These words are adjectives and should not be used as adverbs.

He had a *good* grade on that exam. (correct use of adjective)

He did *good* on that exam. (incorrect use of adjective, adverb needed)

should be:

He did *well* on that exam. (correct use of adverb)

He had a *bad* grade on that exam. (correct use of adjective)

He did *bad* on that exam. (incorrect use of adjective, adverb needed)

should be:

He did *badly* on that exam. (correct use of adverb)

The comparative and superlative forms of these words are the same.

POSITIVE	COMPARATIVE	SUPERLATIVE
good	better	best
well	better	best
bad	worse	worst
badly	worse	worst

Note: The form *worser* is incorrect; *worse* is already a comparative, so the additional *-er* is not needed.

He did *better* on the next exam.

He did *best* on the final exam.

He did *worse* on the next exam.

He did *worst* on the final exam.

This usage problem is complicated by the fact that linking verbs are followed by adjectives, not adverbs. Following is a list of some of the most common linking verbs.

LINKING VERBS
to be (is, am, are, was, were, been)   seem
smell   became
taste   look
feel   remain

LINKING VERB WITH ADJECTIVE (correct)	LINKING VERB WITH ADVERB (incorrect)
He is *good* at math.	He is *well* at math.
The cake smells *fine*.	The cake smells *finely*.
The pie tastes *delicious*.	The pie tastes *deliciously*.
He felt *bad*.	He felt *badly*.
She became *angry*.	She became *angrily*.
He seemed *happy*.	He seemed *happily*.
She looked *pretty*.	She looked *prettily*.
He remained *stubborn*.	He remained *stubbornly*.

Adverbs can be used without linking verbs in sentences such as these:

The ice cream melted *deliciously* in my mouth.

He smiled *happily*.

He spoke *angrily*.

She argued *stubbornly*.

He *angrily* banged the door.

She sat *quietly* in the corner.

PRACTICE

Copy the following paragraphs, inserting the appropriate adjectives and adverbs. The word in parentheses is an adjective; in some cases, the adverb form is needed. When the adjective is appropriate, retain the form in parentheses; when an adverb is needed, supply the appropriate word. When the word in parentheses is followed by a + symbol and *comp*, insert the comparative form. If the word is followed by a + symbol and *sup*, insert the superlative form.

Although I did not do as (good)1 on the last exam as I had hoped I would, I at least did (good + comp)2 than I did on my first exam. My grade on the first exam was absolutely the (bad + comp)3 I had ever made on an exam in my life. I felt so (bad)4 about my grade than I could not bring myself to tell anyone what I had made.

Of course, I really wasn't feeling (good)5 that day, but after the exam I felt (bad + comp)6. Suddenly, the semester, which had begun so (nice)7, began to look rather (grim)8. I was (serious)9 concerned about my GPA. If my grades got any (bad + comp)10, I risked losing my scholarship. Even more (serious)11 was the blow to my pride, which had been hurt (bad)12.

(Final)13, I realized that I had no course of action available to me except to study (hard + comp)14. I had to become (serious)15 about my school work. Although I (certain)16 did not feel (happy)17 about it, I had to cut back on my (social)18 life (considerable)19.

In high school (good)20 grades had been (easy)21 to get, but in college they would not come so (easy)22; of that, I was beginning to feel (certain)23. My pride (stubborn)24 refused to accept the idea of (bad)25 grades. (Disagreeable)26 as the prospect was, I was not at all (doubtful)27 about what would be required of me. The (good)28 times had been (fine)29, but if I wanted a college degree, the fun could come only after some (hard)30 work.

16.4 INTENSIFIERS AND QUALIFIERS

Intensifiers and **qualifiers** modify adjectives and adverbs. Some common intensifiers and qualifiers are listed here.

INTENSIFIERS/QUALIFIERS

very	really
quite	fairly
rather	too

Some intensifiers are regarded as too casual for Standard Written English and should be avoided.

AVOID

She is *real* nice.
He is *awful* mean.
She is *kind of* pretty.
He is *sort of* nice.

Ordinarily, intensifiers and qualifiers should not be used with absolute adjectives. The logic here is the same as that restricting use of the comparative and superlative. If something cannot be *deader* or *most dead*, it cannot be *quite dead* or *rather dead*. However, this rule is not always observed, particularly in fixed expressions like "*deader* than a doornail" or figurative language like "This town is *deader* on Saturday night than any place I have ever lived." Still, writers should exercise caution about using intensifiers and qualifiers with absolute adjectives, especially with *unique* and *perfect*. Since *unique* means "one of a kind," something cannot be *very* "one of a kind." Presumably, if something is *perfect*, it cannot be *rather perfect*. With the word *unique*, the problem often is that *unique* is not the appropriate word; *unusual* might be a better choice.

PRACTICE

Copy the following paragraphs, eliminating inappropriate intensifiers and qualifiers and substituting appropriate ones. If the intensifier or qualifier is modifying an absolute adjective, eliminate it and do not substitute another.

Joe was kind of a nice person, but he was real lazy and sort of worthless. His apartment was the most perfect mess I have ever seen in my life. As far as being a slob was concerned, Joe was really unique.

Joe usually stayed up real late at night, watching TV, drinking beer, and snacking on junk food. If he spilled anything, he never made any effort to clean it up. By the time he went to bed, his sofa was surrounded by a rather unique obstacle course of beer cans, potato chip bags, and other trash. The sofa itself was real filthy, its cover stained with spilled beer, sour cream dip, and pizza sauce. The coffee table was also a most perfect disaster, its wood real scarred by rings and cigarette burns. The carpet was awful bad too.

Joe always got up real late, about noon, and then spent several more hours watching television and eating donuts, coffee cake, and other kinds of pastries. When it started getting kind of late in the day, he would go out for his evening supply of beer and junk food.

Finally, everybody got real disgusted with Joe. He was living in the most unique filth anyone had ever seen. Even though most people thought he was sort of nice, nobody wanted to sit in the middle of that awful mess. I guess maybe Joe was kind of lonely then, but he sort of brought it on himself.

CHAPTER 17
Homonyms and Near-Homonyms

17.1 INTRODUCTION

Homonyms and near-homonyms cause problems for many writers. **Homonyms** are words that sound exactly alike; **near-homonyms** are words that sound almost alike or that sound alike in some dialects of spoken English but not in others. Although there is little or no difference in the pronunciations of such words, there is considerable difference in the meaning and word form. For example, the words *sail* and *sale* are homonyms; they are pronounced the same, but they are spelled differently and they have different meanings (*sail* refers to a piece of cloth that catches wind to provide movement to a boat or ship, while *sale* refers to the selling of merchandise). Since these two words occur relatively infrequently, this pair of homonyms creates little difficulty for most writers. Other homonyms occur more often and consequently offer many opportunities for errors.

Generally, writers do not actually confuse homonyms in the sense that they reverse them—for example, using *sail* to mean selling of merchandise and *sale* to refer to a piece of cloth that catches wind to provide movement to a boat or ship. In practice, homonym errors usually fall into other patterns.

One such pattern is the **combined spelling**. When writers use combined spelling, they combine part of the spelling of one word form with part of the spelling of the other word form. *Wright* is an example of a combined spelling; in this instance, the *w* has been taken from *write* and combined with *right*.

Another common pattern is that writers make no distinction between the two—or, in some cases, three—homonyms. For example, the combination *wright* might be found in a sentence such as the following:

I have to *wright* a paper, but I can't because I broke my *wright* hand.

The correct use would be:

I have to *write* a paper, but I can't because I broke my *right* hand.

As this example illustrates, there is often an underlying, although erroneous, logic to such errors since most people *write* with their *right* hand; consequently, their *right* hand is their *writing* hand.

In this chapter, we deal with the homonyms and near-homonyms that most often cause problems for writers. A brief explanation and a short practice are provided for each set of words. Needless to say, it will do your writing no good if you make perfect scores on the practices but do not apply what you have learned to your own writing. Making a list of troublesome sets that you frequently misuse in your writing and keeping that list readily available in your dictionary or notebook may be helpful to you.

17.2 THE MOST TROUBLESOME HOMONYMS

There are five sets of homonyms that seem to plague writers consistently. Because these words occur quite frequently, writers who have not mastered their distinctions of meaning and word form have the opportunity to make a large number of errors when they use them in their writing. These words are listed here:

POSSESSIVE PRONOUN	CONTRACTION	OTHER
its	it's	
their	they're	there
theirs	there's	
your	you're	
whose	who's	

In each of these sets, the first word listed is a possessive pronoun and should be used only as follows:

POSSESSIVE PRONOUNS

The dog wagged *its* tail.

They missed *their* turn.

The decision was *theirs* to make.

We saw *your* sister at the movie.

The police did not know *whose* fault the accident was.

The second word listed is a verb contraction. Avoiding the use of verb contractions in formal writing may decrease the number of opportunities for error in your writing, but you should know how to use these contractions correctly in informal writing.

CONTRACTIONS

It's too late to go to the movie tonight.

They're waiting for us at the restaurant.

There's a good chance I'll be late Friday evening.

You're early for class today.

Who's going to be at the party?

The best way to tell the difference between the possessive pronoun and the verb contraction is to attempt to substitute the uncontracted version for the word in question. If you can substitute the uncontracted version, then you need the contraction, and the form with the apostrophe is the one you should use. If you cannot substitute the uncontracted version, then the possessive pronoun is the one you should use. Possessive pronouns are **not** written with apostrophes, although apostrophes are used with possessive nouns (for example, "The red car belongs to *Bill's* brother"). In contractions, apostrophes are employed to signal omitted letters.

OMITTED LETTERS IN CONTRACTIONS
it's (*it is* or *it has*)
they're (*they are*)
there's (*there is* or *there has*)
you're (*you are*)
who's (*who is* or *who has*)

Do the following practices. Each practice concentrates on one set of homonyms. When you go through the set the first time, substitute the uncontracted version whenever it fits. Then, as you go through the set the second time, replace the uncontracted version with the contraction. Remember that the contraction uses the apostrophe, but the possessive pronoun does **not**.

Set 1. *its, it's*

Explanation

Its is the possessive pronoun.

> The dog wagged *its* tail.

It's is the contraction of *it is* or *it has*.

> *It's* too late to go to the movie tonight.
>
> *It's* been a long time since I have read that book.

PRACTICE

Last weekend we went to a movie, and this weekend we are going to see _____(1) sequel. _____(2) a movie that was adapted from a book. Reviewers have complained that _____(3) ending is not what _____(4) supposed to be. _____(5) been changed from the one in the book so _____(6) sequel could be filmed. Of course, the book has _____(7) merits, but I think the critics have ignored the fact that the movie has _____(8) strong points too.

Set 2. *their, they're, there*

This set is particularly troublesome because it includes the word *there*, in addition to the possessive pronoun *their* and the contraction *they're*. The word *there* may refer to location and contrasts with the word *here* (for example, "We told them to meet us *there*, but they came *here* instead"). More often the word *there* serves as a "dummy subject" at the beginning of a sentence or clause (for example, "*There* are many car accidents in bad weather").

Fortunately, most writers do not confuse all of these variations; however, many do have problems with some of them. Most commonly writers adopt either the word *there* or *their* and use it consistently in all circumstances. The various uses are illustrated here.

HOMONYMS AND NEAR-HOMONYMS

Explanation

Their is the possessive pronoun.

    They missed *their* turn.

They're is the contraction of *they are*.

    They're waiting for us at the restaurant.

There refers to location and contrasts with *here*.

    We told them to meet us *there*, but they came *here* instead.

It may also serve as the "dummy subject" of a sentence or clause.

    There are many car accidents in bad weather.

Note: Do **not** use the spelling *thier*.

PRACTICE

Last night I went to a party, and _____ were several
1
people _____ that I didn't know. Finally, I saw an old friend
2
of mine standing _____ by the window. She told me that
3
_____were several mutual friends of ours who were sup-
4
posed to be at the party, but for some reason _____ arrival
5
had been delayed. Soon the host came by to tell us that
_____ had been a phone call from our friends. "_____
6   7
going to be late because _____car won't start," he told us.
8

Set 3. *theirs, there's*

Explanation

Theirs is the possessive pronoun.

    The decision was *theirs* to make.

There's is the contraction of the "dummy subject" *there* and *is* or *has*.

> *There's* a good chance I'll be late Friday evening.

> *There's* been an uncomfortable relationship between those two people for some time.

Note: Do **not** use the spelling *thiers*.

PRACTICE

It seems that _____ always a hassle whenever I travel by plane. First, _____ always a long line in front of me. All of those people seem to want seats in the nonsmoking section, so by the time they have _____, nothing is left for me. Then, _____ always a good chance that my luggage will get lost. On my last trip, the couple standing next to me picked up my suitcase by accident, apparently thinking it was _____.

Set 4. *your, you're*

Explanation

Your is the possessive pronoun.

> We saw *your* sister at the movie.

You're is the contraction of *you are*.

> *You're* early for class today.

PRACTICE

I saw _____ high school English teacher last week. She asked me how _____ doing in college. I told her _____ studying hard. She said she still has some of _____ papers. If _____ no longer interested in them, she plans to throw them away.

Set 5. *whose, who's*

Explanation

Whose is the possessive pronoun.

   The police officer did not know *whose* fault the accident was.

Who's is the contraction of *who is* or *who has*.

   Who's going to be at the party?

   Who's been leaving the lights on?

PRACTICE

Does anyone know _____₁_____ supposed to mow the yard this week? No one knows _____₂_____ turn it is. Certainly, no one will admit _____₃_____ not been taking his or her turn. If we knew _____₄_____ responsibility it was, we could see that the work was done. When no one knows _____₅_____ to do what, nothing ever gets done.

17.3 MORE HOMONYMS

In addition to the five most troublesome sets of homonyms discussed in Section 17.2, several other sets can also cause problems for writers. Although it is unlikely that you have trouble with all of these sets of homonyms, you probably do use some of them incorrectly. Because these homonyms are common, simple, everyday words (most of them only one syllable), continued incorrect use of them may create an unfavorable impression on your readers.

Since homonyms are pronounced exactly alike, you must rely primarily on meaning distinctions to keep them straight, but false pronunciations and other memory devices may enable you to master them more easily.

Do the following practices. Concentrate on learning those homonyms that are problems for you. Keep a list in your dictionary or notebook of the homonyms you are unable to master.

Set 6. *bare, bear*

Explanation

Bare means "lacking cover."

    Her face was *bare* of makeup.

Bear refers to the animal, but is used more frequently as a synonym for endure.

    He couldn't *bear* the pain.

PRACTICE

When my friends came from the East to visit, they complained about how _____ the desert is. They also complained that they couldn't _____ the heat. Within a few hours of their arrival, my refrigerator was _____. Within a few days, my wallet was _____ too. Frankly, their visit was almost more than I could _____. By the time they were ready to leave, I was as grouchy as an old _____.

Set 7. *brake, break*

Explanation

Brake usually refers to the brakes on a vehicle or to the act of putting on the brakes.

    My *brakes* need repair.

    He *braked* quickly when the little boy ran into the street in front of his car.

Break means "to shatter."

    I was afraid I would *break* the lamp.

Break also means "to violate."

I did not want to *break* my promise.

Note: Some confusion in meaning may result in confusion of word form. (If you don't *brake* your car at a stop sign, you will *break* the law and you might *break* some bones if an accident occurs.)

PRACTICE

When the car in front of me stopped abruptly, I had to _____ fast. I slammed on the _____-s so hard that my
₁　　　　　　　　　　　　　　₂
tires squealed. I heard the sound of _____-ing glass. When
　　　　　　　　　　　　　　　　　　　　₃
I got out of the car, I saw that the _____ lights on the other
　　　　　　　　　　　　　　　　　　　₄
car were broken. However, the impact did not _____ my
　　　　　　　　　　　　　　　　　　　　　　　　　　　₅
headlights.

Set 8. *coarse, course*

Explanation

Coarse is the opposite of fine.

　The cloth had a *coarse* texture.

　He used *coarse* language.

Course refers to a unit of study.

　I took a history *course* last semester.

Course is also the form used in the common parenthetical expression.

　Of *course*, I was hungry because I had missed lunch.

PRACTICE

Last summer I decided to take a sewing _____. For my
　　　　　　　　　　　　　　　　　　　　　　　₁
first project, I attempted to make a blouse of rather _____
　　　　　　　　　　　　　　　　　　　　　　　　　　　　₂
material. Of _____, I had some problems with my blouse
　　　　　　　₃

project. When I saw how it turned out, I was tempted to use some _____ language. This summer I think I'll take a
4
_____ on how to manage stress.
5

Set 9. *died, dyed*

Explanation
Died refers to death.

He *died* after a long illness.

Dyed refers to color.

She *dyed* her hair red.

PRACTICE

An elderly neighbor _____ a few months ago. Soon
1
after that, his widow _____ her hair bright red. She told my
2
mother that she thought _____ hair would help her catch
3
another husband. She started chasing a widower who lived a few blocks away, but he _____ too. One of the neighbors
4
said that he probably _____ in order to avoid marrying her.
5

Set 10. *fourth, forth*

Explanation
Fourth is used when referring to the number *4*.

He was *fourth* in line.

Forth is used in all other contexts.

The line moved *forth* quickly.

PRACTICE

During registration I walked back and _____ across
                                          1
campus. I also stood in lines that moved _____ at a snail's
                                              2
pace. Once, when I was _____ from the front, the line
                            3
seemed to stop for hours. Many of us spoke _____ to com-
                                                4
plain. This is my sister's _____ semester, and she says it
                                5
never gets any better.

Set 11. *hear, here*

Explanation

Hear refers to sound.

We could not *hear* the speaker.

Here refers to location.

We left the car *here*.

PRACTICE

I was standing _____ in the hallway when I saw an old
                    1
friend of mine rushing to class. I spoke to her, but she didn't
seem to _____ me. Of course, the hall is very noisy
           2
_____ between classes. No one can _____ anything
    3   4
above the clamor. The next time I see her, I'll shout so that she
can _____ me.
        5

Set 12. *hole, whole*

Explanation

Hole means "opening" or "gap."

There was a *hole* in his shirt.

Whole means "entire."

He ate the *whole* pie.

PRACTICE

My brother used to go around wearing dirty old tee shirts with _____-s in them. His table manners were so bad that he would eat a _____ cheeseburger in one bite. Once he ate a _____ pie that my mother had baked for a family dinner. Then he came to the dinner table wearing no shoes and socks with _____-s in them. Mother was so disgusted with him that she made him stay in his room the _____ evening.

Set 13. *hour, our*

Explanation

Hour refers to the measurement of time.

They were an *hour* late.

Our is a possessive pronoun.

Our friends arrived before we did.

PRACTICE

Last night we went to _____ favorite Italian restaurant. We had to wait an _____ before we were finally seated. Service at _____ table was very poor. We had to wait another _____ before our dinner was served. That Italian restaurant ceased to be one of _____ favorites last night.

Set 14. *knew, new*

Explanation

Knew refers to knowledge (notice that both words begin with *kn*).

He *knew* the answer.

New contrasts with *old*.

Her dress was *new*.

PRACTICE

I had to buy several _____ books this semester. I
  1
_____ the _____ books would be expensive. I tried to
  2   3
get used books, but the bookstore only had _____ ones. I
                                                 4
_____ the used books would sell first. Everyone wants to
  5
buy used books because the _____ ones are so expensive.
                              6

Set 15. *know, no*

Explanation

Know refers to knowledge (notice that both words begin with *kn*).

He did not *know* the answer.

No means "none."

There was *no* reason for him to be angry.

PRACTICE

I had _____ opportunity to study for my history exam.
        1
When I saw the exam, I didn't _____ any of the answers.
                                  2
There's _____ feeling that's worse than going blank on an
          3
exam. I _____ I will have to study hard for the next exam.
          4
Otherwise, there's _____ chance for me to pass history.
                       5

Set 16. *miner, minor*

Explanation

Miner means "one who mines."

He is a copper *miner*.

Minor means "not legally of age."

Because he was a *minor*, he needed a cosigner for a car loan.

Minor also contrasts with *major*.

She made a *minor* error.

PRACTICE

Loretta Lynn was the daughter of a coal _____. When she was still a _____ of fourteen, she got married. Since her husband did not want to be a coal _____, they moved away. For several years she was a _____ country-western singer, performing in small clubs. Her song "I was Born a Coal _____'s Daughter" helped make her a star.

Set 17. *passed, past*

Explanation

Passed is the past tense of the verb *to pass*.

He *passed* us at high rate of speed.

Past is used in all other contexts.

He lives in the *past*.

We drove *past* their house.

PRACTICE

Last night a red car _____ our house several times. In the _____ three days, I have seen that car at least ten times. I never saw that car in our neighborhood in the _____. Last night it _____ several boys riding bicycles down the street. It _____ them much faster than was safe.

Set 18. *peace, piece*

Explanation

Peace refers to the absence of conflict.

> There was *peace* and quiet in the house after the children went to bed.

Piece refers to a part of something.

> He ate a big *piece* of pie.

(Notice that *piece* begins with *pie*.)

PRACTICE

My mother baked a chocolate cake that she cut into several _____. My brother grabbed the biggest _____ and devoured it as if he were starving. My sister, who is always on a diet, ate only a small _____. For a few minutes there was _____ and quiet as they ate. Mother knows that both of them like a _____ of chocolate cake.
      1   2   3   4   5

Set 19. *pedal, peddle*

Explanation

Pedal refers to a lever worked by the foot.

> He had lost a *pedal* off his bicycle.

Pedal also refers to the action of moving the pedals.

> He tried to *pedal* his bike faster.

Peddle refers to selling.

> He *peddled* encyclopedias for extra money.

(If you *peddle* your bike, you are trying to sell it.)

PRACTICE

The right _____ on my bicycle is broken. _____
            1   2
the bicycle is now very tiring. I wish I could _____ my old
                                              3
bike for a good price so I could buy a new one. Of course, a
new _____ is cheaper than a new bike. Perhaps if I repair
      4
the old bike, I will be able to _____ it without getting tired.
                                   5

Set 20. *plain, plane*

Explanation

Plain is the opposite of fancy or attractive.

> We baked a *plain* white cake for dessert.
> She had a very *plain* face.

Plain also refers to flat, treeless terrain.

> We drove through the *plains* for hours.

Plane refers to airplane.

> We caught a *plane* to Denver.

PRACTICE

Last week I took a _____ to Denver. The attendants
                        1
wore uniforms that were very _____. Although I like tai-
                                2
lored clothes, I thought the uniforms were too _____. Of
                                                  3
course, elaborate uniforms would probably not work very well
in the narrow aisles of a _____. Fortunately, most of the
                              4
attendants were attractive enough that they looked nice despite
their _____ outfits.
        5

Set 21. *right, write*

Explanation

Right contrasts with *left* and with *wrong*.

   He turned *right*.

   He knew that telling lies was not *right*.

Write refers to writing.

   He had to *write* a paper.

Note: Do **not** use the combined incorrect spelling *wright*.

PRACTICE

My mother always makes me _____ thank you notes when people send me presents. Sometimes I have a hard time thinking of the _____ thing to say. One of my aunts always sends clothes that never fit _____. One time she knitted a sweater for me, and the _____ sleeve was longer than the left. Trying to _____ a thank you note for that gift required considerable tact.

Set 22. *threw, through*

Explanation

Threw refers to the act of throwing.

   He *threw* the ball.

Through is used in all other contexts.

   The ball went *through* the window.

   He was *through* with his book.

PRACTICE

Last night I _____ a pillow at my brother when we were
                    1
fighting. He tried to catch it, but it slipped _____ his hands
                                                          2
and knocked over a vase. Then he _____ the pillow back
                                            3
at me. As it whizzed _____ the air, it broke a lamp. By the
                              4
time we were _____ with our pillow fight, the living room
                      5
was a disaster area.

Set 23. *to, too, two*

Explanation

To is used as a preposition.

    He went *to* the party.

To is also used as part of the infinitive form of the verb.

    He did not know what *to* say.

Too means "also."

    I spoke to him *too*.

Too also means "excessively."

    He is *too* tall.

Two refers to the number.

    He has *two* brothers and one sister.

PRACTICE

Last night I had _____ work overtime. I stayed _____
                            1   2
hours past quitting time. By the time I finally got home, I was
_____ tired _____ do anything. I was supposed
        3   4

_____ do the dishes, but I didn't. I watched TV for _____
                5   6
hours and then went _____ bed.
                                        7

Set 24. *weak, week*

Explanation

Weak contrasts with *strong*.

> He was *weak* after his operation.
>
> The coffee was *weak*.

Week refers to a period of seven days.

> His first *week* on the job was very frustrating.

PRACTICE

My uncle was in the hospital two _____-s after his operation. For several days he was too _____ to have visitors. At the end of the first _____, he began to feel better. We knew he was going to get well when he began to complain about the poor food and the _____ coffee. His voice was still somewhat _____, but his language certainly wasn't.

17.4 COMMON NEAR-HOMONYMS

Near-homonyms are pronounced almost alike or are pronounced alike in some spoken dialects of English. If you memorize the different pronunciations and then say the correct pronunciation as you write the word, the differences in meaning and word form should be considerably easier to recall.

This section contains several sets of common near-homonyms. In each set, information about pronunciation is provided in addition to an explanation of the context in which each word is used. As you do the practice, concentrate on the sets that cause you the most difficulty. Add to your dictionary or notebook list any sets of near-homonyms you are unable to master.

Set 25. *a, an*

Pronunciation
a
(rhymes with *hay*, but is often pronounced *uh*)

an
(rhymes with *fan*)

Explanation
A is used before words that begin with a consonant sound: *a* book, *a* cat, *a* dog.

An is used before words that begin with a vowel sound: *an* apple, *an* egg, *an* inch, *an* orange, *an* uncle.

Note: Vowels are *a, e, i, o, u.* Consonants are the other letters of the alphabet: *b, c, d, f, g, h, j, k, l, m, n, p, q, r, s, t, v, w, x, y, z.* Some words that are spelled with initial vowels are not pronounced with initial vowel sounds. Words that begin with the letter *u* may be pronounced with a *you* sound; the word *a* should be used before such words, as in *a* union. Some words that begin with initial consonants are not pronounced with an initial consonant sound. Words that begin with the letter *h* often are not pronounced with an *h* sound. The word *an* should be used before such words: *an* hour, *an* honest man, but *a* history exam.

PRACTICE

Last month all of the student groups had _____ unity
                                                                    1
breakfast. Unfortunately, _____ argument arose during the
                                        2
planning. There was _____ unpleasant discussion over
                              3
some of the arrangements. Finally, _____ history major sug-
                                                    4
gested _____ solution. After _____ discussion of over
            5   6
_____ hour, _____ agreement was reached.
    7   8

Set 26. *are, our, or*

Pronunciation
are
(rhymes with *car*)

our
(rhymes with *power*)

Explanation
Are is a verb.
   They *are* late.

Our is the possessive pronoun.
   This is *our* car.

or	*Or* is a conjunction used to
(rhymes with *more*)	indicate alternatives.
	He did not turn left *or* right, but drove straight ahead.

PRACTICE

We _____(1)_____ going out for dinner this evening. We can't decide whether to go to an Italian restaurant _____(2)_____ to a Chinese restaurant. Since we _____(3)_____ both particularly fond of Oriental food, we'll probably go to one of _____(4)_____ favorite restaurants, a small Chinese place not far from _____(5)_____ house. Of course, we'll have to decide whether we want Cantonese _____(6)_____ Szechuan food. We really prefer Szechuan, but both of us _____(7)_____ subject to indigestion if we eat the spicier dishes. Although _____(8)_____ taste buds love Szechuan, _____(9)_____ stomachs do not.

Set 27. *does, dose*

Pronunciation	**Explanation**
does	*Does* is a verb.
(rhymes with *buzz*)	He *does* not know the answer.
dose	*Dose* refers to quantity.
(rhymes with *close*, as in "a *close* fit")	He took a large *dose* of cough syrup.

PRACTICE

My brother said that he _____(1)_____ not feel very well. Grandmother wants to give him a _____(2)_____ of her all-purpose home remedy. He said that he _____(3)_____ not feel that bad. The last time she gave him a _____(4)_____ of her home remedy, he was sick for days. If he _____(5)_____ try another _____(6)_____, I'll be very surprised.

WORD FORM

Set 28. *have, of, off*

Pronunciation
have
(pronounced with an
ae sound like *hand*)

of
(rhymes with *dove*)

off
(rhymes with *cough*)

Explanation
Have is a verb.
   They *have* a new car.

Of is a preposition.
   He is a friend *of* mine.

Off contrasts with *on*.
   The book fell *off* the table.

PRACTICE

    I think someone walked _____ with my history book. I
1
_____ tried to remember where I might _____ left it.
2   3
History is one _____ my hardest classes, and I must
                     4
_____ my textbook. If I try to take one _____ those
5   6
history exams without studying, I know I'll fail it. If I can't borrow a book from someone, I'll _____ to buy a new one.
                                                      7

Set 29. *quit, quite, quiet*

Pronunciation
quit
(rhymes with *bit*)

quite
(rhymes with *bite*)

quiet
(rhymes with *diet*)

Explanation
Quit means "stop."
   He *quit* smoking.

Quite means "very."
   He is *quite* late.

Quiet means "without noise."
   The children were *quiet*.

PRACTICE

    Last night should have been a _____ evening at home.
                                                     1
Unfortunately, my little brother wouldn't _____ pestering
                                                      2
everyone. Sometimes he is _____ obnoxious. My parents
                                                     3
became _____ annoyed with him. Finally, they _____
              4   5
telling him to be _____ and sent him to his room.
                     6

HOMONYMS AND NEAR-HOMONYMS

Set 30. *sense, since*

Pronunciation
sense
(rhymes with *tense*)

since
(rhymes with *rinse*)

Explanation
Sense refers to meaning or judgment.
   That story makes no *sense* to me.
   He has no common *sense*.

Since means "because."
   Since we started late, we arrived late.
Since also refers to time.
   Since then, we have never been late.

PRACTICE

_____ I have been in college, I have been trying to
      1
understand registration. Much of what goes on doesn't seem to
make _____ to me. Sometimes I wonder if some of the
          2
people who set up registration have any common _____ at
                                                     3
all. I guess _____ I'm now a college student, I'll have to
              4
keep trying to understand the registration process. Frankly, I'm
beginning to suspect that the registration process makes no
_____ to anyone.
    5

Set 31. *than, then*

Pronunciation
than
(rhymes with *tan*)

then
(rhymes with *ten*)

Explanation
Than is used to indicate comparison.
   She is taller *than* her sister.

Then indicates time.
   We saw her *then* as she crossed the street.

PRACTICE

My brother is two years younger _____ I am.
                                      1
When we were children, I was taller _____ he was. Back
                                         2

_____ he was the shrimp of the family. I used to beat him
          3
up _____. Now he is a foot taller _____ I am.
       4   5

Set 32. *the, they*

Pronunciation
the
(pronounced "*thee*"
or "*thuh*")

Explanation
The is the definite article; it precedes nouns or adjectives followed by nouns.
    The book is on *the* round table.

they
(pronounced "*thay*")

They is a pronoun.
    They talked to their friends.

PRACTICE

_____ driver lost control of _____ car as he turned
     1   2
_____ corner. His passengers screamed, and _____
     3   4
shouted to him to slow down. He stopped _____ car, and
                                                5
_____ all got out. _____ refused to ride further with
     6   7
him, and _____ called friends to come pick them up.
                8

Set 33. *wear, were, where*

Pronunciation
wear
(rhymes with *care*)

Explanation
Wear refers to clothing.
    She *wears* nice clothes.
Wear can also refer to facial expressions.
    He is *wearing* a frown on his face today.

were
(rhymes with *fur*,
begins with a *w* sound)

Were is a verb.
    They *were* late.

where
(rhymes with *there*,
begins with a *wh* sound)

Where refers to location.
    Where is the library?

PRACTICE

There _____ several people waiting at the stop light. Because it was raining, several of them were _____-ing raincoats. A man _____-ing a blue suit asked the others if they knew _____ he could find the closest bus stop. There _____ several opinions about its location. As they _____ arguing, a bus stopped about a few yards away from _____ they _____ standing. They didn't even see _____ the bus stopped because they _____ still arguing. As the man turned to _____ the bus was stopped, he seemed to _____ a smile on his face.

Set 34. *weather, whether*

Pronunciation
weather
(begins with a
w sound)

whether
(begins with a
wh sound)

Explanation
Weather refers to climate.
　The *weather* was rainy.

Whether means "if."
　He did not know *whether* he
　should go.
Whether can also refer to alternatives.
　He did not know *whether* or not he
　should answer the question.

Note: Do **not** use the combined incorrect spelling *wheather*.

PRACTICE

We wanted to have a birthday party for my father last week, but we didn't know _____ to have a picnic or a barbecue. According to the _____ report, there was a possibility of rain. We couldn't decide _____ to have the party Saturday or Sunday. Finally, we decided to have a picnic on Sunday

_____ it rained or not. If the _____ was rainy, we
           4   5
could move the picnic inside the house.

Set 35. *witch, which*

Pronunciation
witch
(begins with a
w sound)

Explanation
Witch refers to an evil woman, specifically a woman who practices black magic.
  She had a temper like a *witch*.

which
(begins with a
wh sound)

Which is used in all other contexts.
  Which book belongs to you?
  The big white house on the corner, *which* was once a showplace, is now a shabby wreck.

PRACTICE

Do you know _____ costumes each of the other chil-
              1
dren is going to wear for Halloween? Cindy wants to go as a
_____. I wonder _____ stores still have a good selec-
     2   3
tion of costumes. Trying to find a size two _____ costume
                                                4
may be a real problem. Perhaps if we called each store, we
could find out _____ ones still have costumes for tiny
                    5
_____-es.
    6

17.5 MORE NEAR-HOMONYMS

This section contains several more sets of near-homonyms. Most of these sets do not occur quite as often as the ones discussed in Section 17.4, but they too are common, simple, everyday words that you should not misuse.

Concentrate on those sets that cause you the most difficulty. Add to your dictionary or notebook list any words that you are unable to master.

Set 36. (*accept, except*)

Pronunciation
accept
(pronounced with an
ae sound like *hand*)

except
(pronounced with an
eh sound like *met*)

Explanation
Accept is a verb.
   He *accepted* the invitation.

Except is a preposition.
   Everyone was there *except* Joe.

PRACTICE

    My cousin applied to several colleges and was _____-ed
by all _____ one. Naturally, the college that did not
_____ him was the one he wanted most to attend. He
would like to go to college out-of-state _____ for the cost.
His mother wants him to _____ the scholarship he was offered by a local college. Since he wants to get away from home,
he will probably _____ a somewhat smaller scholarship offered by a different school.

Set 37. *advice, advise*

Pronunciation
advice
(pronounced with
an *s* sound)

advise
(pronounced with
a *z* sound)

Explanation
Advice is a noun.
   He gave good *advice*.

Advise is a verb.
   He *advised* me well.

PRACTICE

    I went to the counseling service for _____ about
choosing a major. The counselor _____-d me to consider
changing majors. Based on _____ from my father, I had

decided to major in engineering. According to the counselor, following my father's _____ would have been a mistake. She _____-d me that my math aptitude was not really high enough for me to succeed as an engineer.

Set 38. *affect, effect*

Pronunciation
affect
(pronounced with an
ae sound like *hand*)

effect
(pronounced with an
eh sound like *met*)

Explanation
Affect is a verb.
  The movie *affected* her greatly.

Effect is a noun.
  The movie had a great *effect* on her.

PRACTICE

Recently my sister read a book that _____-ed her greatly. The _____ was so great that she began to act quite differently. Everyone commented about the _____ that the book had on her. One _____ was that she quoted the book continually. Evidently, all of us in the family were _____-ed too because soon we began to repeat her quotations.

Set 39. *choose, chose*

Pronunciation
choose
(rhymes with
snooze)

chose
(rhymes with
nose)

Explanation
Choose is the verb form used with helping verbs.
  He did not *choose* the right answer.
Choose is also the form used in the infinitive.
  He tried to *choose* wisely.

Chose is the past tense form of the verb.
  He *chose* the wrong answer.

HOMONYMS AND NEAR-HOMONYMS

PRACTICE

Trying to _____ a major is a big decision for many entering college students. Many students discover after a few semesters that they _____ the wrong major. Then they have to _____ another major. Some _____ several different majors during the course of their college years. Since I was undecided about a major, I _____ to list myself as unclassified when I entered college.

Set 40. *clothes, cloths*

Pronunciation	Explanation
clothes (rhymes with *doze*, the presence of *e* signals the *oh* sound)	*Clothes* refers to wearing apparel. She bought new *clothes*.
cloths (rhymes with *moths*)	*Cloths* are pieces of material. The dust *cloths* were dirty.

PRACTICE

When I work around the house, I never wear new _____. I always change into old _____ first. When my old _____ become too shabby even for cleaning house, I tear them into cleaning _____. Old shirts make especially good dust _____. I guess you could say that my cleaning _____ are recycled _____.

Set 41. *conscience, conscious*

Pronunciation	Explanation
conscience (pronounced with an *n* sound)	*Conscience* refers to one's sense of right and wrong. Her *conscience* bothered her.

conscious
(pronounced without
an *n* sound)

Conscious refers to awareness.
He was barely *conscious* after the accident.

PRACTICE

As I was driving down the street, I became _____ of
                                                  1
the fact that red lights were flashing behind me. I examined my

_____, but I was certain that I hadn't been speeding.
   2

_____ of my innocence, I pulled over to the side quickly. I
   3
sat there with a clear _____ while the patrolman stopped
                           4
behind me and walked up to the car. Unfortunately, I hadn't

been _____ of the fact that I was driving without my lights
        5
on even though it was dark, so I received a ticket for that.

Set 42. *formally, formerly*

Pronunciation
formally
(pronounced without
an *r* sound)

Explanation
Formally contrasts with *informally*.
He spoke very *formally*.

formerly
(pronounced with
an *r* sound)

Formerly means "previously."
He lived in that house *formerly*.

PRACTICE

Two of our neighbors were _____ very good friends.
                              1
Now they speak to each other only very rarely and then quite

_____. Even their children, who were _____ constant
   2   3
companions, are no longer allowed to play together. The

friendship ended when one family _____ filed a law suit
                                     4
against the other as the result of a minor dispute. Now our

_____ tranquil neighborhood has divided itself into two
   5
camps over their disagreement.

Set 43. *lead, led*

Pronunciation
lead
(rhymes with *reed*)

Explanation
Lead is the form used with helping verbs.
  He should *lead* the parade.
Lead is also the form of the infinitive.
  He wanted to *lead* the parade.

led
(rhymes with *red*)

Led is the past tense of the verb.
  He *led* the parade.

PRACTICE

My sister hopes to _____ the debate team to first place in the state debate tournament. Last year she _____ them to second place, but that didn't satisfy her. She says that a good debater should always _____ with his or her best arguments. In the last debate she _____ her team well, but she hopes to do better this time. She is determined to _____ them to victory.

Set 44. *loose, lose*

Pronunciation
loose
(rhymes with *moose*)

Explanation
Loose contrasts with *tight*.
  The hinge was *loose*.
Loose also contrasts with *secured*.
  The dog got *loose*.

lose
(rhymes with *snooze*)

Lose contrasts with *win*.
  He did not want to *lose* the race.

PRACTICE

My sister went on a diet to _____ weight. She knew she was getting fat when last summer's _____ shorts were so tight that she couldn't wear them this summer. She decided that she wanted to _____ at least twenty pounds. To keep from getting _____ and flabby, she began exercising regularly. My brother told her that by the time those shorts were _____ again, winter would be here.

Set 45. *loss, lost*

Pronunciation
loss
(rhymes with *toss*)

lost
(rhymes with *cost*)

Explanation
Loss is a noun.
    The *loss* hurt the team's record.

Lost is a verb.
    We *lost* the game.
Lost can also be an adjective.
    The *lost* boy cried for his mother.

PRACTICE

Our football team _____ the final game of the season last year. The _____ dropped us below the .500 mark for the first time in a year. The major reason for the _____ was that we _____ our quarterback in the first quarter of the game. His _____ was something the team could not overcome. Several people blamed the _____ of the game on the backup quarterback, but it was really not his fault. The whole team just _____ heart.

Set 46. *precede, proceed*

Pronunciation
precede
(begins with a
pree sound)

proceed
(begins with a
proh sound)

Explanation
Precede means "to come before."
    The usher *preceded* us down the aisle.

Proceed is used in all other contexts.
    The debate *proceeded* loudly.

Note: Do **not** use the combined incorrect form *procede*.

HOMONYMS AND NEAR-HOMONYMS

PRACTICE

The usher _____-d/ed us down the aisle. We _____-d/ed to
               1   2
follow him. As we _____-d/ed down the aisle, we spoke to
                         3
several people that we knew. We were unable to get really good
seats because so many people had _____-d/ed us. After we
                                         4
were seated, we _____-d/ed to enjoy ourselves, even
                       5
though the seats were not the best.

Set 47. *woman, women*

Pronunciation	Explanation
woman (pronounced *wuhmunn*)	*Woman* is the singular form. There was one *woman* at the meeting.
women (pronounced *wimmin*)	*Women* is the plural form. There were two *women* at the last meeting.

PRACTICE

I met three _____ walking into the library. I thought I
                  1
recognized two of the _____. At first, I didn't think I knew
                            2
the third _____. When all three _____ spoke to me at
          3   4
the same time, I realized who the third _____ was. She was
                                              5
the sister of the other two _____.
                                  6

UNIT IV
Writing Conventions

UNIT IV provides information about various writing conventions that writers must observe.

Chapter 18, "Punctuation," presents the marks of punctuation and the rules for their usage. Chapter 19, "Capitalization," covers the rules of capitalization. Chapter 20, "Spelling Basics," discusses common spelling problems, lists frequently misspelled words, and explains spelling rules that often cause writers problems. Finally, each chapter contains practices on the writing convention discussed in that chapter.

CHAPTER 18
Punctuation

18.1 INTRODUCTION

When we speak, our listeners understand the meaning of what we are saying not only by the words we use but also by our intonation. Our pitch rises and falls, we make short pauses, and we vary the stress according to the meaning.

Punctuation represents an attempt to indicate these oral signals by written symbols. The system is a very limited one, much less effective and flexible than what we can do with oral language, but writers must attempt to convey their meaning to their readers as completely and accurately as possible. Writing without punctuation is like oral language delivered in a monotone. Just as listeners may miss the full import of speech delivered in a monotone, so too will readers miss the full import of writing without punctuation.

Although the absence of appropriate punctuation creates difficulties for readers, the presence of unnecessary punctuation creates even more serious difficulties. If writing lacks punctuation to signal meaning, then readers must add their own signals. If writing has unnecessary punctuation, readers must read ahead, and then—after they realize that something is wrong—backtrack, and mentally remove the punctuation. If the punctuation signal is inappropriate—for example, a comma where a semicolon is needed—readers must mentally remove the erroneous punctuation mark and substitute the correct signal. This removing or changing of inappropriate punctuation requires readers to do the writer's work, work that some readers may be unable or unwilling to do.

Since mispunctuated text seems to be more difficult to read than unpunctuated text, a good rule of thumb is, "When in doubt, leave it out."

SIGNALING FULL STOPS

The full stop usually signals a complete entity. A full stop occurs at the end of a complete sentence, most commonly indicated by a capital letter at the beginning and a period at the end.

The boy walking down the street is my brother's best friend.

Question marks, exclamation points, and colons also signal full stops; so do semicolons. Some of these punctuation marks also have other uses that are discussed in the following sections.

Period

1. Use periods, in combination with initial capital letters, to indicate complete sentences.

   He spoke to the man coming down the stairs.

2. Use periods after—and sometimes within—abbreviations.

Mr.	A.M.
Mrs.	P.M.
Ms.	B.A.
Dr.	M.A.
C.O.D.	Ph.D.

Question Mark

Use a question mark to indicate a question. The question mark may be used after different kinds of structures as shown here.

Where have you been? (an information question)

Do you know the answer? (a yes-no question)

You do know the answer, don't you? (statement, then a tag question)

Now is the time for us to leave? (sentence order, question intonation)

On the table? (a phrase with question intonation)

Where? Now? (one word, question intonation)

A context is necessary for phrase and one-word questions to be meaningful, but a context is also necessary for full sentence questions to be meaningful. Questions are found quite often in the dialogue of short stories, novels, and plays, but they occur sparingly in academic writing and somewhat more often in business writing. It is **not** a good idea to begin a composition with a series of questions.

Exclamation Mark

Use the exclamation mark to indicate strong emotion. Following are some examples of exclamatory structures; some are sentences, some are not.

> What a good idea that was!
>
> How hard all of you have worked!
>
> You did a wonderful job!
>
> What a terrific idea!
>
> Wow!

Exclamations occur in the dialogue of short stories, novels, and plays; they can also occur in a short narrative used in a longer piece of expository or persuasive writing. Theoretically, any word, phrase, or sentence can be made exclamatory by the addition of stress, but most academic writing does not lend itself to the use of the exclamation mark. "The whole is equal to the sum of its parts!" looks and sounds absurd. Since a calm, measured tone is ordinarily desirable in academic and professional writing, you should use exclamation marks sparingly—if at all.

Colon

1. Use the colon to signal a formal list; such a list is found only after a complete sentence.

    > We brought several items for the party: paper plates, plastic cups, plastic dinner ware, and paper napkins.

    Do **not** use a colon when a complete sentence does not precede the list. In the following sentence, the phrase "I went shopping for" is not a complete sentence.

I went shopping for paper plates, plastic cups, plastic dinner ware, and paper napkins.

2. Use the colon to introduce a formal quotation preceded by a complete sentence.

Removing himself from the campaign for the presidency, Senator Metcalf made the following statement: "I have decided not to run for the office of President of the United States. The cost of such a campaign, financially and personally, is more than my family and I can bear at this time."

3. Use the colon to separate the hour from the minute when writing time. When indicating very precise time measurements, use the colon to separate seconds from minutes.

2:34 (34 minutes after 2)

2:34:15 (2 hours, 34 minutes, and 15 seconds)

4. In business letters, use the colon after the salutation.

Dear Mr. Jones:

Semicolon

1. Use the semicolon to separate two independent clauses joined together without a conjunction.

The farewell party lasted until 2:00 in the morning; we left before midnight because we had to catch an early flight the next morning.

2. Use a semicolon to separate two independent clauses joined together by a long (four or more letters) transitional conjunction.

The farewell party lasted until 2:00 in the morning; however, we left before midnight because we had to catch an early flight the next morning.

3. Use the semicolon for clarity when the comma would be confusing.

After checking the front door, the back door, and the windows, Suzanne left for work; but she returned when she realized that she had left the patio door unlocked.

Ordinarily, a comma before the word *but* would be sufficient, but there are other commas in the first clause of the preceding example, so the semicolon clarifies the relationship between the two independent clauses.

Sarah's favorite toys were Pooh Bear, a bedraggled brown teddy bear; Miss Mary Mine, a doll given to her on her second birthday; and Mr. Robot, a recent gift from her grandparents.

Without semicolons, the sentence would read:

Sarah's favorite toys were Pooh Bear, a bedraggled brown teddy bear, Miss Mary Mine, a doll given to her on her second birthday, and Mr. Robot, a recent gift from her grandparents.

The phrase "a bedraggled brown teddy bear" could be interpreted as referring to a second toy rather than describing the just-named "Pooh Bear."

PRACTICE

Copy the following letter, inserting appropriate full-stop signals—the period, the question mark, the exclamation point, the colon, and the semicolon.

Note: Some of the abbreviations used in this letter would not be appropriate in business correspondence; they are included here only for practice in punctuation.

1022 Park Dr
[1]
K C, Mo
[2]
April 15, 1989
[3]

Ms Jane Smith, Ed
[4]
Campus Parade
[5]
1112 W College Ave
[6]
Chicago, IL 12345
[7]

Dear Ms Smith
⁸

Several months ago I submitted to you, for publication in your magazine, a ms of my essay, "A Ph D Doesn't Make a Professor a Teacher" On Jan 15, at approximately 10 30, I spoke to your assistant, Mr John Hamilton
⁹

He indicated that you were out of town and would no doubt get in touch with me on your return, Feb 3
¹⁰

It is now Apr 15, and I have received no information from you or anyone else, furthermore, my telephone calls have not been returned.
¹¹

Have you received my ms Are you interested in publishing it
¹²

                                        Yours truly,
                                        ¹³
                                        Connie Washington
                                        ¹⁴

USING COMMAS

Commas are a difficult mark of punctuation to master because they are used in so many different ways. Typically writers at first do not use enough commas; later, they may overuse them.

A comma can be thought of as a partial stop; it is needed to indicate a **meaningful** pause or shift in intonation. If a sentence is confusing without a pause, then a comma is needed.

CONFUSING

Shortly after the children left the adults began to talk about the latest scandal.

REVISED FOR CLARITY

Shortly after the children left, the adults began to talk about the latest scandal.

Without a pause after *left*, this sentence might be read as "Shortly after the children left the adults...."

Using Commas to Separate Simple Elements

Some comma rules are simple and reliable.

1. Use a comma after the saluation in a personal letter (the colon is used in a business letter).

    Dear Joe,

2. Use a comma after the closing of a letter.

    Yours truly,

3. Use a comma to separate the elements in an address.
    a. Do **not** use a comma at the beginning of the address, but do use one to set off the end of the address from what follows in a sentence.

    He lives in Tulsa, Oklahoma, with his family.

    b. Use a comma to separate the the street address from the name of the city and the city from the state. Do **not** use a comma **between** the state and the zip code, but do use one **after** the zip code if the address occurs in the context of a sentence.

    Write to 420 Sheridan Drive, Tulsa, Oklahoma 64399, for further information.

    c. In correspondence, use commas to separate elements on the same line, but do **not** use commas at the end of the line.

    420 Sheridan Drive
    Tulsa, Oklahoma 64399

4. Use commas to separate the elements of a date unless the date is reversed European style; do **not** use commas if only the month and year are given.

    He was born on July 10, 1940, shortly after midnight.

    He was born on 10 July 1940 shortly after midnight.

He took a long vacation in August 1983 before he started college.

5. Use commas to separate direct address from the rest of the sentence.

   Alice, you are wanted on the phone.

   I have spoken to her, Mother, several times about my concern in this matter. (Without commas, the sentence could be read as "her mother.")

6. Use commas around transitions and interruptions.

   We were late to dinner, of course, when Sarah couldn't decide what to wear.

   I will speak to him as soon as I can, perhaps tomorrow morning, about the incident.

7. Use commas to separate a title from a name when the title follows the name, but **not** when the title precedes the name.

   Mary Smith, M.D., specializes in neurosurgery.

   Dr. Smith specializes in neurosurgery.

8. Use commas before abbreviations such as or *Inc.* or *Ltd.* in addresses but **not** before *Co.*

   Jones Brothers, Inc.

   Jones Brothers Co.

PRACTICE

Copy the following letter, inserting commas appropriately. Do not use commas where they are not needed.

302 Palm Drive
1
El Paso TX 76901
2
June 15 1989
3

John Jones President
4
Jones Brothers Inc.
5
1413 Laguna Avenue
6
Phoenix Arizona 85289
7

Dear John
8

   In January 1988 I began a campaign to raise donations for
9
The Little Folks Home Inc.

   I am sure John that you will wish to help me in this noble
10
endeavor as have many others. As a matter of fact several
11
people in your neighborhood John have already contributed to
our cause.

   John I am inviting you to join the list of our charter con-
12
tributors for a donation of only fifty dollars before 15 September
1989.

   We would be grateful of course for a larger contribution.
13
In fact we will accept any contribution no matter how small.

   Please join us John in making The Little Folks Home Inc. a
14
happy place in years to come.

                                        Yours sincerely
                                        15
                                        Mary Smith President
                                        16
                                        Little Folks Home Inc.
                                        17

Using Commas in Pairs and in Series

1. Do **not** put a comma between paired elements unless the paired elements are independent clauses.

   John and Sally went to the movies. (paired subjects)

   John and Sally ate dinner and went to the movies.
   (paired subjects, paired verbs)

John and Sally ate dinner and went to the movies and to a nightclub.
(paired subjects, paired verbs, paired prepositional phrases)

John and Sally thought that they would go to the movies and that afterward they would go to a nightclub.
(paired subjects, paired dependent clauses)

John and Sally ate dinner, and later they went to the movies and to a nightclub.
(paired subjects, paired independent clauses)

Note: Do **not** use a comma alone to separate pairs of independent clauses. This kind of construction is called a "comma splice" (See Chapter 10, Section 10.2).

2. Separate three or more items in a series with commas. Put commas between the items of the series but not after the last item of the series.

John, Sally, and Susan went to dinner.
(series of subjects)

John, Sally, and Susan went to dinner, then to the movies, and finally to a nightclub.
(series of subjects, series of prepositional phrases)

John, Sally, and Susan went to dinner, then they went to the movies, and finally they went to a nightclub.
(series of subjects, series of independent clauses)

Although it is acceptable to omit the comma before the conjunction preceding the last item in a series, particularly in journalistic writing, many prefer that it never be omitted. There are two good reasons for this preference:

a. The omission of the comma can lead to misreading in some instances. The following sentences illustrate this point; the first is clear, the second is not.

He is going to speak about Plato, Aristotle, and Darwin or Freud.

He is going to speak about Plato, Aristotle and Darwin or Freud.

b. The presence of the comma more reliably indicates the intonation and the logical relationships of the elements of a series.

               pause   pause
They walked, talked, and fell in love that summer afternoon.

               pause   no pause
They walked, talked and fell in love that summer afternoon.

3. Use commas to separate pairs or series of adjectives when appropriate. When a noun is preceded by more than one adjective, use commas to separate the adjectives if they are of a similar nature.

    He was a troubled, unhappy man.

There are two helpful tests:

a. The adjectives can be reversed.

    He was an unhappy, troubled man.

b. The word *and* can replace the comma.

    He was a troubled *and* unhappy man.

Do **not** use commas when the adjectives describe different qualities. The same two tests apply here.

    Two tall blond men walked down the street.
    (*two*, number; *tall*, size; *blond*, hair coloring)

We would not say *two blond tall men* or *two and tall and blond men*.

    The *sad little old* man spoke to no one.
    (*sad*, feeling; *little*, size; *old*, age)

We would not say *the old little sad man* or *the sad and little and old man*.

Using Commas After Introductory Elements

1. Use a comma after an introductory phrase unless the phrase is very short.

    Because of the bad weather, the picnic was cancelled.

Realizing her mistake, Susan apologized.

To have the costumes ready in time for the Christmas pageant, Frances began sewing them several weeks in advance.

His voice shaking with fear, Richard scolded his son for running into the street.

In 1957 the Russians launched Sputnik.

Even if the introductory phrase is short, always use a comma if the sentence would be unclear without one.

To organize time, charts are often helpful.

Without a comma after *time*, the preceding sentence might be read as:

To organize time charts. . . .

2. Use a comma after an introductory clause.

   After the movie was over, we went out for pizza.

   Because we were tired and sleepy, we went home early from the party.

   When John has enough money saved, he is going to make a down payment on a car.

   While I was cooking dinner, the phone rang several times.

3. Do **not** use a comma when such a clause comes at the end of the sentence.

   We went out for pizza after the movie was over.

   We went home early from the party because we were tired.

   John is going to make a down payment on a car when he has enough money saved.

   The phone rang several times while I was cooking dinner.

   There is one exception: If the clause occurs at the end of the sentence and is not essential to the action described in the main sentence, use a comma.

We enjoyed ourselves at the family reunion, although we were tired after the long drive.

We did not enjoy the family reunion because we were tired from our long drive.

Clauses beginning with *even though* and *although* are usually preceded by commas; clauses beginning with *if* and *because* are not.

PRACTICE

Copy the following paragraphs, inserting commas appropriately. Do not use commas where they should not be used.

Because so many young people have been killed or injured¹ in alcohol-related car accidents after graduation many communities have begun to organize alcohol-free post-graduation parties. In 1987 there was a serious accident in our community on² graduation night. Although no one was killed or permanently³ crippled several young people spent many weeks in the hospital recuperating from their injuries.

To avoid a recurrence our community decided to arrange a⁴ post-graduation party in 1988. The local PTA found many people⁵ willing to volunteer their help when they were approached. Some of the people volunteered even though they had no chil-⁶dren in school. They decided to help because they were con-⁷cerned about the possibility of a fatal or permanently crippling accident.

In January committees were formed to collect money and⁸ begin planning although graduation was four months away. Meeting every week the committees worked through February⁹ March and April. By the end of April the committee charged¹⁰ with the responsibility for collecting donations had achieved its goal. Reservations for a large hall having been made several weeks ago the committee made a substantial deposit.

To keep the young people occupied a band was hired to play from 10 P.M. to 4 A.M. With disk jockeys from a local radio station playing during breaks there would be eight hours of music to dance to. If some did not want to dance games and prizes could keep them busy.

At one end of the hall hot dogs hamburgers french fries pizza and other hot food would be served. Lying in tubs of crushed ice dozens of cans and bottles of every conceivable nonalcoholic beverage would be kept cold. Scattered around the floor small bistro tables with chairs awaited the hungry the thirsty and the tired.

After the last dance was played at 4 A.M. busses took the participants to an elegant hotel for a lavish buffet breakfast. Exhausted but well-fed they were returned to the school parking lot where their parents waited to pick them up and drive them home. To conclude the party was definitely a success.

Using Commas to Separate Nonrestrictive Elements

Perhaps the most difficult comma rules to master are those concerning **restrictive** and **nonrestrictive** elements. Many find the terms themselves confusing and, in consequence, cannot distinguish between the two with any great reliability.

Commas are placed around nonrestrictive elements but not restrictive elements. The two can be distinguished if the following are remembered:

NONRESTRICTIVE	RESTRICTIVE
Not essential to the meaning of the sentence	Essential to the meaning of the sentence
Commenting	Defining

Extra to the meaning = extra punctuation marks (commas)	Not extra to the meaning = no extra punctuation (no commas)
Proper nouns	Common nouns

Restrictive and nonrestrictive elements may be words, phrases, or clauses.

Note: Clauses beginning with *that* are always restrictive, so no commas are used. Clauses beginning with *which* are usually nonrestrictive and thus need commas.

NONRESTRICTIVE	RESTRICTIVE
Her husband, John, manages a supermarket. (not necessary to the meaning of the sentence; presumably she has only one husband)	Her daughter Susan lives in Detroit. (necessary to the meaning; presumably she has one or more daughters who do **not** live in Detroit)
The weight lifter, with his muscles bulging, lifted the bar bell over his head. (not necessary)	The woman with the little girl was waiting in line. (necessary)
The detective, standing in the corner, heard the burglars sneak into the room. (only one detective)	The boy standing in the corner was being disciplined for unruly behavior. (several boys)
Senator Jones, who was running for reelection, campaigned vigorously. (only one Senator Jones— thus extra—so extra commas.)	Most of the senators who were running for reelection campaigned vigorously. (some were not running for reelection, and some were not campaigning vigorously; necessary—not extra, therefore no extra commas)
John, whose car I bought, gave me a good deal. (John's identity already specified)	The man whose car I bought gave me a good deal. (necessary to specify which man)

The old Chevy, which runs beautifully, just had a tune-up. (a specific Chevy, as suggested by the use of *the* with the proper noun Chevy)	I bought an old Chevy that runs beautifully. (the use of the indefinite article *an* with the proper noun Chevy makes the noun phrase nonspecific, "an old Chevy," but the clause "that runs beautifully" specifies that the car was not just "any old Chevy")

PRACTICE

Copy the following paragraphs, inserting commas appropriately. Put commas around nonrestrictive (extra) elements; do not put commas around restrictive (necessary) elements.

Thomas Fullerton who was an incredibly difficult man to live
1
with was married to a woman who had more patience than anyone I have ever known. Martha Fullerton whose family and
2
friends had objected loudly and long to her incomprehensible decision to marry a man that everyone knew would make her life miserable suffered patiently from his abuse for years.

Although Tom was a man who never struck his wife, he
3
wounded her emotionally every chance he had. When dinner
4
was a few minutes late, Tom was the kind of man who would clear the table with one sweep of his arms, throwing the dishes and the food on the floor. His long-suffering wife who had
5
worked hours preparing a pleasant meal for a husband that could not be pleased then spent more hours clearing up the mess on the floor. Tom hungry and in a foul mood would leave
6
the house and eat dinner at a local bar named Clancy's the one on Derby Lane.

Then he would come home drunk and terrorize his wife
Martha and his children three small boys who lived in a constant
state of fear. Finally one evening in an even worse temper than
usual Tom struck Martha.

The next day Martha whose patience had finally snapped
went to the bank where John had their joint checking and savings accounts and safety deposit box. She transferred the savings account which had several thousand dollars in it to a bank
in another city. She cashed a check for several hundred dollars
that closed out the checking account. Next she went to the
safety deposit box which contained John's prized collection of
gold coins that was worth several thousand dollars. She also
took all of the cash over fifty thousand dollars.

Then she went home and packed suitcases for herself and
her children who were in school, and she made reservations on
a plane that would leave for Hawaii that afternoon. Since she
wanted to make certain that her husband would not follow her,
she also reported that all of his credit cards had been stolen.
Later that day she picked up her children who were delighted
to hear that they were going on a trip to Hawaii.

18.4 USING OTHER PUNCTUATION MARKS

There are several other marks of punctuation writers use, although not as often as the full-stop signals and commas.

Apostrophe

1. Use the apostrophe to indicate omitted letters in contractions.

    She *doesn't* know the answer.

(*Doesn't* is a contraction for *does not*.)

She *won't* be with us today.

(*Won't* is a contraction for *will not*.) (See Section 17.2, "The Most Troublesome Homonyms," for further discussion of apostrophes in contractions.)

2. Use the apostrophe to signal possession and similar relationships. Note the following rules for the placement of the apostrophe.

a. Place the apostrophe after the noun and before the *s* when the noun is singular.

Laura's new dress was expensive.

b. Place the apostrophe after the *s* when the noun is a regular plural.

The brothers' lawsuit against their parents was a local scandal.

c. Place the apostrophe after the noun and before the *s* when the noun is an irregular plural.

The children's cries frightened the kitten.

(See Section 13.5, "Possessive Nouns," for further discussion of the use of the apostrophe to indicate possession and other relationships.)

Hyphen

Note: Do **not** add space before or after the hyphen.

1. Use hyphens when writing fractions.

I have paid off one-fifth of the mortgage on my house.

2. Use hyphens in some—but not all—compound words. Consult a dictionary for hyphenation of individual words.

She is a real know-it-all.

3. Use hyphens to divide words at the end of a line, but consult a dictionary to determine proper placement of the hyphen.

Sarah proofread her paper and then spent hours carefully retyping it.

4. Use hyphens when two or more words preceding the noun modify the noun.

It was a vine-covered building.

She had a well-thought-out plan.

Do **not** use hyphens when a word ending in -*ly* modifies the word(s) preceding the noun.

She had a carefully organized schedule.

Dash

Note: Dashes may be typed using two hyphens; do not space before or after the dash.

1. Use the dash to indicate an abrupt change in structure or thought.

He had a perfectly wonderful scheme for getting rich—or so he thought.

Do **not** overuse the dash.

He was a good man—and a better friend than I ever knew. I never realized how much I admired him—but I really did. Then he was killed in a freak accident—and it was too late to tell him.

Parentheses

1. Use parentheses around numbers or letters in a series.

The school sent home a list requiring the following items: (1) a notebook, (2) pencils, (3) an eraser, and (4) a box of crayons.

2. Use parentheses for information incidental to the meaning of the sentence.

Aunt Sarah's youngest son was born in 1983 (the same year I graduated from high school).

Do **not** overuse parentheses.

> Mr. Jones (who is really a rough teacher) gave me a bad grade (in fact, the worst I have ever received in my entire life) on my last exam (the midterm).

A much better sentence would be the following, revised and punctuated differently.

> Mr. Jones, who is really a rough teacher, gave me the worst grade I have ever received in my entire life on the midterm exam.

Underline

1. Underline titles of books, movies, magazines, newspapers, and television shows to indicate italics.

   The Shining is a novel by Stephen King.
   Casablanca is one of my favorite movies.
   He reads *Newsweek* and *Time* every week.
   The New York Times is a famous newspaper.
   60 Minutes has won many awards.

2. The underline can be used to show emphasis.

   He had a *really* bad night after his operation.

   Do **not** overuse the underline.

   I had a *really great* time visiting with you. Everything was *just* wonderful, *absolutely* terrific.

Quotation Marks

1. Use quotation marks for the titles of songs, short stories, articles in magazines or newspapers, and episodes of television shows.

   "Stardust" is the title of a famous song.

Professor Jones' article, "A New Approach to the Research Paper," appeared in the journal, Teaching Writing.

2. Use quotation marks around quoted material.

One of Shakespeare's most widely quoted lines occurs at the beginning of Hamlet's famous soliloquy: "To be, or not to be: that is the question."

18.5 REVIEW ON PUNCTUATION

Copy the following letter, inserting appropriate punctuation. Use as many types of punctuation marks as you can.

1333 March Dr
¹
Austin Texas 76958
²
Jan 13 1989
³

Professor Angela Larkin
⁴
Dept of English
⁵
University of Texas at El Paso
⁶
El Paso Texas 79968
⁷

Dear Professor Larkin
⁸

Thank you for meeting with me on Jan 8 to discuss my application for a position as a part time tutor in your composition program Obviously your program is carefully organized with a well planned schedule
⁹

Although I am sure I would have enjoyed working in your program I must withdraw my application I have decided to be a full time student next semester My advisor Mr Scott Dalby has helped me obtain a loan one large enough that I will not need to work
¹⁰

Please convey my regards to Professor James Myers who spent considerable time talking with me and provided me with several dittos a professional resource I am certain that I will have occasion to use in the future His book How Writers Think has been a source of inspiration to me in the past I also am looking forward to reading his latest article When Writers Fail which I understand will appear in the September 1989 issue of College English

Again thank you for the interview

Yours truly

Mary Beth Yorkston

CHAPTER 19 Capitalization

19.1 INTRODUCTION

In Standard Written English, certain conventions of capitalization are observed. In handwritten work, writers sometimes use a mixture of printed and cursive capital and lowercase (small) letters that violates these conventions. The result is that they may seem not to know the rules of capitalization when, in fact, they do. Although writers ordinarily do not mix capital and lowercase letters in the same way when they type their own papers, someone else typing their papers for them — either a friend or a professional typist — may misinterpret their handwritten draft.

If your papers are frequently marked for capitalization errors, you need to ensure that you are not sending teachers and typists the wrong signals simply because of handwriting quirks.

19.2 RULES OF CAPITALIZATION

1. Capitalize the first letter of the first word of a sentence.

    The boy rode his bicycle down the street.

2. Capitalize the word *I*.

    He and I enjoyed the movie.

3. Capitalize proper nouns. Proper nouns are the names of specific persons, places, or things.

CAPITALIZED (specific)	NOT CAPITALIZED (general)
John Smith	the man in the street
Palm Street	across the street
Lake Tahoe	fishing in the lake

Some proper nouns include articles, prepositions, and/or conjunctions that are not capitalized; these words are usually quite short — two or three letters.

    Lake *of the* Ozarks

    Truth *or* Consequences, New Mexico

In foreign names, equivalent small words are also left uncapitalized.

    Alexis *de* Tocqueville

    Canyon *de* Chelly

However, many cities in the United States begin with the Spanish equivalent of *the*, which is capitalized.

    Los Angeles

    Las Cruces

    El Paso

4. Capitalize brand names and the names of companies, but not general terms for products or industries.

CAPITALIZED	NOT CAPITALIZED
Kleenex	tissues
General Motors	auto industry
Chevrolet	sedan
Pinto	compact car

5. Capitalize the first and last word and all important words in titles of poems, short stories, books, movies, and television shows.

    The Decline and Fall of the Roman Empire

    Meet the Press

6. In writing abbreviations, you may sometimes choose to use either capital letters or lowercase (small) letters. You may use a combination of capital letters and lowercase letters in some abbreviations but not in others.

ACCEPTABLE	NOT ACCEPTABLE
C.O.D.	C.o.D.
P.M. or pm	Pm
Ph.D.	PH.D.

7. Capitalize the days of the week and the months of the year, but not the seasons. In academia, however, the seasons are sometimes capitalized when the reference is to a specific term.

CAPITALIZED	NOT CAPITALIZED
January	spring
Sunday	

   EXCEPTION
   Registration for the Fall 1990 semester is scheduled for the last week of August.

8. In correspondence, capitalize the first word of salutations and closings.

SALUTATIONS	CLOSINGS
Dear Mr. Jones:	Sincerely,
Dear sir or madam:	Very truly yours,

9. Capitalize titles when they refer to specific persons.

CAPITALIZED	NOT CAPITALIZED
Professor Thomas Jones is a retired history professor.	I do not like my history professor.

10. Capitalize the names of specific courses but not the general names of subjects unless they would otherwise be capitalized.

CAPITALIZED	NOT CAPITALIZED
American History I meets in room 301 at 9:00.	I have to write a paper for my history class.
The section of Political Science 302 that I was scheduled to take was cancelled.	I need another three hours of political science.
One of my least favorite classes was English 101.	I have an exam Monday in my English class. (English is the name of a language and thus would ordinarily be capitalized.)

My advisor suggested that I take African History 304.

I think African history is fascinating.
(Africa is the name of a continent and thus would ordinarily be capitalized.)

REVIEW ON CAPITALIZATION

1. Copy the following letter, inserting capital letters appropriately. Do not use capitals where they are not needed.

1020 lake drive
¹
las cruces, new mexico
²
october 10, 1990
³

professor katherine mahoney
⁴
department of english and philosophy
⁵
university of texas at el paso
⁶
el paso, texas 79968
⁷

dear professor mahoney:
⁸

    i was in your english composition class in the fall 1988
⁹
semester. since then i have transferred to texas tech university,
¹⁰
and i am scheduled to graduate in the spring semester.

    in order for me to receive credit for the english composi-
¹¹
tion course that i took from you, i need to show the catalog description and a copy of the course syllabus to the people here at texas tech university who evaluate transcripts.

    could you please send me a copy of the catalog description
¹²
and your course syllabus?

CAPITALIZATION

thank you very much. i really enjoyed your class, and i
    13   14
learned a lot about writing in it.

                                          sincerely yours,
                                                15
                                          thomas wilson
                                          16

2. Copy the following letter, inserting capital letters appropriately. Do not use capitals where they are not needed.

                                          2330 desert place
                                          1
                                          el paso, texas
                                          2
                                          february 12, 1990
                                          3

mr. rogelio avila, general manager
  4
solar power company
  5
1844 presidio drive
  6
el paso, texas 79023
  7
dear mr. avila:
  8

    i am very interested in learning more about solar energy,
    9
and i am writing a research paper on the subject for my english class this spring.

    my english professor, dr. johnathan riddle, suggested that
    10
i write to you about some materials that your company has published. would you send me copies of the following: a book
                            11
called solar energy for the future by thomas jones, a pamphlet by george adams called solar energy today, and a article in the magazine solar titled solar energy homes?

    if there is any charge for these materials, please send them
    12
c.o.d. my paper is not due until may 1, but i am trying to gather
      13
as much information as i can well in advance.

would it be possible for me to visit your company sometime in march? i have classes all day monday, wednesday, and friday, but i am free on tuesday and thursday p.m. i understand that you have solar energy homes in various parts of el paso and that it is possible to arrange to see these homes on saturday and sunday.

    thank you very much.

                                                  yours truly,
                                                  rick garcia

CHAPTER 20 Spelling Basics

20.1 INTRODUCTION

Many people regard themselves as poor writers because they are poor spellers. Actually, spelling is not an important part of the creative process of writing, except when it becomes such an obsession that it intrudes itself into the creative process, blocking the flow of thought.

If you find yourself consistently worrying about how to spell a word when you are writing a paper or an exam, then it is true that poor spelling can make you a poor writer—but only because you are concerning yourself with spelling at the wrong time. When you are writing a paper or an exam, you should concentrate first on **what** you want to say. After you have expressed your ideas to the very best of your ability, then you should look at **how** you expressed them. Looking at the **how** and then correcting whatever weaknesses you find is not actually a part of the creative process of writing. It is, however, an important part of revision, and careful revision is often the difference between good writing and poor writing. If you are a poor speller, then checking for misspelled words should be an essential step in your revision process. In coursework assignments such as papers and exams, numerous spelling errors sometimes make the difference between a passing grade and a failing grade. In other writing situations—for example, a letter of application—one or two misspelled words may eliminate the writer from consideration.

Writers who consider themselves poor spellers often seem to abandon hope about their spelling. "I can't spell," they say to their teachers, particularly their English teachers, or "I'm a lousy speller." Implicit in statements like these is the idea that being a better speller is just not possible for them so there is no point in trying. This assumption is simply not true. If you are a poor speller, you may never become a spelling champion, but you can learn how to deal with the problem so that it no longer handicaps you seriously as a writer. To achieve this goal, you must approach the spelling problem in a systematic manner.

The first step is to recognize which words you misspell frequently in your writing. You do not need to learn how to spell every word in the English language, but you do need to know which words you consistently misspell in your own writing. Sometimes writers ask, "How do I know which words to look up in the dictionary?" Or they complain, "I look up **dozens** of words, but my writing is still filled with spelling errors." In many such cases, the problem is that the writer looked up all the "big" words or "hard" words, but did not look up common words which he or she uses frequently—and misspells every time. To improve your spelling, you need to recognize which common words you misspell; then either learn how to spell them correctly, or look them up in a dictionary. Carry a small pocket dictionary with you. When you are writing essay exams or in-class assignments, many teachers will permit you to use a dictionary.

In this chapter, various kinds of common spelling problems are discussed. You should concentrate on recognizing patterns in your own spelling and then consistently work on your spelling problems with each writing assignment. Within a reasonable period of time, you should make considerable progress.

20.2 PHONETIC SPELLING

One reason many writers are poor spellers is that they are spelling "phonetically"; that is, according to the **sound** of a word. Although phonetic spelling works for some words, the English spelling system is not truly phonetic.

The unphonetic nature of the English spelling system creates many problems for writers of English, particularly for individuals whose auditory memory is better than their visual memory. Good spellers "see" the word as they spell it; if a good speller cannot remember the exact spelling of a word, he or she may write down two or three different spellings and, in most cases, will instantly recognize the correct one. Many times a good speller, when asked how to spell a word, will need to write it down first before being able to give the correct spelling. For such a person, the **shape** of the word is, in many respect, more meaningful than its **sound.**

In contrast, the poor speller remembers the **sound** of the word, not its **shape**, relying on auditory memory rather than visual memory. In many situations — for example, in learning how to play a musical instrument — the individual who relies more on auditory memory has the advantage over the individual who relies on visual memory. However, spelling is an area where the individual whose auditory memory is superior to his or her visual memory is at a disadvantage.

Obviously, you cannot switch from being one kind of person to being another any more easily than people who write right-handed can switch to writing with their left hand, but there are certain techniques than can help you to compensate for a weak visual memory.

Often words are misspelled because they are mispronounced; for example, the word *athlete* is often incorrectly spelled as *athalete* because it is not correctly pronounced. There should be no sound between *ath-* and *-lete*. If you remember how to pronounce the word correctly, you will remember how to spell it correctly.

On the other hand, writers sometimes misspell words for exactly the opposite reason; that is, they omit certain sounds when they pronounce some words. For example, the words *mathematics* and *sophomore* are often misspelled as *mathmatics* and *sophmore* because the sound between *math-* and *-matics* and the sound between *soph-* and *-more* are omitted in the pronunciations. If you pronounce these words carefully as you write them, you should also be able to spell them correctly.

No doubt you will hear words like these pronounced both ways; the pronunciation used by national radio and television news broadcasters is usually the best spelling guide.

In spelling such words as *athlete, mathematics,* and *sophomore,* accurate pronunciation can help you spell accurately. In other cases, words are not misspelled because they are mispronounced but because their spelling does not accurately reflect their pronunciation. For example, writers often misspell words like *knowledge* and *psychology* because these words contain letters that are not pronounced. In cases where the spelling and the pronunciation are different, one useful technique is to develop a **false pronunciation.** As you spell *knowledge* and *psychology*, say the word to yourself, sounding each letter of the correct spelling. If you fix the false pronunciation in your auditory memory, then you will no longer need to rely only on your visual memory.

Such artificial spelling pronunciations are also useful to the phonetic speller dealing with words that sound alike or similar. For example, the words *accept* and *except* are often confused. In ordinary speech, these words are virtually identical. If you can fix two artificial pronunciations in your auditory memory for the two different spellings, then remembering both spellings will be easier.

Mnemonic devices are also useful to the poor speller. These are memory devices, sometimes in rhyme, that help you remember certain spelling rules. If you memorize these devices so you can repeat them aloud to yourself whenever you are uncertain about particular spelling situations, they can be very helpful. The following rhyme is an example of a mnemonic device.

> **I** before **E**
> Except after **C**
> Or when sounded like **A**
> As in *neighbor* and *weigh*.

COLLEGE-RELATED WORDS OFTEN MISSPELLED

College students inevitably find themselves using certain school-related words again and again in their conversation; often they use these same words in their writing. Knowing how to spell such words is particularly important, primarily because misspelling them creates such a negative impression on readers.

Following is a list of thirty school-related words that are often misspelled. Quiz yourself on these thirty words. Either have a friend dictate the words to you, or dictate them yourself slowly into a tape recorder and then play the tape back while you write the words. When you have isolated the words that you misspell, concentrate on only those words, drilling until you know how to spell them correctly. Remember to check particularly troublesome words in a dictionary when you use them in your writing.

1. absence
2. answer
3. athletics
4. attendance
5. author
6. dictionary
7. dormitories
8. government
9. grammar
10. holiday
11. knowledge
12. laboratory
13. language
14. libraries
15. literature
16. mathematics
17. misspelled
18. professor
19. reference
20. registration
21. research
22. roommate
23. schedule
24. semester
25. senior
26. sophomore
27. speech
28. studying
29. writing
30. written

COMMON WORDS OFTEN MISSPELLED

Following is a list of 150 commonly used words that are often mispelled. Quiz yourself on these words to determine which ones you misspell. Either have a friend dictate the words to you or dictate them yourself slowly into a tape recorder and then play back the tape while you write the words. Then concentrate on the words that you misspell, particularly the ones that you use the most frequently. Drill yourself on those words until you can spell them correctly.

Remember to look up particularly troublesome words in a dictionary when you use them in your writing. If you have trouble with several words, making an alphabetical list of those words for easy reference may be helpful to you. You might want to write this list on the inside cover of your pocket dictionary or on a card you can keep in your dictionary or notebook.

Note: You will accomplish more in less time if you concentrate on a few words every day rather than trying to master all of them at once.

1. accidentally
2. across
3. actually
4. against
5. agreement
6. a lot
7. all right
8. always
9. amateur
10. among
11. analyze
12. apparently
13. appearance
14. argument
15. article
16. attacked
17. audience
18. awkward
19. basically
20. beginning
21. belief
22. business
23. calendar
24. career
25. category
26. certain
27. committee
28. conference
29. confidence
30. consistent
31. controlling
32. convenient
33. countries
34. criticize
35. curiosity
36. dealt
37. decision
38. definitely
39. democracy
40. description
41. desperate
42. difference
43. difficulty
44. dining room
45. disappear
46. disappoint
47. disastrous
48. disease
49. dissatisfied
50. efficient
51. eighteen
52. eighth
53. embarrassed
54. equipment
55. equipped
56. especially
57. excellent
58. exercise
59. experience
60. explanation
61. familiar
62. February
63. finally

64. financially
65. foreign
66. forty
67. friend
68. gradually
69. grateful
70. handicapped
71. height
72. hoping
73. humorous
74. hundred
75. illiterate
76. immediately
77. independent
78. intelligence
79. interesting
80. introduction
81. length
82. license
83. loneliness
84. miscellaneous
85. mischievous
86. naturally
87. necessary
88. negative
89. neighborhood
90. neither
91. nickel
92. niece
93. nineteen
94. ninety
95. ninth
96. nonsense
97. nuclear
98. numerous
99. operation
100. opinion
101. opportunity
102. optimistic
103. ordinarily
104. originally
105. paid
106. particularly
107. pastime
108. peculiar
109. performance
110. persistent
111. personally
112. persuade
113. planning
114. pleasant
115. possession
116. possibility
117. potential
118. practically
119. predict
120. prejudice
121. prescription
122. privilege
123. probably
124. process
125. professional
126. quantity
127. receive
128. recognize
129. religious
130. restaurant
131. safety
132. sandwich
133. secretary
134. separate
135. shining
136. similar
137. sincerely
138. strength
139. strictly
140. surprised
141. temperature
142. together
143. truly
144. twelfth
145. until
146. used to
147. useful
148. using
149. Wednesday
150. welcome

20.5 SPELLING RULES

If you look at the words you misspelled in the spelling lists and at the words you frequently misspell in your papers, you will probably find that there are certain patterns to these misspellings. Learning the following spelling rules should help you to master most of the words that you misspell frequently. Quiz yourself to determine which spelling rules you do not know. Either have a friend dictate the words to you, or dictate them yourself slowly into a tape recorder and then play back the tape while you write the words.

Note: Follow the order suggested by the numbers in parentheses to determine which rules you know and which ones you don't.

Rule 1. *ie* and *ei*

There is a familiar little jingle that can help you remember how to spell words with the **ie** or **ei** sequence.

I before E
Except after C
Or when sounded like A
As in *neighbor* and *weigh*

I Before E Words

niece (1)
hygiene (2)

-ief *words*
chief (3)
grief (4)
handkerchief (5)
mischief (6)
relief (7)

-iev *words*
achieve (8)
aggrieve (9)
grievous (10)
mischievous (11)
reprieve (12)
relieve (13)

-ier *words*
cashier (14)
chandelier (15)

Except After C Words

-ceive *words*
conceive (16)
deceive (17)
perceive (18)
receive (19)

-ei(p)t *words*
conceit (20)
deceit (21)
receipt (22)

When Sounded Like A Words

-eigh *words*
eight (23)
freight (24)
neighbor (25)
weight (26)

-ei(g)n *words*
rein (27)
vein (28)
reign (29)

Exceptions

either (30)	protein (36)
foreign (31)	science (37)
forfeit (32)	seize (38)
height (33)	their (39)
leisure (34)	weird (40)

Rule 2. Adding Prefixes Without Change

When a prefix (word beginning) ends with the same letter that the rest of the word begins with, include both letters.

dis + satisfied = dissatisfied (1)
mis + spelled = misspelled (2)
un + necessary = unnecessary (3)
im + moderate = immoderate (4)
in + numerable = innumerable (5)
il + legal = illegal (6)
ir + responsible = irresponsible (7)

Note that the prefixes themselves do not end in double letters. Consequently, when a prefix precedes a base word that does not begin with the same letter that the prefix ends with, no double consonant appears.

dis + appear = disappear (8)
dis + appoint = disappoint (9)
mis + chief = mischief (10)
un + usual = unusual (11)
im + possible = impossible (12)
in + sincere = insincere (13)

Rule 3. Adding Suffixes Without Change

When the main part of the word ends with the same letter that the suffix (word ending) begins with, include both letters. (This rule operates like the prefix rule described previously.)

accidental + ly = accidentally (1)
book + keeper = bookkeeper (2)
real + ly = really (3)

room + mate = roommate (4)
Exception: eighteen (5)

Rule 4. Doubling Final Consonants Before Suffixes

When a word consists of only one syllable and if that word ends with a single consonant preceded by a single vowel, then the final consonant is doubled.

(CVC) run + n + ing = running (1)
(CVC) hop + p + ing = hopping (2)
(CVC) hit + t + ing = hitting (3)

The final consonant is not doubled if it is preceded by another consonant.

(CVCC) gasp + ing = gasping (4)
(CVCC) part + ing = parting (5)
(CVCC) help + ing = helping (6)
(CVCC) walk + ing = walking (7)

The final consonant is also not doubled if it is preceded by two vowels.

(CVVC) leap + ing = leaping (8)
(CVVC) meet + ing = meeting (9)
(CVVC) read + ing = reading (10)
(CVVC) rain + ing = raining (11)

If a word is more than one syllable and the final consonant is preceded by a single vowel, then the final consonant is doubled if the stress is on the final syllable.

begin + n + ing = beginning (12)
control + l + ing = controlling (13)

If the stress is not on the final syllable, then the consonant is not doubled. One set of words often misspelled as a result of this rule is *occur*, *prefer*, and *refer*. All three double the consonant preceding the *-ed* and *-ing* suffixes.

occur + r + ed = occurred (14)
       + ing = ocurring (15)
prefer + r + ed = preferred (16)
        + ing = preferring (17)

refer + r + ed = referred (18)
       + ing = referring (19)

When the -*ence* suffix is added, the stress remains on the final syllable in *occurrence* but not in *preference* and *reference*.

occur + r + ence = occurrence (20)
prefer + ence = preference (21)
refer + ence = reference (22)

Rule 5. Changing *y* to *i* Before Suffixes

When a word ends in **y** preceded by a consonant, change the **y** to **i** before all suffixes except *-ing*.

(CY) try (1)   tries (6)   trying (11)
(CY) study (2)   studied (7)   studying (12)
(CY) happy (3)   happier (8)
(CY) beauty (4)   beautiful (9)
(CY) busy (5)   business (10)

Do **not** change the **y** to **i** if the **y** is preceeded by a vowel.

(VY) buy (13)   buyer (16)   buying (19)
(VY) stay (14)   stayed (17)   staying (20)
(VY) joy (15)   joyful (18)

Exceptions

(CY) shy (21)   shyly (22)
(VY) day (23)   daily (24)
(VY) lay (25)   laid (26)
(VY) pay (27)   paid (28)
(VY) say (29)   said (30)

Rule 6. Dropping Final e Before Suffixes

Many common English words end with a silent **e**. Although the **e** is not pronounced, its presence or absence affects the pronunciation of many words. The presence of the final **e** indicates that the vowel sound of that syllable is long; its absence indicates a short vowel sound.

SHORT VOWEL	LONG VOWEL
not	note
bit	bite
hat	hate

The final **e** should be dropped if it precedes a suffix beginning with a vowel, but it should not be dropped if it precedes a suffix beginning with a consonant.

BASE WORD	VOWEL SUFFIX	CONSONANT SUFFIX
amuse	amuse + ing = amusing (1)	amuse + ment = amusement (2)
care	care + ing = caring (3)	care + ful = careful (4) care + less = careless (5)
love	love + able = lovable (6) love + ing = loving (7)	love + ly = lovely (8) love + less = loveless (9)
use	use + able = usable (10) use + ing = using (11)	use + less = useless (12)
move	move + able = movable (13) move + ing = moving (14)	
arrive	arrive + al = arrival (15) arrive + ing = arriving (16)	
fame	fame + ous = famous (17)	
safe		safe + ly = safely (18) safe + ty = safety (19)
whole		whole + some = wholesome (20)

Exceptions

BASE WORD	VOWEL SUFFIX	CONSONANT SUFFIX
argue		argue + ment = argument (21)
awe		awe + ful = awful (22)
true		true + ly = truly (23)
notice	notice + able = noticeable (soft **c** sound) (24)	
service	service + able = servi**c**eable (soft **c** sound) (25)	
change	change + able = chan**g**eable (soft **g** sound) (26)	
courage	courage + ous = coura**g**eous (soft **g** sound) (27)	
knowledge	knowledge + able = knowled**g**eable (soft **g** sound) (28)	

20.6 REVIEW ON SPELLING BASICS

1. Proofread the following letter for spelling errors. Then copy the letter, inserting the appropriate spellings.

Febuary 9, 1989
[1]

Dear Susan,
[2]

    Well, colege is now in the third week of the semestir, and
[3]
I haven't had alot of time for writting letters. Registration was
[4]
aweful, as usual. I am taking mathmatics and goverment, and I
hate both of them. The proffessors are so boreing, and they
[5]
seam to think school is nothing but studing, writting papers,
and doing reserch.

    At least my math prof doesn't take atendence so I cut class
[6]
whenever I can, and the goverment prof just lectures so I
don't have to anser any questions in class.

I am also studing Spanish and I have langage labratory twice
            7
a week.

When I'm a sophmore, I'll have to take speach, and I am
         8
realy dreading it. I can't wait to be a senoir so I can graduate
                    9
and get away from libaries and literture classes where you allways have to read boreing authors, amoung other things.

I read an articel the other day saying that basicly the job
  10
market for busness majors was begining to get better, so I am
sertain to get a good job when I graduate. I've defanatley made
                                                 11
a decisson to go into busness. I'm hopping that finaly I'll be
                                12
making alot of money.

I just need the right opurtunity, where I can get payed well.
  13
I'm serten that if I'm persistant, I'll do well when they see my
    14
performense on the job. There's a posibillity I might recieve a
                             15
large salary as a proffessional.

I am disatisfied with eating sandwishes. I want to eat lunch
   16   17
in the executive dinning room and have dinner at expensave
restaurants. I also want a secertary who fells priviledged to work
                          18
for me. I'm sure I could get use to that realy fast.
                                        19

Probly it will take a year or two, but if I'm carefull I might
20
become rich and fameous.

I'll call you Wensday about geting togeather on the
              21
twealfth.

Sincearely and truely,
22

Brenda
23

2. Proofread the following letter for spelling errors. Then copy the letter, inserting the appropriate spellings.

Novemver 11, 1989

Dear Jo,

    Thanks for the nice long letter. I was hopping to hear from you but suprized that you were writting so soon.

    Not alot is going on here. I had a conferrence with my English proffessor last Wensday. Basicly I hated to go becuase all she ever dose in criticise my writting. According to her my last paper was truely disasterous from begining to end.

    I acidently ran across an old freind of ours from the nineth grade a few days ago. It was Sarah Johnson, and she was eating in the dinning room of a nieghborhood resturant. I allmost didn't reconize her becuase her apearence had changed so much, but I knew this woman looked familair to me. Finaly my curoisity was so persistant that I walked over to her table. I was practicly there before I knew who she was. She imediatley knew me, and we had a plesant disscusion over sanwishes.

    Aparently she has a proffesional job in a bussiness in Seattle, and her carreer has excelent potenshul. She was very optomistick about her future. She was going to a comitee meeting and then to a conferrence when she was giving a paper that attacked an article she had read, but she was not certiam that the audeince would like what she had writen. She thought they might have dificultey imediatley understanding her opinons and be negitive if they were not knowledgable about the subject. I read the interduction and told her I personly liked it and thought it was intersting.

    We walked to casheir's counter, payed our bills, and got our reciepts. Then we went our seperate ways.

I hope everything is alright with you. You allways wright
                18   19
such intersting letters, and I can never think of annything to say.

                                                           Your greatfull freiend,
                                                           20
                                                           Rosie
                                                           21

Word Index

a/an, 304
-able, 359–360
accept/except, 311
advice/advise, 311
affect/effect, 312
an/a, 304
and, 121, 145–146
are/our/or, 304–305
army, 178
asked, 201
ate, 243
auto, 179
awful, 283

baby, 178
bad/badly, 280–281
bad/worse/worst, 155, 274, 280–281
bare/bear, 292
bass, 190
be, 118–120, 251–252
bear, 190
bear/bare, 292
bear/bore/born, 238
beautiful, 154–155
begin/began/begun, 229
best, 155, 274, 280–281
bet, 221
better, 155, 274, 280–281
between you and me*, 263–264
bid, 221
bite/bit/bitten, 232
bleed/bled, 215
blow/blew/blown, 240
boy, 177
brake/break, 292–293
brang*, 206, 209
break/brake, 292–293

break/broke/broken, 235
breed/bred, 215
bring/brought, 207
brung*, 206, 209
buffalo, 179
build/built, 213
burst, 221
buy/bought, 207

calf, 181
can/could, 253
came, 243
catch/caught, 207
cello, 179
chief, 181
child/children, 184
Chinese, 190
choose/chose, 312
choose/chose/chosen, 235
clothes/cloths, 313
coarse/course, 293
combo, 179
come/came/come, 243
conscience/conscious, 313
could, 253
course/coarse, 293
cut, 221

day, 177
dead, 274
deal/dealt, 210
deer, 190
died/dyed, 294
do/does/did/done, 248, 252
does/dose, 305
domino, 179
dose/does, 305
draw/drew/drawn, 240
drink/drank/drunk, 229

drive/drove/driven, 232
duo, 179
dwarf, 181
dyed/died, 294

-e, 358–360
early/earlier/earliest, 279
eat/ate/eaten, 243
echo, 180
-ed, 200–202
effect/affect, 312
ego, 179
-ei-/-ie-, 355–356
elf, 181
enemy, 178
-er/-est, 154–155, 273
-es, 174
except/accept, 311

fairly, 283
fall/fell/fallen, 235
far/farther/farthest, 274
fartherest*, 274
fast/faster/fastest, 279
feed/fed, 215
feel/felt, 210
few/fewer/fewest, 276–277
fight/fought, 207
find/found, 218
fish, 190
fly, 178
fly/flew/flown, 240
foot, 186
formally/formerly, 314
forth/fourth, 294
freeze/froze/frozen, 235
further/furthest, 274
furtherest*, 274

*The asterisk indicates forms that should not be used.

364

get/got/gotten, 243
give/gave/given, 243
go/went/gone, 243
good/better/best, 155, 274, 280–281
good/well, 280–281
goose, 186
got, 243
gotten, 243
grind/ground, 218
grow/grew/grown, 240

half, 181
hard/harder/hardest, 279
have/of/off, 306
he/him/his, 256
hear/here, 295
held, 222
here, 125–126
here/hear, 295
hero, 180
her/hers, 256, 262
herself, 268–269
hide/hid/hidden, 232
him, 256
himself, 268–269
his, 256, 262
hisself*, 268–269
hit, 221
hold/held, 222
hole/whole, 295–296
hour/our, 296
hurt, 221

I, 256
-ie-/-ei-, 355–356
-ing, 358–359
it, 256
its, 256, 262
its/it's, 286–288
itself, 268–269

Japanese, 190

keep/kept, 210
key, 177
kind of, 283
kneel/knelt, 210
knew/new, 296–297

knife, 181
know/knew/known, 240
know/no, 297

lasso, 179
lain, 243
late/later/latest, 279
lay, 243
lead/led, 215, 315
leaf, 181
least/less, 276–277
leave/left, 210
led/lead, 215, 315
lend/lent, 213
less/least, 276–277
liberty, 178
lie/lay/lain, 243
life, 181
little/less/least, 276–277
long/longer/longest, 279
loose/lose, 315
lose/lost, 210
loss/lost, 316
louse, 188
low/lower/lowest, 279

make/made, 222
man/men, 184
many/much, 276
may/might, 253
me, 256
meet/met, 215
men, 184
might, 253
mine/my, 256
miner/minor, 297–298
moose, 190
more/most, 154–155, 273, 276
mosquito, 179
most/more, 154–155, 273, 276
mouse, 188
much/many, 276
my/mine, 256
myself, 268–269

new/knew, 296–297
no/know, 297
nor, 121

of/off/have, 306
or, 121
or/our/are, 305–306
our, 256
our/hour, 296
our/or/are, 305–306
ours, 256, 262
ourselves, 268–269
-ous, 359–360

passed/past, 298
patio, 179
peace/piece, 299
pedal/peddle, 299
perch, 190
perfect, 274
photo, 179
piano, 179
piece/peace, 299
plain/plane, 300
poor/poorly, 280
potato, 180
precede/proceed, 316
pretty, 154–155
procede*, 316
proceed/precede, 316

quiet/quit/quite, 306
quite, 283

radio, 179
rather, 283
ran, 243
read, 215
real, 283
really, 283
ride/rode/ridden, 232
right/write, 301
ring/rang/rung, 229
rise/rose/risen, 232
round, 274
run/ran/run, 243

safe, 181
said, 222
sat, 222
satisfied, 201
saw, 243
say/said, 222
see/saw/seen, 243
seek/sought, 207

seen, 243
self, 181
sell/sold, 222
send/sent, 213
sense/since, 307
set, 221
shake/shook/shaken, 235
shall/should, 253
she/her/hers, 256
sheep, 190
shelf, 181
should, 253
shrink/shrank/shrunk, 229
since/sense, 307
sing/sang/sung, 229
sink/sank/sunk, 229
sit/sat, 222
sky, 178
sleep/slept, 210
sold, 222
solo, 179
soprano, 179
sort of, 283
speak/spoke/spoken, 235
species, 190
spend/spent, 213
spring/sprang/sprung, 229
stand/stood, 222
sting/stung, 218
stood, 222
strike/struck, 218
studio, 179
supposed to, 201
surprised, 201
swear/swore/sworn, 238
sweep/swept, 210
swim/swam/swum, 229
swing/swung, 218

take/took/taken, 235
teach/taught, 207
tear/tore/torn, 238

tell/told, 222
than/then, 307
that, 133–135
the/they, 308
their, 256
their/there/they're, 286–289
theirs, 256, 262
theirs/there's, 286–287, 289–290
theirselves*, 269
them, 256
themselves, 268–269
then/than, 307
there, 125–126
there/their/they're, 286–289
there's/theirs, 286–287, 289–290
they/the, 308
they/them/their/theirs, 256
thief, 181
think/thought, 207
they're/their/there, 286–289
threw/through, 301
throw/threw/thrown, 240
to/too/two, 302
told, 222
tomato, 180
too, 283
too/to/two, 302
tooth/teeth, 186
trout, 190
two/too/to, 302

unique, 274
us, 256
used to, 201

very, 283

we, 256
weak/week, 303
wear/were/where, 308
wear/wore/worn, 238
weather/whether, 309
week/weak, 303
weep/wept, 210
well/better/best, 280–281
well/good, 280–281
went, 243
were/wear/where, 303
wheather*, 309
where/wear/were, 308
whether/weather, 309
which, 133–135
which/witch, 310
who, 133–135
whole/hole, 295–296
who's/whose, 286–287, 291
wife, 181
will/would, 253
win/won, 218
witch/which, 310
wolf, 181
woman/women, 184, 317
worse/worst, 155, 274, 280–281
worser*, 280
would, 253
wright*, 301
wring/wrung, 218
write/right, 301
write/wrote/written, 232

-y, 358
you/your/yours, 256
your/yours, 256, 262
your/you're, 286–287, 290
yourself, yourselves, 268–269

zero, 179

Subject Index

Adjectives, 272–284
  absolute, 274
  after linking verbs, 281
  comparatives, 273–274
  definition of, 272–273
  intensifiers/qualifiers, 283
  superlatives, 273–274
Adverbs, 278–281
  definition of, 278–279
Antecedent, pronouns, 256–257
Apostrophe, 337–338
Audience, 7–8
Auxiliary verbs, 250–254
  dummy *do*, 248, 252
  modals, 253–254

Base form of verbs, 247–248

Capitalization, 343–348
Clause, dependent, 129–135
Clause, independent, 129–135
Clause boundaries, 138–150
College-related words often misspelled, 352
Colon, 323–324
Combined spelling, 285–286
Comma splices, 139–141
  revising 144–150
Commas, 326–337
Common nouns, 173
Common words often misspelled, 353–354
Comparatives, 273–274
  double, 154–155
  irregular, 155, 273–274

Comparison-contrast, 46–47
  half-and-half, 47
  point-by-point, 47
Complex sentences, 146–147
Compound pronouns, 262–263
Compound sentences, 145–146
Conjunctions
  coordinating, 145–146, 149–150
  subordinating, 130–131
  transitional, 146, 149–150
Connectives, 147–150
Contractions, 286–287
Count nouns, 276–277

Dangling modifiers, 165–167
Dash, 339
Dependent clause, 129–135
Description, 21–23
Development, 22
Double comparatives, 154–155, 273–274
Double negatives, 157
Double subjects, 152
Double superlatives, 154–155, 273–274
Dummy auxiliary *do*, 248, 252

Editing, 5
Exclamation mark, 323

Faulty parallelism, 163–164
Feminine pronouns, 259

Fragments, sentence 129–137
  dependent clause, 129–135
  phrase, 135–137
Full stops, 322–325

Gender, pronoun, 259–260
Generation of text, 4–5

Helping verbs, 250–254
Homonyms, 285–303
Hyphen, 338–339

Illogical structures, 165–167
Italics, 340
Independent clause, 129–135
Intensifiers, 283
Intransitive verbs, 247
Invention, 4
Irregular comparatives, 155, 273–274
Irregular noun plurals, 183–190
  overcorrection, 184
  regularization, 183
  simplification, 183
Irregular plural possessive nouns, 194
Irregular superlatives, 155, 273–274
Irregular verbs, 225–245
  overcorrection, 228
  regularization, 227–228
  simplification, 226–227

Linking verbs, 246
  before adjectives, 281
  before pronouns, 264

Markers, noun, 173
Masculine pronouns, 259
Mass nouns, 276–277
Misclassification of verbs, 206
Mnemonic devices, 352
Modal auxiliary verbs, 253–254
Modifiers, dangling, 165–167
Most troublesome homonyms, 286–291
Multiple negatives, 157

Near-homonyms, 303–317
Negatives, double/multiple, 157
Neuter pronouns, 259
Noun markers, 173
Nouns, 173–195
  common, 173
  count, 276–277
  definition of, 173
  irregular, 183–191
    overcorrection, 184
    regularization, 183
    simplification, 183
  mass, 276–277
  plural, 174–191
  plural possessive, 193–194
    irregular, 194
    regular, 193
  possessive, 191–195
  proper, 173
  regular, 174–175
    overcorrection, 175
    simplification, 175
  singular possessive, 191
  variations on the regular pattern, 177–183
    ending in *f*, 181
    ending in *o*, 179–180
    ending in *y*, 177–178

Object of the preposition, 122–123, 263–264
Objective pronouns, 261–264
Organization, 4

Overcorrection
  of noun plurals, irregular, 184
  of noun plurals, regular, 175
  of verbs, irregular, 228
  of verbs, regular, 198, 201–202
  of verbs, variant regular, 206

Parallelism, faulty, 163–164
Parentheses, 339–340
Passive verb forms, 251–252
Past participle of verbs, 249
Past perfect verb forms, 251
Past progressive verb forms, 251
Past tense verb forms, 248–249
Period, 322
Personal pronouns, 255–256
Persuasion, 65–66
Phonetic spelling, 350
Phrase fragments, 135–137
Phrases as connectives, 149–150
Plural nouns, 174–191
  irregular 183–191
    overcorrection, 184
    regularization, 183
    simplification, 183
  regular, 174–175
    overcorrection, 175
    simplification, 175
  variations on the regular pattern, 177–183
    ending in *f*, 181
    ending in *o*, 179–180
    ending in *y*, 177–178
Plural possessive nouns, 193–194
  irregular, 194
  regular, 193
Positive, 273–274
Possessive nouns, 191–195
  irregular plural, 194

  regular plural, 193
  singular, 191
Possessive pronouns, 261–262, 286–287
Prefixes, 356
Prepositional phrases, 122–125
  object of preposition, 122–125, 263–264
  prepositions, 122–123
Present participle of verbs, 249
Present perfect verb forms, 250–251
Present progressive verb forms, 251
Principal parts of verbs, 247–250
Process, 32–33
Progressive verb forms, 251
  past, 251
  present, 6
Proofreading, 6
Pronouns, 255–271
  after linking verbs, 264
  antecedent, 256–257
  avoiding sexist usage, 259–260
  definition of, 255–256
  function, 261–264
    objective, 261–264
    possessive, 261–262, 286–287
    subjective, 261–264
  gender, 259–260
    feminine, 259
    masculine, 259
    neuter, 259
  personal, 255–256
  reference, 255–257
  reflexives, 268–269
  relative, 133–135
  shifts in number, 258–259
  shifts in person, 257–258
Proper nouns, 173
Process, 32–33
Punctuation, 321–342
  apostrophe, 337–338
  colon, 323–324
  commas, 326–337

Punctuation *(Continued)*
  dash, 339
  exclamation mark, 323
  hyphen, 338–339
  italics, 340
  parentheses, 339–340
  period, 322
  question mark, 322–323
  quotation marks, 340–341
  semicolon, 324–325
  underline, 340
Purpose, 8–9

Qualifiers, 283
Question mark, 322–323
Quotation marks, 340–341

Reference, pronoun, 255–257
Reflexive pronouns, 268–269
Regular noun plurals, 174–175
  overcorrection, 175
  simplification, 175
  variations on the regular pattern, 177–183
    ending in *f*, 181
    ending in *o*, 179–180
    ending in *y*, 177–178
Regular plural possessive nouns, 193
Regular verbs, 197–202
  overcorrection, 198, 201–202
  simplification, 198, 200–201
  when to add -*ed*, 200–203
  when to add -*s*, 197–198
Regular verbs, variants, 205–224
  misclassification, 206
  overcorrection, 206
  regularization, 205
  simplification, 205
Regularization
  of irregular noun plurals, 183

of irregular verbs, 227–228
of variant regular verbs, 205
Relative pronouns, 133–135
Restrictive and nonrestrictive elements, 334–336
Revision, 5–6
Rewriting, 5
Run-together sentences, 142–144
  revising, 144–150

Semicolon, 324–325
Sentence boundaries, 129–137
Sentence fragments, 129–137
  dependent clause, 129–135
  phrase, 135–137
Sentences, complex, 146–147
Sentences, compound, 145–146
Sexist language, pronouns, 259–260
Shifting pronoun reference, 257–259
  shifts in number, 258–259
  shifts in person, 257–258
Simplification
  of irregular noun plurals, 183
  of irregular verbs, 226–227
  of regular noun plurals, 175
  of regular verbs, 198, 200–201
  of variant regular verbs, 205
Singular possessive nouns, 191
Spelling, 349–363
  college-related words often misspelled, 352
  combined, 285–286

common words often misspelled, 353–354
false pronounciation, 351–352
mnemonic devices, 352
phonetic, 350–351
Subject, 6–7
Subjective pronouns, 261–264
Subjects, 113–128
  agreement with verb, 117–128
  double, 152
  recognizing, 114
Subordinating conjunctions, 130–131
Suffixes, 356–360
  changing *y* to *i*, 358
  dropping final *e*, 358–360
  doubling final consonants, 357–358
Summaries, 80–81
Superlatives, 273–274
  double, 154–155
  irregular, 155, 273–274

Text, generation of, 4–5
Thesis, 7
Third person singular verbs, 248
Transitional conjunctions, 149–150
  overuse of, 146
Transitive verbs, 246
Troublesome homonyms, 286–291

Unbalanced structures, 163–164
Underline, 340

Vague pronoun reference, 256–257
Variant regular verbs, 205–244
  misclassification, 206
  overcorrection, 206
  regularization, 205
  simplification, 205
Verb terminology, 245–254

Verbs, 196–254
  auxiliary, 250–254
    dummy *do*, 248, 252
    modals, 253–254
  base form, 247–248
  definition of, 245–246
  intransitive, 247
  irregular, 225–245
    overcorrection, 228
    regularization, 227–228
    simplification, 226–227
  linking, 246
    before adjectives, 281
    before pronouns, 264
  passive, 251–252
  past participle, 249
  past perfect forms, 251
  past progressive, 251
  past tense, 248–249
  present participle, 249
  present perfect, 250–251
  present progressive, 251
  principal parts, 247–250
  progressive
    past, 251
    present, 251
  recognizing, 114–115
  regular, 197–202
    overcorrection, 198, 201–202
    simplification, 198, 200–201
    when to add *-ed*, 200–203
    when to add *-s*, 197–198
  regular, variant, 205–224
    misclassification, 206
    overcorrection, 206
    regularization, 205
    simplification, 205
  third person singular, 248
  transitive, 246

Writing process, 3–6